RECOGNITION AND THE SELF IN HEGEL'S *PHENOMENOLOGY OF SPIRIT*

Hegel's *Phenomenology of Spirit* is famed for its account of the problem of recognition. Yet while readers agree about the importance of its influential accounts of the struggle to the death and the master/slave relation in developing that problem, there is no consensus regarding what sorts of relations among subjects would count as successful forms of recognition. Timothy L. Brownlee articulates the essential connections between Hegel's concepts of recognition and the self, and presents a novel interpretation of the *Phenomenology* that traces the emergence of actual relations of reciprocal recognition through the work as a whole. He focuses on the distinctive social constitution conception of the self that Hegel develops in his account of "spirit," and demonstrates that the primary significance of recognition lies in its contribution to self-knowledge. His book will be valuable for scholars and students interested in Hegel, German Idealism, and philosophical conceptions of recognition.

TIMOTHY L. BROWNLEE is Professor of Philosophy at Xavier University where he also directs the Philosophy, Politics, and the Public Honors Program. He is the author of numerous articles on Hegel's practical philosophy and aesthetics, German idealism, and social and political philosophy.

RECOGNITION AND THE SELF IN HEGEL'S *PHENOMENOLOGY OF SPIRIT*

TIMOTHY L. BROWNLEE

Xavier University, Cincinnati

CAMBRIDGE
UNIVERSITY PRESS

Shaftesbury Road, Cambridge CB2 8EA, United Kingdom

One Liberty Plaza, 20th Floor, New York, NY 10006, USA

477 Williamstown Road, Port Melbourne, VIC 3207, Australia

314–321, 3rd Floor, Plot 3, Splendor Forum, Jasola District Centre,
New Delhi – 110025, India

103 Penang Road, #05–06/07, Visioncrest Commercial, Singapore 238467

Cambridge University Press is part of Cambridge University Press & Assessment,
a department of the University of Cambridge.

We share the University's mission to contribute to society through the pursuit of
education, learning and research at the highest international levels of excellence.

www.cambridge.org
Information on this title: www.cambridge.org/9781009098236

DOI: 10.1017/9781009099141

First published 2023

A catalogue record for this publication is available from the British Library.

ISBN 978-1-009-09823-6 Hardback

For my parents, J. Hugh and Janet Brownlee

Then Polemarchus said, Socrates, you seem to me to be headed
   towards town, as though you're leaving.
You don't opine badly, I said.
Do you see us, he said, how many we are?
How couldn't I?
So become stronger than these men, he said, or stay here.
Isn't there, I said, still the option that we persuade you it's
   necessary for us to leave?
Would you really be able, he said, to persuade us if we don't listen?

Plato, Republic, 327c

The position is this: This is my first appearance in a lawcourt, at the age
of seventy; I am therefore simply a stranger to the manner of speaking
here. Just as if I were really a stranger, you would certainly excuse me if
I spoke in that dialect and manner in which I had been brought up, so
too my present request seems a just one, for you to pay no attention to
my manner of speech—be it better or worse—but to concentrate your
attention on whether what I say is just or not, for the excellence of a
judge lies in this, as that of a speaker lies in telling the truth.

Plato, Apology, trans. G. M. A. Grube, rev. John Cooper, 17d-18a

Contents

Preface and Acknowledgments

This book addresses two of the principal themes of G. W. F. Hegel's 1807 *Phenomenology of Spirit*, those of recognition and the self. It aims to demonstrate that, for Hegel, these two phenomena are tightly intertwined.

You and I stand in the relation of recognition (*Anerkennen*) to one another when my activities of "recognizing" you are guided by a conception of what you are, so that those activities generate a new condition for you, being-recognized. Recognition is, Hegel argues, a vital need for creatures like ourselves. But that need is not, like our needs for food and shelter, rooted in features of ours that are merely natural. Rather, the activities of recognizing and being recognized by others are so important because they make it possible for us to arrive at a specific kind of knowledge, *self*-knowledge.

Our capacity to recognize and be recognized by others is grounded in a basic element of our constitution, the fact that we are *self-conscious*. Self-knowledge is possible only for self-conscious beings like you and me. As a self-conscious being, I am able to learn and know about myself by taking up distinct relations to various objects that are different from me. For example, I learn my tastes in music, what I find satisfying to hear, by listening to different types of music and reflecting on my experiences of them. Among the most important sorts of objects that can contribute to self-knowledge are other self-conscious beings, beings like you. While there is a variety of different ways in which we can relate to others – for example, loving or hating them, dominating or venerating them, obsessing over them or ignoring them, among a myriad of others – Hegel singles out relations of recognition between self-conscious beings as the most significant for arriving at self-knowledge. The self-knowledge that relations of recognition make possible is unique because it is not just the knowledge that I might come to have of my particular attitudes and states, or even my particular tastes or interests, but rather a much more general sort of knowledge, knowledge of the sort of being that I am.

Of course, in some sense, it's easy enough to identify the sort of being that I am. After all, I've already stated that I am a being who is self-conscious. But I've also acknowledged that I'm not the only being who is like that, since you are self-conscious too. One reason that recognition comprises such an important form of knowledge is because it entails an acknowledgment of a deep and important kind of equality between us, the fact that we are both self-conscious beings. Indeed, Hegel thinks that part of the essence of recognition lies in the fact that it is a relation that is, in principle, reciprocal: When I recognize you, you can also recognize me. We might object that there are various forms of recognition that are not and cannot be reciprocal, for instance forms of recognition in which I honor you for your superior achievement and abilities, or, to take Hegel's famous example, the sort of recognition that a bondsman gives to their lord. However, there is an important sense in which these forms of one-sided recognition are actually dependent for their significance on an implicit equality of the parties involved. It would be silly for me to care about the recognition of my musical abilities from nonmusicians (what do they really know about shredding?), just as the recognition of the bondsman is, in an important sense, meaningless for the lord, coming as it does from a being he deems inferior. What the lord really seeks from the bondsman (and the musician from the nonmusician) is probably not recognition, but rather easy pleasure, or a sense of power, or some other such good.

The link between recognition, on the one hand, and reciprocity or equality, on the other, stems from an important connection between practices of recognition and the existence of *the self*. The equality implicit in relations of recognition is ultimately an equality grounded in our shared constitution as selves. I will succeed in recognizing you only to the extent that my activities reflect a correct understanding of who you are. For this reason, I say more when I identify you as a self than I do when I simply identify you as a self-conscious being. Being self-conscious is, of course, essential to you. You would be a very – we could say entirely – different sort of creature if you were not self-conscious. But self-consciousness alone by no means exhausts what you are, and it does not, by itself, give me much guidance in determining how I might successfully recognize you. Indeed, Hegel goes so far as to say that self-consciousness alone is an empty form that is nothing positive in itself, only an "absolute negativity." To be sure, this absolute negativity is very important for you to be the sort of being that you are, since in a sense it elevates you above everything that you encounter, enabling you to separate and distinguish yourself from everything else. Of course, it may not be a comforting thought to acknowledge that we all harbor a sort of abyss, a basically negative and destructive capacity, at the heart of our very being. But your capacity to distance yourself from what is merely given and positive is at once the source of your capacity for transformation, not only of the world as you merely find it, but also of yourself. Because of this negativity, both you and your world can become something they are not yet.

The fact that we are self-conscious beings is the source of our need for recognition, since it is through establishing the right sorts of relations to others that we are capable of positive self-knowledge. But that fact is also the source of one of the greatest challenges to achieving recognition, since it is unclear how we ought to go about recognizing a being that is, at its core, nothing positive. Of course, we are never – or almost never – in a situation where we are faced only with this radical negativity of the other. Instead, we find ourselves along with others sharing a world. And that world is not merely a collection of objects, but is rather a human world, structured by shared norms that establish joint expectations for how we will and ought to act, and that provide the terms through which we make sense of ourselves and one another. That world is also a sort of project, a shared venture whose continued existence depends on us all taking its demands seriously, producing and reproducing it through our joint activity. Hegel's idea of "spirit" (*Geist*) is, initially at least, just the idea of the unity (or rather reciprocal dependence) comprising self-conscious beings and their shared social world. And because of the ways in which our shared practices help us to make sense of and understand ourselves, Hegel reserves the term "the self" (*das Selbst*) to refer to the sorts of beings who understand themselves through that shared participation.

In understanding the self in this way – to use the terminology that I develop in what follows, in understanding the self as socially constituted – Hegel is pushing against what is I think a common, intuitive understanding of what the self is. According to this understanding, the self is something that exists independent of and prior to the shared social world, a secure property belonging to the individual, that may appear in social form in particular instances, but whose existence doesn't depend on those appearances. By contrast, for Hegel, we do have a sort of existence independent of relations to others, but that is our existence as self-conscious beings, which, as we've seen, Hegel thinks is grounded in nothing positive. Instead, we become selves only through our engagement in shared practices, even the mundane and prosaic practices of day-to-day social life. But that entails that my existence as a self is not an invulnerable guarantee, but rather a product of a shared activity that also requires you.

You and I both become selves through engagement in the shared social world, which means that we both assume a unique equal or universal status as participants in that world, even as we each seek the unique forms of engagement in which we find individual fulfillment, that is, meaningful activities that give adequate expression to the things that we think are important.

As I've described it so far, this might not sound like the social world that you know. Many of the activities in which we are required to engage might seem to be completely meaningless, or nearly so, so that it can be challenging to see how they could be sources of fulfillment. Moreover, many of the central institutions of social life are exclusive, unjustly limiting participation on the basis of arbitrary distinctions of gender, race, ability, or class, or instituting basic inequalities on the basis of those distinctions. Instead of linking the existence of the self to any particular institution – like that of the state, or a profession, or the market, or the family – Hegel instead shows that it is through participation in moral discourse, the practice of giving expression to the deeply held convictions that we realize through our actions, that we come to exist as selves. Moral discourse gives expression to concerns that matter to me, and to my own insight and knowledge, so that I can find myself expressed in moral action and speech. At the same time, what distinguishes moral discourse from the expression of my particular tastes or idiosyncratic interests is the fact that I expect others to agree with what I express, since morality concerns matters that are (or ought to be) of importance to everyone. Hegel designates this moral conception of the self, in which you exist as a self through acting on and expressing your convictions to others, "conscience."

We can now see that the two principal phenomena on which this book will dwell, recognition and the self, actually presuppose one another. First, it is only when you and I share a common conception of the self – in particular, it is only when we both orient our activities according to the norms implicit in the idea of conscience – that it is possible for us to recognize one another. So recognition depends on a shared conception of the self. Of course, it is always possible for us to fail to act according to those norms. When I ignore the claims that you make on and before me about what it is right to do, or when I dismiss you as not fully competent to make those claims, I fail to treat you as conscientious, and so make it impossible for you to be recognized. However, second, we can also see that the existence of the self actually depends on the recognition of others. This dependence is most visible in cases where we treat one another as conscientious, but still fail to come to agreement with respect to the convictions that we express in our actions and speech. The failure to reach agreement on matters of the highest importance, moral matters, drives a wedge between us, and undermines the equality that is central to the idea of the self. In such cases, I might have a profound experience of the singularity of selfhood, of the inescapable fact that I am (as Hegel says) *this* self. However, what is lacking is the other essential pole of selfhood, its being shared with others who are also selves, or (as Hegel puts it) the "continuity" with others that arises from the shared or "universal" dimension of our being.

The practices of recognizing and being recognized by others and our existence as selves therefore depend on one another. As a result, we can see why Hegel would link recognition and self-knowledge in the way that he does. What you are is not simply a natural or transcendental fact about you, one that holds irrespective of your relations to others. Instead, your existence as a self is something that is made and remade through your joint engagement in a shared social world. And since my existence as a self is only secured through my own participation in moral discourse – of giving expression to my convictions about what is right, realizing those convictions in action, and judging conscientiously the like actions and expressions of others – I can only arrive at self-knowledge, knowledge not only of my particular existence as this singular self, but knowledge of the general sort of being that I am, through the practices of recognizing and being recognized by others.

This fundamental link between recognition and selfhood means that our existence as selves is subject to a very basic ontological vulnerability. We might rue that vulnerability and seek refuge from it by attempting to carve off a dimension of the self that is insulated from the doubt and desolation that can arise when we find ourselves at odds with and so cut off from others. If Hegel is right, such efforts are bound to fail. To be sure, there is an important dimension of my being that is not so dependent on others; but there is nothing "positive" there, nothing that could, by itself, lend direction and meaning to my life. Instead, being a self requires that we embrace our relations to others, even with the knowledge of the risks attendant on that embrace. Just as importantly, being conscientious requires acknowledging our answerability to the requirements of morality, both in our actions but also in our judgments of others. Being a self, for Hegel, means endeavoring to answer in earnest to those requirements, an endeavor that will require transformation, both of the world, when we find that the way things are falls short of the way that they should be, and of ourselves, when we find that we have failed to live up to our highest aspirations.

***

This book took me a long time to write. Quill Kukla was my first teacher of Hegel, and their semester-long seminar on the *Phenomenology* at Carleton University in winter 2001 likely did more than anything else to shape the direction that my work in philosophy would take.

I began to engage seriously with the themes of conscience and recognition as a graduate student at Boston University, where I found an outstanding community of philosophers interested in Hegel. Dan Dahlstrom has been an ideal mentor in every way, and I owe him a great debt. Allen Speight has been a model teacher and scholar. The late Klaus Brinkmann was a careful reader and critic. I am incredibly grateful for all their consistent encouragement and support.

I am also grateful to the members of the Department of Philosophy at Xavier University. Gabe Gottlieb, in particular, has been an unstinting source of encouragement and a patient and generous reader. I feel very fortunate to call him a colleague and friend. My department chairs, Richard Polt, Tim Quinn, and Michelle Brady, have all been outstanding advocates and supporters. Steven Frankel has been an able mentor. I would also like to thank the office of the Dean of the College of Arts and Sciences and the office of the Provost, most recently for support in the form of a research leave in fall 2021. Finally, thanks to students in seminar courses that I have taught on the *Phenomenology* and to all the students in the Philosophy, Politics, and the Public honors program.

I have presented aspects of the reading that I offer in what follows at various talks and conferences over the years. I am particularly grateful for discussions with Joe Arel, James Clarke, Iain Macdonald, Wayne Martin, Michael Rosen, Joe Saunders, Robert Stern, and Kevin Thompson. I have had the good fortune to work through many of the ideas that I set out here with a variety of informal organizations and working groups. I am grateful to the participants in the various Ontario Hegel Organization meetings over the years, especially to John Burbidge, David Ciavatta, Bruce Gilbert, Jeffrey Reid, and John Russon. More recently, I've benefitted greatly from conversations at the meetings of the Ohio Hegel Roundtable, in particular with Mark Alznauer, Stefan Bird-Pollan, Olga Lyanda Geller, and Vladimir Marchenkov.

My great thanks to Hilary Gaskin of Cambridge University Press for her encouragement for my project and patience as I've completed it. Thanks also to Abi Sears for her help in the project's latter stages. I am deeply grateful to the work's two anonymous reviewers for their reflections, suggestions, and criticisms. They have helped me to improve it considerably.

Portions of Chapters 2 and 3 appeared in two articles, "Ethicality and the Movement of Recognition in Hegel's *Phenomenology of Spirit*," *International Philosophical Quarterly* Vol. 56, No. 2 (June 2016): 187–201 and "Alienation and Recognition in Hegel's *Phenomenology of Spirit*," *Philosophical Forum* Vol. 46, No. 4 (Winter 2015): 377–396. My thanks to those publications for their permission to reproduce those selections.

This book is dedicated to my parents, J. Hugh and Janet Brownlee, in gratitude. Thanks also to my brothers, Ken and Mark, and to their families.

I am grateful for the friendship and good cheer of Jeff DeButte and Jason Karamchandani, and of David Jennings (who generously translated the book's first Platonic epigraph), Jamie Kelly, Tony Reeves, and Matt Schaffer.

Day to day, no one has been more important for me during the completion of this project than my wife and daughters. To Joanna, thank you for your conversation and for your care and concern for everyone around you. To Sarah, who arrived mid-way through the work's completion, thank you for your enthusiasm and persistence in everything (and for your patience on our many runs). And thanks most of all to Amy, without whom not.

Abbreviations

I have used the following abbreviations for works by Hegel:

PhG   G. W. F. Hegel, *Die Phänomenologie des Geistes*, ed.
Wolfgang Bonsiepen and Reinhard Heede. *Gesammelte
Werke*, Band 9. References cite the page number in the
Gesammelte Werke edition, followed by the paragraph
number in Hegel, *The Phenomenology of Spirit*, ed. and trans.
Terry Pinkard (New York: Cambridge University Press,
2018). I have benefitted greatly from consulting Pinkard's
translation.

GW   G. W. F. Hegel, *Gesammelte Werke* (Hamburg: Felix Meiner,
1968–). References cite the volume and page number.

TW   G. W. F. Hegel, *Theorie Werkausgabe*, 20 vols, ed. E.
Moldenauer and K. M. Michel (Frankfurt a.M.: Suhrkamp,
1970). References cite the volume and page number.

I have used the following abbreviations for works by other authors:

AA   Immanuel Kant, *Kants gesammelte Schriften: Herausgegeben
von der Deutschen Akademie der Wissenschaften*, 29 vols.
(Berlin and Leipzig: De Gruyter, 1902–). References cite the
volume and page number.

SW   J. G. Fichte, *Sämmtliche Werke*, 8 vols, ed. I. H. Fichte (New
York: De Gruyter, 1971). (Original Berlin: Veit, 1845–6.)
References cite the volume and page number.

Unless otherwise noted, translations from the German are my own.

Introduction

I

J. M. Coetzee's *The Lives of Animals* dramatizes a unique challenge raised by the fact of moral disagreement. Such disagreement presents a range of challenges to moral understanding. Some philosophers have appealed to the fact of moral disagreement to challenge the possibility of moral knowledge, and so to argue for a form of moral relativism. However, Coetzee's stories identify a different challenge: Moral disagreement threatens the integrity of the self. Coetzee's work presents a unique and important failure of *recognition*, arising in situations where shared participation in moral discourse does not generate moral agreement.

Initially delivered as the 1997 Tanner lectures, and published along with a set of replies,[1] Coetzee's two stories, subtitled "The Philosophers and the Animals" and "The Poets and the Animals," were subsequently included in the 2003 novel *Elizabeth Costello*. In Coetzee's stories, the titular character, Elizabeth Costello, an aging Australian novelist, has been invited to the fictional Appleton College, where her son is a professor of physics, to deliver an invited lecture in honor of her achievements on a topic of her choosing. In her lecture, Costello raises a series of challenges to predominant modes of treatment of and thinking about nonhuman animals.

That Costello takes her topic of concern to be one of moral significance is indubitable.[2] She identifies the human treatment of animals, in

---

[1] Coetzee 1999.
[2] There is some debate about what the *primary* issue of significance is in Coetzee's text. Cora Diamond juxtaposes two approaches to *The Lives of Animals*. The first approach sees the story's primary aim as being to advance "arguments which are meant to support one way of resolving" "the ethical issue of how human beings should treat animals." Diamond 2003, 4. The second approach, which Diamond endorses, sees the story as primarily presenting "a woman haunted by what we do to animals," or "as presenting a kind of woundedness or hauntedness, a terrible rawness of nerves." 2, 3. So for Diamond the core question is whether the story aims primarily to narrativize a moral argument, or to portray a woman wounded by the human treatment of animals, grappling with "the difficulty of

particular the industrial production, harvest, and slaughter of animals, as
"an enterprise of degradation, cruelty, and killing."[3] However, her mode of
responding to this moral problem eschews some prominent philosophical
models.

First, in her skeptical attitude toward the role of reason in moral practice, Costello denies the centrality of argument and rational insight to
responding to moral challenges. Costello challenges the claim that reason
and shared reasoning might contribute to the resolution of moral disagree-
ments.[4] She claims that others have often appealed to the possession of
reason – or its absence – to justify the maltreatment of nonanimals, establishing that reason and reasoning can exacerbate moral failures.[5] And she
points instead to sympathy, the capacity "to share at times the being of
another" through imagination and thinking, and whose "seat" lies instead
in the "heart," as a more reliable guide with respect to the moral failures that we find in the Holocaust and in our treatment of nonhuman
animals – Costello does not shy away from claiming a deep similarity
between these failings.[6]

Second, Costello rejects the suggestion that her actions and concerns
are best understood to be the effects or expressions of "moral conviction":

> "But your own vegetarianism, Mrs. Costello," says President Garrard, pour-
> ing oil on troubled waters: "it comes out of moral conviction, does it not?"
> "No, I don't think so," says his mother [Costello]. "It comes out of a
> desire to save my soul."[7]

Instead of understanding her actions simply to be the expressions of convictions or beliefs – convictions or beliefs that she could possibly have or
not, and still remain the same person – Costello identifies the roots of her
concern in something more fundamental, her "soul," where the fate of that
soul – its possible salvation – depends on what she does in response to the
challenge of our treatment of animals. One way of putting this suggestion
would be to say that, for Costello, these concerns are constitutive of her
very selfhood. To be sure, she no doubt *has* what we would acknowledge
as moral convictions and beliefs. Her point, however, seems to be that her

reality," as Diamond puts it throughout. By contrast, interpreters like Karen Dawn and Peter Singer
(2010) argue that Diamond overstates the unsuitability of Coetzee's stories to contribute to a moral
discourse concerning the specific "issue" of our treatment of nonhuman animals.
[3] Coetzee 2004, 65.
[4] Coetzee 2004, 112.
[5] Coetzee 2004, 78–79.
[6] Coetzee 2004, 79–80.
[7] Coetzee 2004, 88–89.

actions are themselves ultimately rooted in – they "come[...] out of" – something more fundamental, which she identifies as herself.

Given her rejection of certain forms of moral discourse, namely those that rest on reason and reasoning, and her identification of the sources of moral concern with her very self, we might expect Costello not to devote significant care to the intersubjective dimensions of moral practice. One might imagine an alternative Costello who, certain of the depth and importance of her concerns, and dismissive of the need to argue those concerns to others, is confident in her moral pursuits, and indifferent to the competing claims of others, or the need to reach an agreement with them. However, Coetzee's Costello is far from this sort of moral individualist. The very fact that Costello feels the need to engage with others suggests that the theory of recognition might provide the appropriate lens through which to consider her distinctive struggle.

Of course, it might seem far-fetched to claim that the specific failure at issue in "The Lives of Animals" is a failure of recognition, in particular in the absence of some clarification about the nature of that relation. To be sure, Coetzee's stories highlight at least two senses in which Costello *is* recognized. The prominence of the human mistreatment of nonhuman animals in the stories highlights a first sense in which Costello is not denied recognition, namely that her *rights* – be they legal or moral – are in no way violated. She is not subject to violent attack or threat. She is not prevented from speaking publicly regarding her convictions, and nor is she subject to persecution for holding and expressing them. The general situation that Coetzee portrays in the stories highlights a second sense in which Costello is the object of appropriate recognition: She has been invited to Appleton College to deliver a talk as an *honor*, a form of recognition for her distinctive achievements as a novelist. There are, then, at least two important senses in which Costello is recognized in Coetzee's stories. Based on the theory of recognition that Stephen Darwall defends, these seem to be the only two forms that recognition can take: the ascription of authority to another as a being possessing dignity (recognition respect), and the ascription of value to a person in virtue of their distinctive nonmoral achievements (honor respect).[8]

---

[8] On recognition respect, see Darwall 2006. For the distinction between recognition respect and honor respect, see Darwall 2013. Of course, Darwall also thinks we can distinguish a third form of respect, moral esteem, from these others. See Darwall 1977. But unlike recognition respect and honor respect, he does not identify esteem as a kind of recognition. The ground for this distinction seems to be that esteem is merely an "attitude," not "something we broadly *do*," while, presumably, the other forms of recognition are things that "we broadly do." Darwall 2013, 17.

However, the specific failure of recognition that the stories dramatize is rather one of a distinctive sort of *moral* recognition that Darwall does not countenance, the failure to achieve a unique standing as a participant in moral discourse. Of course, there are many different ways in which individuals can be denied recognition as participants in the practice of moral discourse. One would be when individuals are excluded generally from participation in moral discourse, for example when they are deemed not competent to make claims and engage with others in moral discussion. Darwall might account for this failure as the failure to ascribe appropriate moral authority to another participant in discourse, and so as a failure of what he calls recognition respect. However, this failure is not the one that we find in Coetzee's story: Costello is not only welcomed as a participant in moral discourse, she is given a particularly prominent role within that discourse.

Instead, Coetzee's story dramatizes and makes one of its primary objects the meaning of moral disagreement. And actual moral disagreement is possible only if the others with whom we disagree actually admit us into the practice of moral discourse. Indeed, we ought to read Coetzee's story as exploring the importance of moral discourse to moral practice more generally. In so doing, we can draw on a helpful distinction that Cheshire Calhoun sets out between two sorts of moral failure. On her account, morality is driven by two "ideals."[9] According to the first ideal, the aim of moral thinking is to "get things right," to articulate the standards for appropriate action. According to the second, the aim of morality is to make possible participation in a shared scheme of social cooperation. On the basis of this latter ideal, morality consists of a kind of social practice whose aim is the achievement of a likemindedness with others that enables us to live together. Calhoun dwells on the example of moral revolutionaries to identify cases where these two ideals conflict: In arguing that the predominant standards for "getting it right" are morally flawed, the moral revolutionary undermines the possibility of realizing the second ideal, since they appeal to standards for action that others fail to acknowledge. In Calhoun's picture, success in "getting things right" morally can itself produce a (second) kind of moral failure, since it can undermine our ability to achieve a condition of likemindedness with others.

We might understand Costello's evident concern with engaging in moral discourse – even if that discourse eschews the norms of reason and rationality – to be an expression of her attachment to this second ideal.

[9] Calhoun 2016.

Indeed, it is evident throughout Coetzee's story that Costello experiences the interpersonal tensions that arise when others do not share our moral concerns, or criticize or dismiss them. Moreover, her case presents a powerful claim about the *source* of the need for achieved likemindedness with others. That is, for Costello, that likemindedness does not seem to be important primarily for consequentialist reasons, connected to the benefits of or instrumental necessity for cooperation. Instead, that likemindedness derives its importance from its contribution to the integrity of the self.

For Costello, the issue is not simply the experience of a harmony between her own convictions and those of others. Instead, the challenge stems from the significance of *others'* failure to acknowledge and value appropriately what she takes to be objects of moral importance. She expresses the sense of disorientation that such disagreement can generate to her son as follows:

> "It's that I no longer know where I am. I seem to move around perfectly easily among people, to have perfectly normal relations with them. Is it possible, I ask myself, that all of them are participants in a crime of stupefying proportions? Am I fantasizing it all? I must be mad! Yet every day I see the evidences. The very people I suspect produce the evidence, exhibit it, offer it to me. Corpses. Fragments of corpses that they have bought for money."
>
> "It is as if I were to visit friends, and to make some polite remark about the lamp in their living room, and they were to say, 'Yes, it's nice, isn't it? Polish-Jewish skin it's made of, we find that's best, the skins of young Polish-Jewish virgins.' And then I go to the bathroom and the soap wrapper says, 'Treblinka – 100% human stearate.' Am I dreaming, I say to myself? What kind of house is this?"
>
> "Yet I'm not dreaming. I look into your eyes, into Norma's, into the children's, and I see only kindness, human kindness. Calm down, I tell myself, you are making a mountain out of a molehill. This is life. Everyone comes to terms with it, why can't you? *Why can't you?*"[10]

So for Costello, this experience of disagreement does not simply prompt an attitude of accusation against others for failing to see the moral truth as she does. Instead, it undermines the possibility of a coherent experience of her own self. The challenge that she issues to herself – "*Why can't you?*" – indicates the persistence of this experience of a contradiction within herself: It is directed to herself ("Why can't *you*?"), but the fact that the challenge expresses her *failure* to "come to terms with it" ("Why *can't* you?"), indicates her inability to separate herself from the objects of her moral concern, even in the face of such disagreement.

---

[10] Coetzee 2004, 114–115. Italics in original.

This specific failure that Coetzee's stories dramatize – one in which the failure to achieve likemindedness with others threatens the integrity of the self – can therefore be understood as a failure to achieve *recognition*. Recognition is a relation between subjects that shapes, or in some cases, even constitutes, the selfhood of one or more of them. And when others fail to recognize me, that failure can itself threaten or undermine the integrity of my selfhood. Coetzee's stories point to the distinctiveness of what we can call moral recognition, the sort of recognition that is afforded to us as full participants in moral discourse, in distinction from the perhaps more-familiar forms of recognition that we enjoy as the bearers of rights or as the recipients of honor. Situations of moral disagreement of the kind that Coetzee portrays, in which this recognition is lacking, highlight its significance and importance for securing the selfhood of its recipients.

We have in view, at this point, at least two significant questions: What is the self if it can be undermined by the absence of moral recognition, and that it can be secured through it? And what are the conditions in which moral recognition is actually possible? One worry that we might have in linking moral recognition and selfhood in this way is that we seem to undermine the possibility of a consistent experience of selfhood. Given the persistence and ubiquity of moral disagreement, and if recognition requires *actual agreement* on moral questions, it seems we would rob individuals of the basis for a coherent self in linking it to recognition in this way.

Of course, it may very well be that such coherence and consistency is a rare achievement; perhaps the typical reality of being a self is the one that Coetzee's stories present in the figure of Costello. But even if such coherence is not as common as we might be inclined to expect, it still need not be the case that moral recognition – and so selfhood – depend on actual moral agreement. That is, there may be forms of moral discourse that secure relations of reciprocal recognition, but that do not require full agreement.

Among the core commitments of the following study is that these issues – the distinctively moral shape of recognition and its contribution to selfhood – are at the heart of G. W. F. Hegel's 1807 *Phenomenology of Spirit*. And, I shall argue, Hegel directly faces the challenge that moral disagreement poses to this achievement. On his account, some forms of moral disagreement will prove intractable. However, instead of identifying complete moral agreement as necessary for moral recognition, Hegel explores forms of moral discourse in which agents can be participants who can nonetheless achieve shared understanding, even if that shared understanding of themselves and one another falls short of complete agreement on moral questions.

In considering the significance of moral recognition, Hegel also emphasizes the vulnerability of the self to others. Coetzee's stories explore the threat to selfhood that profound moral disagreement poses, and Hegel's text provides us with a framework for understanding that threat, a framework provided by the concept of recognition. Arguably, Coetzee's stories present us with no ultimate resolution to this challenge. But they do point, in a negative way, to such a resolution: Through the recognition of others, we become ourselves.

2

Through the recognition of others, we become ourselves. This statement has the air of paradox about it, and it is, by itself, ambiguous. How might "we" "become ourselves"? Aren't "we," in an important if not fundamental sense, already "ourselves"? Of course, I – presumably I count among this "we" – have depended on others in myriad ways to become who I am now. But why highlight *recognition* as the unique relation to others that is so important for this coming to be? "Recognition of others" itself bears a deep ambiguity. Especially if we think of human development, we might be inclined to think that it is being recognized *by* others that is essential to becoming ourselves. But that thought often obscures the importance of *recognizing* others. Consider an analogy with love: Being loved is no doubt essential to upbringing, but coming to be able to love another is, while deeply different, arguably just as important to human development. Likewise, being recognized by others is important to becoming ourselves. But equally important are the sorts of relations that we develop when we learn to recognize others.

We find these same ambiguities in one of the core claims of Hegel's *Phenomenology of Spirit*: "Self-consciousness is *in* and *for itself* when and because it is in and for itself for an other; that is, it is only as something recognized [*ein Anerkanntes*]."[11] What is "self-consciousness" that it can exist "in and for itself" only when it is recognized? Why highlight recognition as the distinctive relation that is necessary for this self-consciousness? Even if this passage points to the importance of being recognized for the achievement of self-consciousness, it bears noting that throughout the text, Hegel identifies the relevant *relation* as the act of "recognizing" (*Anerkennen*). (By contrast, contemporary scholarship focuses much more on the *condition*

---

[11] *PhG* 109/¶178

of "recognition" [*Anerkennung*], a term that actually appears only once in Hegel's text, and not in the famous account of "Self-Consciousness.")[12]

The following study aims to resolve these ambiguities through a close reading of Hegel's *Phenomenology*. I say more about the method that I follow in presenting that reading in what follows. But I can set out in broad strokes the main argument that I take Hegel to be advancing in the text.

For Hegel, recognizing and being recognized are essential to *self-knowledge*. Considered from the side of activity – recognizing – I can only recognize another when my act is guided by an accurate understanding of that other. And likewise, considered from the side of the condition – being-recognized – I can be recognized by another only when they recognize *me*, which in turn presupposes an accurate understanding on their part of what I am. In the terms that Hegel introduces in *Phenomenology*, recognition requires a true conception of "the self" (*das Selbst*), a term that Hegel first introduces around the work's mid-point, and a concept that structures much of his account of "spirit."[13]

What sort of idea is the idea of "the self" and what sort of knowledge is self-knowledge? The idea of the self has what we can identify as two essential poles in Hegel's account. On the one hand, I am always "*this* self," a singular individual, with my own "particular thoughts, sensations, perceptual experiences, physical properties, and actions," and indeed my own desires, interests, tastes, and convictions. One dimension of self-knowledge is the project of coming to understand these aspects of my constitution. On the other, I also know that there are other selves, so that selfhood is a status that is universal, that I share with you and others. There is another dimension of self-knowledge that will be concerned with understanding "the kind of thing that we are."[14] And both of these dimensions of selfhood will be significant for my efforts to recognize you, which will succeed only to the extent that they acknowledge both of these poles.[15]

---

[12] *PhG* 248/¶456
[13] Beyond the Preface (which Hegel wrote only after completing the rest of the work) we find the first explicit mention of the self in the treatment of phrenology. (*PhG* 191/¶344) From the conclusion of the discussion of reason to the end of the text, the expression becomes ubiquitous.
[14] On the two poles of selfhood – being "*this* self" and a "universal" self – see, e.g., *PhG* 286/¶525, 351/¶652. The distinction between knowledge of "the kind of things we are" and "*particular* self-knowledge" is from Cassam 1994, 1.
[15] The question of what the self is is therefore distinct from the question of personal identity, at least in one of its formulations. The latter question often focuses narrowly on the persistence conditions of my existence – how I can remain the same being over time – and need not concern itself with the question of what makes me the particular individual I am, or the more general question of the sorts of beings we all are.

Of course, even if we grant that recognition will succeed only if it is guided by a true conception of the other whom we recognize, a true conception of "the self," why is this recognition necessary for me to know myself? Why isn't it possible for me to begin with an accurate conception of what I am, and then simply apply that to others in my acts of recognition? Why does selfhood depend on others in this way?

A significant part of Hegel's argument about "the self" in *Phenomenology* is negative or skeptical, directed against the claim that I can be conscious of myself as I am of objects outside of me, or that I can intuit myself directly through immediate reflection, or that I can know myself through passive observation. While I shall consider some of these skeptical arguments in what follows, Hegel ultimately holds that my inability to know myself in separation from distinctive relations to others lies in part in my distinctive nature as a self-conscious being. In Hegel's phrase, the "essence of self-consciousness" consists of "absolute negativity, *pure being-for-self*," "pure universal movement, absolute becoming-fluid of every continuing existence."[16] Absent determinate relations to others, I am unable to know myself because, as a self-conscious being, my "essence" is nothing positive, but rather this "absolute negativity," my *not*-being any determinate object, but instead the capacity to dissolve any fixed characteristic or relation through self-conscious activity. The problem with individualistic models of self-knowledge is not simply epistemic, but rather ontological: the purported object of self-knowledge is, by itself, something negative, and not a positive being that might be given to these sorts of knowledge (immediate awareness, reflection, observation).

We might be inclined to think that, given these robust claims about the essence of self-consciousness, it is unreasonable to expect that relations of recognition will provide much help in arriving at self-knowledge. However, Hegel argues instead that the project of self-knowledge is itself guided by the same dialectical movement that animates the series of forms of consciousness that the text as a whole tracks. The negativity of self-consciousness need not simply be the empty abstraction of nothingness, whose "movement" is a "mere *negative* movement."[17] Instead, the negativity that belongs to the essence of self-consciousness is better understood as a negativity that gives rise to content, a "*determinate* negation." And it is at this point that the activity and condition of recognizing and being recognized are significant for the issue of self-knowledge. Even if immediate

[16] *PhG* 114/¶194.
[17] *PhG* 57/¶79.

awareness, reflection, or passive observation will not yield knowledge of what I am, the activity of taking others to be selves and of others so taking me can yield a stable self-relation that amounts to self-knowledge.

We can appreciate what is distinctive in Hegel's appeal to recognition in this connection by contrasting it with Cavell's well-known idea of "acknowledgment." For Cavell, the demand for acknowledgment arises in response to a skeptical worry about our capacity to know others' minds. In the absence of that knowledge, Cavell proposes that acknowledgment should take the place of knowledge in establishing appropriate relations with others.[18] By contrast, for Hegel, the epistemic challenge that recognition addresses is not simply that of knowing *others*, but rather *self-knowledge*. And recognition does not take the place of that knowledge. Instead, the activity of recognizing is itself partially constitutive of self-knowledge, a specific intentional relation to others whose ultimate aim is the achievement of a specific cognitive relation to myself.

A determinate idea of the self is necessary because it structures relations among self-conscious beings so that those are relations of recognition. For Hegel, the concept of the self is a determination of "spirit" (*Geist*). This means that conceptions of the self are essentially social.[19] Instead of understanding the self, for example, as a simple substance that exists independent of relations to others and to the world, conceptions of the self are complex, comprised of a constellation of constituent concepts: namely self-conscious agents and the shared worlds that guide their actions and that they sustain through their activity.[20] In addition to being social and complex, conceptions of the self are, for Hegel, normative. That is, I exist as a self only when I participate in specific shared social practices. And I succeed in satisfying the criteria that are constitutive of the self when my activities fulfill a set of norms that are themselves complex. Different conceptions of the self involve different criteria that identify different features of the agent as significant, mandate different understandings of the relation between the agent and their deeds

---

[18] Cavell 1969.
[19] In general, the account of spirit that I offer focuses on Hegel's use of that term through chapter VI of *Phenomenology*. By consequence, my primary interest is in understanding its implications for his social theory, especially as that bears on his account of relations between subjects. By consequence, I do not dwell much – beyond a brief reflection in §5.3 – on the well-known controversies concerning the religious and metaphysical dimensions of this idea. Throughout, I refer to the chapters in the *Phenomenology* with the uncapitalized "chapter," as in "chapter VI" above. I refer to sections of this book using "§" and Arabic numerals as in "§5.3" above. And I refer to chapters in this book using the capitalized "Chapter," as in "Chapter 1: Self-Consciousness."
[20] See Bykova's (2009) account of the relation between spirit and the self in terms of a conception of "concrete subjectivity."

and entail different conceptions of the proper role of language in mediating these elements. Because of its rootedness in practice, the self, therefore, has a normative foundation: selves exist when self-conscious agents determine their deeds and language in accordance with the specific standards inherent to particular practices. As a determination of spirit, the self depends on the shared acknowledgment of a set of commonly binding norms.[21]

While there are different conceptions of what it means to be a self, not all of them make possible relations of recognition among self-conscious agents. In particular, in order to make possible relations of recognition, a conception of the self must satisfy two criteria. First, Hegel argues that relations of recognition are essentially *reciprocal* (*gegenseitig*) – in Hegel's terms, the idea of reciprocity belongs to the "pure concept" of recognition.[22] That reciprocity depends on an idea of the self that can be affirmed equally of all who might be parties to relations of recognition. So the first criterion that a conception of the self must satisfy is an *equality* criterion. Second, for a relation to count as one of recognition, the description under which I am recognized must be one that I can affirm of myself. When your activities are guided by a determinate conception of the self, that conception of the self must accord with what I take myself to be in order for you to recognize *me*. Conceptions of the self that fail to do this entrench an experience and condition of *alienation*. Charles Taylor rightly identifies one of the central challenges for the theory of recognition to lie in addressing problems of misrecognition: "A person or group can suffer real damage, real distortion, if the people or society around them mirror back to them a confining or demeaning or contemptible picture of themselves."[23]

---

21 In the terms that I employ in what follows, relations of reciprocal intersubjective recognition among subjects depend on their mutual recognition of a set of shared norms. I agree with Bykova's (2019, 165) assertion that Hegel's account of the self is "not limited solely to mutual recognition." This claim is true both in that the self stems from "social" relations that are not directly determinate relations between subjects, and that its implications extend beyond his account of the conditions for recognition. At the same time, in *Phenomenology*, the idea of the self is at the core of Hegel's account of recognition, and its *primary* significance in that text lies in its contribution to that account.

22 *PhG* 110/¶¶184–185. I present Hegel's argument for the claim that recognition is essentially reciprocal in §1.2.

23 C. Taylor 1994, 25. At the same time, Taylor's account is distinct from Hegel's in at least two ways. First, Taylor understands recognition primarily in terms of a conception of identity, which he links to the experience of having a certain sort of culture. By contrast, for Hegel, recognition shapes and determines not just an individual's particular identity, but the more basic conception of what it means to be a self that is shared in a given social form. And Hegel understands the importance of ethical life to lie not simply in the contribution that it makes to shaping one's identity, but more importantly in its role in establishing relations of *reciprocity* among individuals. Second, Taylor seems to treat "nonrecognition" and "misrecognition" in basically the same terms. By contrast, for Hegel, these constitute importantly different failures of recognition.

So the second criterion that a conception of the self must satisfy to make recognition possible is a *nonalienation* criterion.

These criteria have an important bearing on the issue of what is distinctive about Hegel's account of recognition in *Phenomenology*. The idea that recognition requires participation in specific normatively governed social practices might suggest that the ultimate requirement of a theory of recognition lies in spelling out those specific institutions that make it possible.[24] That is, it might sound like the theory of recognition requires an account of the institutions comprising a specific form of *Sittlichkeit*, or "ethical life."[25] Indeed, this suggestion has provided the basis for a common criticism that, in the absence of an account of such institutions, the conception of recognition that we find in *Phenomenology* is incomplete.[26] For interpreters

[24] We can distinguish between normatively governed social practices and specific institutions, such as the family, civil society, or the state. In my reading, Hegel's account of recognition in *Phenomenology* depends on the idea of social practices, but not on a specific theory of institutions.

[25] While I am drawn to the more literal translation of *Sittlichkeit* as "ethicality," I also acknowledge that this term poses a deep challenge for translation, in particular since neither choice adequately conveys the term's link to the German *Sitte*, custom, which, as we shall see, is central to Hegel's conception.

[26] We find the roots of this idea in Habermas's "Labor and Interaction," perhaps the most influential text for understanding Hegel's theory of recognition, aside from Kojève's lectures. Habermas advances the claim that recognition's primary importance lies in its contribution to the *Bildung* of self-consciousness. Habermas 1967/1968, 13. According to Habermas, in *Phenomenology*, Hegel abandons the social model of the *Bildung* of self-consciousness that we find in the earlier Jena lectures in favor of a monological philosophy of reflection. Ludwig Siep takes up Habermas's claim that recognition is essential to the *Bildung* of self-consciousness, while rejecting the claim that *Phenomenology* depends on a monological conception of spirit, instead arguing that the latter develops through forms of interaction. However, because he links recognition so tightly to the idea of *Bildung*, Siep is prompted to regard the theory of recognition that we find in *Phenomenology* as essentially *incomplete*. He looks instead to the Jena philosophy of spirit for an account of the institutions on which such a complete theory ultimately depends. Siep 2014, chapter 4. We find a similar move in the prominent recent interpretations of Robert Pippin and Dean Moyar. For Pippin, *Phenomenology*'s primary task lies in undermining accounts of the individual as independent of relations of recognition. The mature *Philosophy of Right* takes over the task that Siep assigns to the Jena philosophy of spirit, in presenting a theory of the institutions in which recognition is actual: "The ethical life theory *is* an account of successful recognition, or a mutuality based on a kind of rational acknowledgement." Pippin 2008, 185. Likewise, Moyar argues that *Phenomenology* presents a picture of the *process* of recognition through which society's structures are transformed over time, promoting what he calls *direct* relations of recognition. By contrast, he looks to the mature philosophy of objective spirit to find an account of the *relation* of recognition through determinate norms and values, through which subjects are objects of *indirect* recognition through their participation in free institutions. Moyar 2011, 144ff. In what follows, I challenge the claims that Hegel's theory of recognition in *Phenomenology* is incomplete because it is primarily concerned with the *Bildung* of self-consciousness or relations of recognition, and that it therefore depends on a theory of the specific institutions of a form of ethical life for its completion. Instead, I argue that we find a complete account of recognition in the text, and that that account does not depend on a theory of institutions of the kind that we find in the *Philosophy of Right*. I expand on these competing interpretations in §1.3.

like Pippin, such an institutional theory is required since institutions provide the terms on the basis of which individuals justify their actions one to another, and so are conditions for being recognized as such an agent.[27]

By contrast, in pursuing the question of the conception of the self adequate to the achievement of relations of reciprocal recognition, Hegel is not engaged in an inquiry into those specific institutions that make such recognition possible. Instead, he considers how those bound by relations of recognition must understand themselves and one another in order for those relations to be possible. I shall have only a little to say about the compatibility between the approach that Hegel takes to these issues in *Phenomenology of Spirit*, and the status of recognition in the mature philosophy of objective spirit in what follows. In general, I take him to be engaged in a *different* project in the early work, so that we find there a distinctive conception of recognition and the conditions for its success. Instead of attending primarily to different conceptions of the plural and particular institutions that make recognition possible, Hegel is instead concerned with the question of what unified and universal conception of the self individuals must share in order to recognize and be recognized by others, and so to be themselves. Hegel's account of "Spirit" in chapter VI of the text resembles less the mature philosophy of right, the Jena accounts of ethical life, or the philosophy of spirit, which all do focus on specific institutions, than it does the sort of inquiry into different conceptions of the self that have animated (at least western European) self-understanding from ancient Greece to the present that we find in Charles Taylor's *Sources of the Self*.[28] One of the central contentions of the following study is that this attention to the question of the self is inseparable from the theory of recognition that we find in Hegel's text.[29]

---

[27] See in particular Pippin's remarks on "institutional rationality" in Pippin 2008, 262–266 especially. For Honneth, institutions play an analogous role in contributing to the achievement of recognition and social freedom. See Honneth 2011, 93: "The institutions of recognition are not merely appendages or external presuppositions of intersubjective freedom; because without them subjects would not be able to know their reciprocal dependence on one another, they form at once the ground and site of the actualization of this freedom."

[28] Cobben notes that Hegel offers not only a historical account of the emergence of the self, but rather "a systematic, conceptual development of the self." Cobben 2009, 1. Siep rightly points out that, in *Phenomenology*, the concerns of social and moral philosophy are "subordinated to epistemological and ontological questions." Siep 2000, 81–82. Hegel's concern with the self – and, I shall argue, his account of recognition – in the text are addressed primarily to ontological questions about what we are, rather than to moral or political claims about how we ought to act or live.

[29] By consequence, I disagree with the approach to questions of recognition taken by interpreters like Stekeler-Weithofer, who seem to aim to deny the significance of recognition for directly interpersonal interactions. Instead, for Stekeler-Weithofer, recognition is primarily of "institutions" (2014, 2, 243) or "actions" (645), but not directly of other individuals. ("It is completely unclear what it would mean in general to recognize persons as persons." [683]) By contrast, I argue that such

Hegel identifies three conceptions of the self that emerge in the course of the experience of "spirit" – that of the legal "person," that of "absolute freedom," and that of "conscience" – each having its place in a specific "world" of spirit – the ethical world, the world of culture, and that of morality, respectively.[30] In each case, Hegel suggests that a determinate conception of the self emerges as a "totality or actuality" comprising the "truth" of that given world. So the articulation of a conception of the self is a sort of achievement that emerges within the dialectical process of experience. Moreover, Hegel identifies each of these conceptions of the self in terms of the issue of recognition, where the self's existence consists of "being-recognized" (*Anerkanntsein*). In so doing, he aims to highlight two features of a conception of the self. First, it is a norm whose existence depends on its recognition by agents within that specific social world. And second, as such a norm, it is supposed to make it possible for agents within that world to be recognized by others.

At the same time, Hegel argues that we find a sort of progressive development from the first conception of the self to the last, arguing that the first two conceptions, those of the person and absolute freedom, are inadequate for the achievement of relations of fully reciprocal recognition. In the terms that I've introduced, personhood satisfies the *equality* criterion that reciprocal recognition requires, since it is a conception of the self that can apply to all participants in a given social world. However, personhood alone is insufficient to secure relations of recognition, because, Hegel contends, being recognized *solely* as a person is *alienating*, since it cannot take account of the ways in which I make myself through those deeds and actions that I take to matter. By contrast, absolute freedom satisfies the *nonalienation* requirement, since it acknowledges the authoritativeness of my own will. However, it cannot satisfy the *equality* requirement, since it undermines the shared bases for reciprocity in intersubjective relations. In Hegel's terms, it is incapable of generating the shared social "world" that is necessary for such reciprocity.

Tracking the genesis and development of the self within Hegel's account indicates important distinctions between what I call different

---

directly interpersonal encounters are central to Hegel's account of recognition, and that we clarify what it means to recognize another individual by treating them in accordance with the demands stemming from a distinctive conception of the self, so that, for example, recognizing the other as a (legal) person is obviously different from recognizing them as a conscientious individual who addresses distinctively moral claims to me.

[30] *PhG* 341–342/¶633. Others have acknowledged the significance of this passage for making sense of the argument of the "Spirit" chapter as a whole. See especially Cobben 2009, but also Wildt 1982, 384 and Siep 2014, 132.

"models" of recognition to which these conceptions of the self correspond. "Personhood" corresponds to what I call an "automatic" model of recognition, according to which recognition is something that we owe to others simply in virtue of being the sorts of creatures they always already are. In indicting "personhood" as an alienating conception of the self, Hegel also indicates the need to adopt a new model of recognition, which I call the "achievement" model, in which I come to merit recognition not in virtue of what I always already *am*, but rather in virtue of what I *become*. In his discussion of "culture" (*Bildung*), Hegel considers different conceptions of the end that I might adopt to merit recognition in this way.[31] The failure of "absolute freedom" to make possible relations of reciprocal recognition points to a deep similarity between the models of recognition corresponding to it and to "personhood." Both are instances of *responsive* models of recognition, according to which recognition is essentially a response to the possession of a determinate trait, either one that I always already possess (as in the case of personhood) or one that I come to achieve as a result of my own activity (as in the case of culture).

By contrast, with the introduction of the third conception of the self, "conscience," Hegel points to the need for a new model of recognition that is not responsive, but *constitutive*. In *Phenomenology*, Hegel shows that it is only when I recognize others and am recognized by them as "conscience" that fully reciprocal relations of recognition are possible. In the text, conscience identifies a conception of the self, a norm that requires a specific relation between my attitudes, actions, and speech, so that conscientiousness is not a simple property that inheres in me, but is instead the product of my engagement in a concrete practice that I identify as that of "moral discourse." That practice is one in which my actions are understood to be the realization of my convictions about what is right, and which is a form of discourse because it holds that the act of expressing my convictions to others and of addressing the claims that others make on and before me are both essential. Conscience satisfies the *equality* criterion necessary for the achievement of reciprocal recognition because it is a norm that can equally bind all participants in the practice of moral discourse. And it satisfies the *nonalienation* criterion because I can only recognize you as conscientious

---

[31] Throughout, I translate "*Bildung*" as "culture." This translation is imperfect. *Bildung*, from the verb *bilden*, "to form," refers first and foremost to a process of "formation" or "enculturation." So we are better off thinking of "culture" as a process of culturing, of growth and development. Hegel's account of the world of *Bildung* tracks the "coming to be" of the self as a result of a process of self-transformation on the part of the individual. For an able account of Hegel's concept of *Bildung*, see Bykova 2020.

through engagement with the concrete claims that you make on and before me, claims that give expression to what you take to matter. (Of course, as Coetzee's stories about Elizabeth Costello make plain, because it requires engagement with the concrete claims that we make on and before one another, actually recognizing and being recognized by one another as conscientious is a particularly fraught matter.) This recognition entails a constitutive model of recognition, since it is only through participation in the shared practice of moral discourse that I come to have the status of conscientiousness: Moral practice is actually constitutive of the self.[32]

Of course, given this presentation, my conclusions may sound familiar to those that we find in Axel Honneth's *Struggle for Recognition*. There, Honneth argues that the concept of recognition provides the "moral grammar of social conflict." For Honneth, recognition derives its significance from its contribution to the achievement of appropriate self-relations. Social conflict, in turn, stems from situations where individuals are denied recognition, and so are unable to achieve those self-relations. The concept of recognition is therefore essential for understanding the different shapes that social conflict can assume: "It is through the morally motivated struggles of social groups, their collective attempt to help themselves institutionally and collectively to the assertion of more extensive forms of reciprocal recognition, that the normatively directed transformation of societies takes place practically."[33] Honneth's account is similar to the one that I am ascribing to Hegel in *Phenomenology of Spirit* in that both identify the core contribution of recognition to the achievement of a distinctive sort of "selfhood," and that they both interpret the primary significance of recognition in moral terms.

However, the *Phenomenology of Spirit* view differs in significant respects from Honneth's. Most importantly, for Honneth, the relevant moral claims are claims *to recognition*, where recognition comprises the content of the claims that social groups make on and before others.[34] By contrast, it is not necessary for recognition to provide the normative content of

---

[32] The moral dimension of our constitution is essential for being a self, then. Moreover, Hegel aims to demonstrate that morality is not optional because it is through addressing and responding to the demands of others that we secure one of the essential poles of our existence as selves, its universal dimension, shared with others. To be sure, Hegel argues that it is essential that recognition not ignore our particularity, the things that matter to me as "*this* self." But he will argue that I cannot coherently anchor my selfhood solely in terms of a "ground project" whose importance I cannot justify to others, since I would thereby neglect the other essential pole of selfhood. The phrase is, of course, that of B. Williams 1981.

[33] Honneth 1992, 149.

[34] For criticism of the suggestion that the concept of recognition can also provide the content for the claims at the heart of social struggle, see Fraser 2003.

moral claims in Hegel's account. Consider, again, the case of Elizabeth Costello. Costello does not explicitly frame her moral challenge regarding our treatment of nonhuman animals as a challenge about recognition or its absence.³⁵ Recognition does not enter into the content of her engagement in moral discourse. And that means that moral discourse can be significant for the achievement of recognition, even if the content of that discourse does not itself include appeals to recognition. Engagement with Costello's claims is essential to recognizing her successfully. But her claims need not themselves be understood as claims about recognition or its denial.

This aspect of the conception of recognition that Hegel advances in *Phenomenology* is significant because it indicates a diminished role for institutions in that conception. While Hegel does think that recognition depends on a shared "world," we can make sense of that shared world in terms of normatively governed social practices, rather than in terms of a set of fixed institutions. To Hegel, recognition will be possible as long as those practices support moral discourse. But that means that recognition can be an engine for institutional transformation: As long as the conditions for participation in moral discourse remain, moral discourse and the recognition that it makes possible can be sites of criticism and change.³⁶ That is, the conception of recognition that Hegel defends in *Phenomenology* is suited to the "time of birth and transition to a new period" in which "The spirit has broken with the previous world of its existence and representation, and it is about to sink it back into the past, in the labor of [spirit's] own transfiguration. Because spirit is grasped never in rest but always in progressive movement."³⁷ And one of Hegel's aims in the text is to present an account of recognition according to which those transformations in the world of spirit need not undermine spirit itself, and the relations of reciprocal recognition in which it is actual.

3

I have claimed that the *Phenomenology of Spirit* account of recognition is neither incomplete nor dependent on a theory of rational institutions that we ought to seek elsewhere. These substantive claims about the character

---

³⁵ Of course, one *might* try to argue that the idea of recognition can play such a role for making sense of our treatment of nonhuman animals. See, for example, M. J. Thompson 2011. However, it is significant that, both in Coetzee's stories and in Hegel's *Phenomenology*, that role need not be fulfilled by recognition.

³⁶ So we find here another significant link to Honneth, for whom the struggle for recognition is significant in making sense of social transformation. Of course, again, for Hegel, that transformation can be rooted in moral claims generally, rather than in specific claims to recognition.

³⁷ *PhG* 14/¶11.

of the concept of recognition that we find in the text grow out of the approach that I take in the following work.

This book concerns the idea of recognition as it emerges and develops in *Phenomenology of Spirit*. I do not include among my *primary* tasks relating that concept to its emergence in Hegel's early writings,[38] or to considering its fate in his mature philosophy.[39] Instead, I begin in earnest where Hegel introduces the idea of recognition in the text, namely the account of "Self-Consciousness." There, Hegel identifies a specific configuration of recognition – reciprocal recognition (*gegenseitiges Anerkennen*) – as necessary for a certain kind of knowledge, consciousness's knowledge of itself. However, this reciprocal recognition is initially announced only as the goal of a specific "movement" or "process" (or "trial" [*Prozeß*]),[40] a movement that only resolves itself at the conclusion of Hegel's account of "spirit" in the text, in the treatment of "conscience."[41] If we, therefore, focus our investigation on Hegel's text itself, rather than on earlier or later works, we find a clear and distinctive account of the roots of the appeal to recognition, and of the resolution of its movement.

There is a second sense in which this study takes its orientation from the text of *Phenomenology of Spirit*. That is, throughout, I attend closely to the specific terms that Hegel employs in connection with the thematic of recognition – *Anerkennen* and its cognates, "counting" (*gelten*) as an individual, reciprocity (recognition that is *gegenseitig*), and equality (*Gleichheit*). Since I demonstrate that the concept of "the self" is at the core of Hegel's account of successful reciprocal recognition, I devote equal attention to distinguishing between different terms whose meanings we might be inclined to elide in thinking about the self – most centrally, *das Selbst*, but also consciousness of itself (*Bewußtsein seiner selbst*), self-consciousness (*Selbstbewußtsein*), self-conscious reason, and self-conscious spirit. Finally, I dwell significantly on understanding *why* Hegel would treat relations of reciprocal recognition as impossible for certain standpoints (like those of "self-consciousness" or "reason"), but not others. This close attention to the text itself is important because it helps to clarify when the idea of recognition is relevant to Hegel's account in the text, and when it is not. My account is guided by the axiom that, if Hegel wants us to understand a specific development or concept in terms of the idea of recognition, he

---

[38] For studies that do, see Habermas 1967/1968, Siep 2014, and Honneth 1992.
[39] See most notably Pippin 2008, but also R. Williams 1997.
[40] *PhG* 109/¶178, 110/¶185.
[41] *PhG* 361/¶670. This development is noted clearly by Brinkmann 2003, 243. See also Siep 1998, 118–119; Siep 2008, 182–184; and Siep 2010, 112–113.

will himself establish or signal that connection. In this way, my reading of the text is a *de dicto* reading, oriented to making sense of what Hegel actually says, that contextualizes what he says in light of the other things that he says in the book.[42]

This study takes as its primary focus the issue of recognition in *Phenomenology of Spirit*. As such, it is not concerned with unpacking the overall argument of the work as a whole. Instead, I direct my attention primarily to those portions of the text in which recognition is at issue. Of course, given the importance of the dynamic of recognition to the general tasks that Hegel sets for himself in the book, the arguments that I consider are not irrelevant to its overall significance.[43] Likewise, this study is not a commentary on the text, oriented toward identifying specific historical referents for the specific details Hegel considers.[44] Of course, I don't hesitate to point to some of these when doing so is helpful to grasp Hegel's aims and intentions. However, my primary aim here is to reconstruct the argument that Hegel offers regarding the issue of recognition in the text.

Prior studies of the issue of recognition fail to take seriously the argument that Hegel advances throughout the book. Many scholars focus their attention on the emergence of the idea of recognition in Hegel's account of self-consciousness, but fail to follow through to consider the conditions for the achievement of relations of reciprocal recognition in Hegel's account of spirit. The political account of recognition that Kojève made famous, for example, reads the entire development of the book in chapters IV–VI through the lens of the struggle to the death that generates the relationship between lord and bondsman. But there is little evidence that Hegel ascribes to *that* relationship the sort of significance for the rest of the book that interpreters like Kojève do.[45] And Kojève ultimately understands the resolution of that struggle in a specific political doctrine.[46] However,

---

[42] This methodological commitment basically distinguishes my approach to the text from that of Brandom 2019. Throughout, I identify some of the principal ways that I believe that Brandom's competing *de re* approach generates some basic confusions about Hegel's core concepts.
[43] I offer a few considerations regarding that overall significance in my conclusion.
[44] For extensive commentaries, see Harris 1997 and Stekeler-Weithofer 2014. For clear accounts of the work as a whole, see Siep 2000, Stern 2002, and Russon 2004 and 2015.
[45] See Kelly 1972 and Siep 1974. Nor is it clear how Kojève's claims about the relation between Hegel and Napoleon would resolve the problem of recognition as Kojève construes it, namely as a struggle for "prestige." Kojève 1980, 51. Or how that "mutual" struggle for prestige might be resolved by a relation between an acting statesman and a contemplative philosopher.
[46] "Man can be truly 'satisfied,' History can end, only in and by the formation of a Society, of a State, in which the strictly particular, personal, individual value of each is recognized as such, in its very particularity, by *all*, by Universality incarnated in the State as such; and in which the universal value of the State is recognized and realized by the Particular as such, by *all* the Particulars." Kojève 1980, 58.

since we find no account of "the State" in which relations of reciprocal recognition would be actual in the text, we are therefore obliged to treat the *Phenomenology* account as incomplete in this reading. Accounts like Kojève's fail to grasp the fact that the resolution to the movement of recognition in the text is not political, but moral.

We find a similar failure in interpreters who consider the movement of recognition in the text as deriving its ultimate significance from its contribution to "culture" or "formation" (*Bildung*). Habermas's account of recognition in "Labor and Interaction" is perhaps second in influence only to Kojève's famous account. In Habermas's reading, recognition derives its importance from its contribution to the formation or *Bildung* of self-consciousness.[47] While Habermas's account is based primarily on a reading of the other Jena-era writings, a range of scholars, most notable among them Ludwig Siep, have taken up the claim that, in *Phenomenology of Spirit*, too, the primary importance of recognition lies in the role it plays in *Bildung*.[48] However, interpreters of this stripe fail to identify the fact that Hegel sets out the conditions for the achievement of relations of reciprocal recognition *within Phenomenology* itself. While, in the account that I offer in what follows, he considers a specific model of recognition in his account of *Bildung* or "culture," that model of recognition is not the one that serves to make sense of the possibility of actual relations of reciprocal recognition. In the terms that I introduce, the model of recognition that we find in the account of culture is a *responsive* one – when I recognize you in virtue of your distinctive achievements, I am responding to a fact that exists independent of my recognition of it, for example, your success in besting me in a duel (to take an example of Moyar's).[49] By contrast, Hegel ultimately argues that the model of recognition within which relations of *reciprocal* recognition are possible is a *constitutive* one, in which the act of recognition constitutes the equal status that makes possible relations of reciprocity. In *Phenomenology*, we find this model of recognition in Hegel's account of *morality*, not of culture.

The idea that acts of recognizing might be constitutive of the shared status in virtue of which relations of *reciprocal* recognition might be possible should be familiar from Pippin's account of Hegel's practical philosophy. In that

---

[47] "On the basis of reciprocal recognition [*wechselseitiger Anerkennung*] self-consciousness, which must be secured through the mirroring of my own consciousness in the consciousness of another subject, forms itself [*bildet sich*]." Habermas 1967/1968, 13.
[48] For Siep, the "theory of consciousness" that Hegel develops in the text is "a theory of a process of the formation [*Bildung*] of consciousness in forms of interaction and institutions," where the "unity" of "the 'basic model' of this process [of formation] is the 'principle' of recognition." Siep 2014, 71. For similar accounts see again Moyar 2011, 144–145, Quante 2010, and Pinkard 2012.
[49] Moyar 2011, 145.

account, the relevant status is that of being an "agent," and Pippin contends that, for Hegel, agency is not a given natural or metaphysical fact about us, but instead a status that we achieve by standing in the appropriate relations to others: being recognized as an agent is partially constitutive of what it means to be an agent.[50] The claim that I defend in what follows, that we ought to understand the idea of "the self" in similarly constitutive terms, is thus deeply similar and indebted to the account of agency that Pippin defends.

At the same time, I argue that Pippin's own reading of *Phenomenology*, in particular of the concept of recognition that Hegel develops there, is flawed in important ways. In terms of approach, Pippin treats the mature philosophy of objective spirit as continuous with the *Phenomenology* account of recognition.[51] Specifically, in his reading, the primary task of *Phenomenology* is the *negative* one of undermining the opposed "liberal" account of individuals as existing independent of institutionally mediated relations of recognition.[52] Given these commitments, Pippin's interpretation fits within the broader interpretive trend of considering the *Phenomenology* account of recognition as by itself incomplete. However, when Pippin turns to consider those passages in *Phenomenology* where we *do* find achieved relations of reciprocal recognition, his interpretations are spurious. Indeed, when Pippin considers the discussion of recognition in "Conscience," on which my own account will dwell at length, he claims that Hegel "leaves his narrative 'hanging' at the end of the chapter on *Geist*" because he "does not suggest any institutional resolution" of the problem of recognition. Pippin dismisses Hegel's treatment of recognition in terms of "moral and religious practices," claiming that the problem is actually the "proper subject for political remedy" within a constitutional state.[53] However, Pippin's argument is a non sequitur. The fact that Hegel does not provide an institutional remedy to the problem of recognition does not mean that the argument of the text is irrelevant to politics. And

---

[50] According to what Pippin calls "the basic sociality claim in Hegel's practical philosophy": "[B]eing a free agent is a kind of normative status, the content and very possibility of which depends on *being recognized as*, taken to be such, a free agent within a community of mutually recognizing agents." Pippin 2008, 27–28.

[51] See again Pippin 2008, 185.

[52] See Pippin 2008, chapter 8.

[53] Pippin 2004, 264. Interpreters like Farneth follow the course that Pippin recommends avoiding, in pursuing the resolution to the account of recognition in specific religious practices and theological ideas. See Farneth 2017. On the account that I offer, the achievement of reciprocal recognition depends ultimately on shared participation in moral discourse. While certain religious views may be more germane to that practice, I argue that it need not require a shared faith, and that the account of religion that Hegel offers in chapter VII of the book does not significantly affect the picture of achieved reciprocal recognition that we find at the conclusion of chapter VI.

regardless of that relevance, it is interpretive malpractice to judge the significance of the argument that Hegel traces in the account of conscience on the basis of a set of expectations about its importance for politics that are not drawn from the text itself. On the account that I offer in what follows, Hegel does not present an "institutional" remedy to the problem of recognition because that problem is not one that institutions can resolve.

These particular features that distinguish my own approach from those of other commentators point to a fundamental difference in our understandings of the significance of recognition in *Phenomenology*. In it, Hegel does not seek to provide an account of the foundations of political life, a "practical philosophy,"[54] or a theory of freedom or agency. Instead, he appeals to the idea of recognition in trying to answer a different basic question about the achievement of self-knowledge. In the terms that I introduce in what follows, recognition's primary significance in the text lies in its contribution to an *ontology of the self*. Since, as I have been suggesting, Hegel understands the self to be in part constituted through the recognition of others, the ontology of the self will be a social ontology.[55] To be sure, this account of the self draws on experiences that are significant for politics and moral life, and it may also generate relevant implications for practical philosophy or conceptions of agency. But recognition concerns a different fundamental question about the basic character of the self.[56]

4

My account follows the emergence of the concept of recognition in *Phenomenology of Spirit*'s account of "self-consciousness" through to the achievement of fully reciprocal recognition at the conclusion of the book's

[54] For Siep, Hegel is engaged in "practical philosophy," that is, the attempt to articulate a theory of human practice that is both normatively rich (and so not merely a description of existing institutions) and also substantive and concrete (and so not dependent on a procedure of "deducing" specific actions or institutions from an abstract principle). See Siep 2014, Introduction. Compare Farneth's "social ethics." Farneth 2017, ix.

[55] A range of recent studies explore Hegel's views through the lens of the idea of social ontology. See in this connection Ikäheimo and Laitinen's (2011b) helpful overview, and the contributions in their (2011a) collection, especially Ikäheimo's (2011) account of the social ontology of Hegel's later system. See also Testa 2008; and Bykova 2008.

[56] Throughout, I link the views and arguments that we find in *Phenomenology* to those of figures in contemporary philosophy. I do this for two reasons. First, in many cases, those figures' views are more accessible to contemporary readers. Second, while Hegel's work is now over 200 years old, its core ideas are not limited in scope to its immediate surroundings. Of course, my approach may raise for some the worry that I've misconstrued those ideas, reading them through a distorting contemporary lens. I leave it to the reader to assess whether my reading of the text is an accurate one.

discussion of "spirit." It falls into two broad parts. In the first, I consider the concept of recognition, and trace Hegel's argument that successful recognition requires an adequate conception of the self. In the second, I examine the different conceptions of the self that Hegel considers in chapter VI of the text, focusing ultimately on his treatment of conscience.

Part I: Recognition: I begin, in Chapter 1, by tracing the emergence of the concept of recognition from Hegel's account of self-consciousness. I argue that, for Hegel, what is distinctive about self-consciousness is not that it is a shape of consciousness that is apperceptive, since he understands all shapes of consciousness to involve a consciousness of the specific mode in which the knower relates to the object known. Instead, I show that what is distinctive of self-consciousness is a specific structure, namely that it has a "double-object." Self-consciousness is a shape of consciousness – of the relation of a knower to an object distinct from the knower – where the first object relation mediates a second relation to the knower. So, for example, desire is a shape of self-consciousness because it involves a determinate relation to the objects of desire, which are separate from the knowing subject (the first object), but where the ultimate point of that relation is to secure a relation to the desiring subject (the second "object"). Just as the implicit aim of any shape of consciousness is to achieve knowledge of its object, so the implicit aim of a shape of self-consciousness is to achieve knowledge of its (ultimate) object, namely itself.

I argue that this structural account of self-consciousness helps to address some thorny interpretive questions about the structure of chapter IV that have proven particularly puzzling for readers. Identifying the primary aim of self-consciousness to be the achievement of adequate self-knowledge helps us to understand why recognition emerges where it does in Hegel's account: it is a more sophisticated embodiment of the same double-object structure that characterizes desire. It also helps us to correct some common interpretive errors that emerge in connection with the roots of recognition. While recognition and desire are both shapes of self-consciousness, they are distinct shapes, so it does not make sense to hold that Hegel posits the existence of a desire for recognition. Likewise, recognition is just one shape of self-consciousness among many others, so it also does not make sense to say that recognition is necessary for the achievement of self-consciousness. Instead, the implicit aim of recognition is the achievement of *self-knowledge*. Finally, my account is also uniquely capable of showing why recognition is, according to its "pure concept," reciprocal. That is, a relation of recognition between subjects has the "double-object" structure characteristic of self-consciousness only when both individuals relate to one another in the specific mode of recognition. The shape of one-sided recognition that Hegel considers in the relation between lord and bondsman points to the necessity of reciprocity for the achievement of self-knowledge. But it also raises a separate question about the conditions under which fully reciprocal recognition is actually possible.

In Chapter 2, I show that Hegel believes that a shared form of social life, of ethical life (*Sittlichkeit*) is necessary for the achievement of reciprocal recognition. I argue that Hegel understands social practices to be important not only because of the role that they play in shaping the individual's identity, but also because of the contribution that they can make to securing relations of equality among individuals: When everyone is subject to the same norms in the same way, relations of "one-sided" recognition will be impossible. That is, the achievement of *reciprocal intersubjective recognition* depends on *mutual norm recognition*. So understanding the development of Hegel's theory of recognition requires, in turn, attention to his social theory. I devote some time to considering what is distinctive of understanding ethical life as a configuration of "spirit" (*Geist*). I argue that Hegel rejects conceptions of ethical life according to which it can be understood (1) merely *instrumentally*, as a means for the achievement of aims and purposes originating solely in the individual, or (2) as *expressive* of independently grounded rational standards. Instead, in construing ethical life as a shape of spirit, Hegel is committed to the idea that ethical life is, at once, generated and sustained through the deeds of individuals, but also the source of direction for the activities of those subjects. In construing ethical life in terms of the idea of a "world," Hegel aims to make sense of the distinctive kind of existence that social practices have. While they are produced and reproduced through the deeds of individual subjects, they have a standing and existence over and above any one individual. So while Hegel holds that self-conscious subjectivity retains the possibility of transcending the world by means of this "negativity," the capacity to "dissolve" the ethical world is limited to the domain of thinking, and it can be the source of no independent standards for the rational assessment and critique of that world. Instead, the engine and justification for change will have to stem from possibilities inherent in the world itself.

Having set out these elements of Hegel's social theory, I then turn to his argument for the claim that reciprocal intersubjective recognition is not possible in *every* form of ethical life. Instead, it depends on a specific configuration of ethical life and a specific set of norm-governed practices. In particular, I show that Hegel considers, in *Phenomenology of Spirit*, a unique *failure* of recognition. This failure of recognition owes its existence to specific forms of ethical life in which the terms necessary for reciprocity are absent. However, I argue that the distinctive problem that Hegel considers in chapter VIA.a–b of the text does not arise from a situation in which normatively governed practices make it possible for some to be recognized while others are not. Instead, the problem with that scheme of ethical life is, in a sense, more deeply rooted. That is, Hegel contends that it is possible for a scheme of ethical life to exist in which *no one* can be recognized: Instead of the asymmetrical relation of recognition that we find, for example, in the relation of lord and bondsman, the problem with such a social order is that it lacks the normative resources for *anyone* to be an agent or object of recognition.

In particular, he considers a form of ethical life in which the responsibilities necessary for sustaining the social world are divvied up on the basis of differences that are understood to be *natural*, and argues that an ethical world that lacks a socially and normatively articulate self-conception that is shared universally among its members will be fundamentally unstable. Configurations of a social world depend on a diverse range of forms of activity for their continued existence, but it is possible for worlds to be structured so that the normative resources are lacking for acknowledging those diverse forms of activity. A social world that attributes that sustenance to nature will therefore fail to acknowledge one of its constitutive conditions, namely the *agency* of self-conscious individuals in making and remaking it. Instead of counting as an individual in such a social world, self-conscious agents are limited, on Hegel's terms, to being mere "shadows." Put otherwise, mutual norm recognition alone is not sufficient for reciprocal intersubjective recognition, since it is possible for everyone to recognize the same norms but for no one actually to *be recognized*. In the interpretation I offer, Hegel is offering a kind of *reductio* argument: In the absence of a conception of "the self" that is shared universally among the participants in a social world, it will be impossible for anyone to be recognized or to recognize others.

Part I, then, clarifies the central question that the study considers: What are the social conditions under which reciprocal intersubjective recognition is possible? Part II pursues Hegel's response to this question by considering the role that his social ontology of the self plays in the establishment of relations of reciprocal recognition.

The central claim of Part II: The Self is that Hegel defends a social constitution account of the self on the grounds that only this conception of the self can make possible relations of reciprocal recognition. In Hegel's account, the existence of the self is not grounded in a fact – either transcendent or natural – that exists independent of human attitudes and practices. Instead, the self owes its being to the practices in which human beings take one another to be and treat one another as selves. In Hegel's terms, this kind of being possessed by the self is "being-recognized" (*Anerkanntsein*).

Of course, this claim about the socially constituted character of the self pushes against a range of competing accounts that aim to identify the self in terms of some fact that exists independent of our attitudes and practices: that the self is really the soul, or the body, or some other bit of material nature, or the transcendental ego. In Chapter 3, I set out the contrasting account of the self as a determination of "spirit," the normatively structured social world produced and reproduced by self-conscious subjects. On this account, the idea of the self is a linking idea that links individuals to their actions, and to one another. Determinate conceptions of the self are distinguished in virtue of the particular ways that they establish these links.

Having provided the broad outlines of this "social constitution" account of the self, I turn to the first concrete conception of the self that emerges in Hegel's discussion of "The Condition of Right." (*Rechtszustand*) There, Hegel considers the possibility that the self is the (legal) person. Construing the self as the person addresses the central challenge to the possibility of recognition that Hegel identified in the "ethical world," where no one is recognized. First, being a person means possessing a normative status that is explicitly acknowledged within the social order. So, in contrast to the "shadow" existence of the prior ethical world, personhood is, we can say, a publicly acknowledged norm. Second, the person is a universal conception of the self, applying equally to every participant in the social order. So unlike the status of "lord," where recognition is necessarily one-sided and so not reciprocal, personhood is a status that can be possessed equally by all, and so permits a kind of reciprocal recognition.

However, Hegel also presents a powerful criticism of the idea of the person and what I call the model of recognition corresponding to it. He argues that personhood is a merely formal conception of the self that includes only those generic and self-standing features that individuals always already share. This conception of the self means that recognition is fundamentally a *responsive* act: I recognize you as a person when I respond appropriately to the relevant generic trait that you cannot fail to possess. I call this particular model of recognition the *automatic* model, since recognition should follow simply from the identification of the trait that makes you a person. The problem with these conceptions of the self and of recognition lies in the fact that, because the "person" excludes concrete "content," when I am recognized as a person, that recognition does not take account of those specific features that distinguish me from others and that are actually necessary for the production and reproduction of the social order. Hegel identifies this distinctive failure of recognition as the condition of "alienation" (*Entfremdung*).[57] Alienation names the condition in which the conception of the self that predominates in a social order fails to comprehend those concrete aspects of our constitution that distinguish us one from another. What is needed is a conception of the self that can *both* be affirmed equally of everyone – so guaranteeing the possibility of reciprocal recognition – and that comprehends those features of my constitution that distinguish me from others – so that I can find "fulfillment" in it when others recognize me.

I argue that, in chapter VIB, "Culture," Hegel considers the possibility of a different model of recognition. In place of the automatic model, where I merit recognition simply in virtue of a generic trait that I cannot fail to possess, Hegel presents the elements of a second model of recognition, which I call the *achievement* model of recognition. In this model, I only come to *merit* the recognition of others in virtue of some activity of my own, through which I transform my merely given being so that I bring about a commonly acknowledged set of purposes. Instead of meriting recognition simply for what I always already *am*, on the achievement model, I am deserving of recognition in virtue of what I *become*.

This new model of recognition addresses the key shortcoming in the automatic model of recognition and the conception of the self, the person, operative within it. Since the project of achieving some commonly acknowledged purpose draws on, as Hegel says, my "determinate individuality," when I am recognized for this achievement of becoming a self, that recognition takes account of what distinguishes me from others.

At the same time, there remains an important open question for this model of recognition: What are those commonly acknowledged purposes that we can justifiably deem to be the ultimate ends of our activity? What sort of life is it in terms of which I can come legitimately to expect the recognition of others? I show that the central argument that Hegel advances in his discussion of "Culture" aims to demonstrate that we cannot consistently construe these ultimate ends of our action as natural givens. Instead, we must come to understand them as purposes that are actually *constituted*

---

[57] Chapter VIB considers "spirit alienated from itself" (*Der sich entfremdete Geist*); *PhG* 264.

through our collective acknowledgment, or as *norms* that we mutually recognize. But that entails that recognition can no longer be understood to be merely a *responsive* act, but instead a *constitutive* one.

In Chapter 4, I show that Hegel finds the resolution of this challenge in "Morality." I argue that Hegel believes that the achievement of reciprocal recognition requires bringing together two notions – recognition and conscience – that Fichte held belong to different domains, those of right and morality. I show that the conception of the self that predominates in "Morality," that of "conscience," is one that can accommodate both of the requirements necessary for reciprocal recognition. On the one hand, conscience is a conception of the self that can be affirmed universally of every participant in moral discourse. On the other hand, conscience can address the "fulfillment" requirement since recognizing another individual as conscientious requires directly addressing the specific claims that they make on and before others.

At the same time, elements of this account of conscience may seem counterintuitive. First, Hegel construes conscience as a sort of public norm, rather than as a private faculty for moral judgment or an inner oracle specifying the moral truth. That is, being conscientious is, for Hegel, primarily a matter of being treated by others in a certain way, namely when others affirm or contest those convictions concerning what is right and true that we express before them and realize through our actions. Second, being conscientious requires taking seriously the concrete claims that individuals make. Instead of understanding conscience simply to be a capacity to make claims, or a uniform faculty possessed by every subject, Hegel instead holds that we exist as conscience only when we give voice to our convictions and realize them in action, *and* when others respond directly to those concrete claims.

Unlike with the person, the model of recognition that corresponds to conscience as a conception of the self is an *achievement* model, since I exist as conscience when I am so recognized by others, by virtue of my participation in moral practice. Moreover, conscience explicitly acknowledges that recognition is not merely a responsive act, but is constitutive of the self. In considering cases of moral disagreement, Hegel argues that the "experience" of conscience is one in which my own selfhood is only restored through the "forgiveness" of the other. So conscience is the only conception of the self that we find in *Phenomenology of Spirit* that is, we might say, a shape of "self-conscious spirit," that acknowledges the radically self-productive character of human forms of life.

I conclude by addressing some of the implications of my account of reciprocal recognition for our understanding of *Phenomenology* as a whole. I argue that, in drawing attention to the importance of moral discourse, *Phenomenology* offers a distinctive account of the ways in which reciprocal recognition need not depend on shared institutions, so that recognition and moral discourse might play a significant role in personal and societal transformation.

Recognition

CHAPTER I

Self-Consciousness

Why does the dynamic of recognition emerge within Hegel's account of "self-consciousness" in chapter IV of *Phenomenology of Spirit*? In spite of the fame and depth of Hegel's discussions of desire, life, recognition, the struggle to the death, lordship and bondage, and labor, we find scant agreement regarding the specific role of recognition in Hegel's account.

In one prominent account, Hegel believes that self-consciousness is necessarily social, an achievement dependent on being recognized by others.[1] This Fichtean account makes sense of the emergence of recognition in chapter IV by identifying it as a necessary condition for self-consciousness.[2] We might be concerned that this account requires too robust a concept of self-consciousness, since it is not obvious that all forms of self-consciousness require this specific relation to others. However, there is another powerful interpretive trend that considers Hegel's account of self-consciousness through a Kantian lens, so that Hegel is taken to be concerned with the achievement of a distinctive sort of self-consciousness, analogous to the transcendental unity of apperception. What is distinctive of this account is that it treats self-consciousness as a necessarily *practical* achievement, where relations of recognition are necessary to secure that achievement.[3]

---

[1] "I cannot properly be self-conscious (recognize myself) except in the context of a recognition structure that is *reciprocal*: insofar as I am recognized by those I recognize." (All emphases in quotes are from the originals, unless otherwise noted.) Brandom 2007, 137. Bernstein ascribes to Hegel "a conception of self-consciousness as mediated through, and so dependent on, the recognition of others." Bernstein 2015, 178.

[2] In the *Grundlage des Naturrechts*, Fichte argues that the concept of right, the concept of a relation of reciprocal recognition among rational beings, is a necessary condition for self-consciousness. On the emergence of the concept of recognition in German idealism, see Gottlieb 2018. On the relation between Fichte's and Hegel's concepts of recognition see Siep 2014 and Williams 1992.

[3] Of course, Fichte is equally interested in the practical conditions for the achievement of self-consciousness. So these interpreters' concerns with Kantian apperception are ultimately addressed in a Fichtean register: "It is asserted that the practical *Ich* is the *Ich* of original self-consciousness; that a rational being immediately perceives itself only in willing, and would not perceive itself, and thus the world, and would not be intelligence if it were not a practical being. Willing is the properly essential

33

Among my primary aims in this chapter is to argue that interpreters over-burden chapter IV in a number of ways and that this tendency obscures the central argument that Hegel aims to advance concerning the relation between self-consciousness and recognition. First and foremost, accounts of recognition in *Phenomenology of Spirit* not only frequently make chapter IV their point of departure for considering Hegel's concept of recognition, but also try to draw an account of the full conditions for the achievement of recognition from it.[4] However, the account of recognition that we find in chapter IV is importantly limited. The only actual configuration of recognition that we find there is "one-sided recognition," and not the "reciprocal recognition" that belongs to the "pure concept" of recognition.[5] Moreover, the account of the famed relation of lord and bondsman resolves itself with a decidedly antisocial (and, indeed, antiworldly) stance, that of "Stoicism." My aim in this book is to demonstrate that we can understand Hegel's concept of recognition only by attending to the broader argument that he advances in chapters IV–VI of *Phenomenology*, rather than focusing exclusively on the initial account that we find in chapter IV.

Second, I argue that interpreters over-burden the discussion in chapter IV in another way, by holding that Hegel is offering a Kantian account of the nature of self-consciousness, and a Fichtean account of its dependence on relations to others.[6] I argue that interpreters exploit an ambiguity in the idea of "apperception" to establish this Kantian interpretation. While Hegel no doubt does defend a sort of idealistic view, where the self-conscious activity of the "I" is an indispensable condition for experience, he only presents a defense of idealism in his account of reason, whose central claim is that reason is "the certainty of being all reality."[7] The aims of the discussion of "self-consciousness" are much more modest.[8]

In general, I argue that Hegel appeals to the idea of recognition as a possible source of *self-knowledge*. And one of the principal conclusions that he

---

character of reason..." *SW* III, 20–21. "Hegel ... treats self-consciousness as (i) a practical *achievement* of some sort... the *result of an attempt*... And (ii) Hegel sees such an attempt and achievement as necessarily involving a relation to other people, as inherently social." Pippin 2011, 15–16, 19.

[4] See, for example, Brandom 2019, chapter 9.

[5] *PhG* 113/¶191, 110/¶184, 110/¶185.

[6] In what follows, I dwell most extensively on Pippin 2011.

[7] *PhG* 132/¶231.

[8] I by no means intend to deny the centrality of self-consciousness to the structure and development of the work as a whole, or the ways in which chapter IV, "Self-Consciousness," establishes a set of core questions and problems that Hegel pursues through the remainder of the work. In this connection, see Düsing 1993 and Pöggeler 2006. However, we err in expecting this introductory discussion to offer a complete account of all of the issues at stake in understanding what self-consciousness is or why it is important. I am grateful to an anonymous reviewer for requesting that I clarify this issue.

aims to defend in the book as a whole is that self-knowledge depends on specific recognitive relations to others. However, saying that self-knowledge depends on recognition is very different from saying that self-consciousness depends on recognition. I show that Hegel is committed to the former claim, but not the latter, since there are configurations of self-consciousness (for example, desire) that do not require recognitive relations. Hegel's famous claim, which we've already encountered in this work's introduction, is that "Self-consciousness is *in* and *for itself* when and because it is in and for itself for an other; that is, it is only as something recognized [*ein Anerkanntes*]."[9] The specific condition of self-consciousness that recognition makes possible is its being *in and for itself*, which is just the achievement of self-knowledge.[10] But that does not preclude the existence of myriad other shapes of self-consciousness that might be deficient as sources of self-knowledge, but remain nonetheless shapes of self-consciousness.

I begin by reviewing the subject matter and method of *Phenomenology* as a whole, to set up an argument that Hegel's approach does not undergo a substantive change in the move from his treatment of "consciousness" to "self-consciousness" (§1.1). In my reading, the account of self-consciousness is continuous with that of consciousness, where self-consciousness is simply the shape of consciousness that takes itself to be the object of its knowledge. At the same time, self-consciousness remains distinctive for Hegel, but this distinctiveness does not stem from a robust claim about the necessarily self-conscious character of experience. Instead, I argue that self-consciousness derives its distinctiveness from object-consciousness in virtue of its unique *structure* (§1.2). Hegel's account is continuous in the sense that it focuses throughout on the issue of *knowledge*, so we should not be too distracted by the shift in subject matter from more traditional epistemological concerns in chapters I-III to the apparently "practical" ones in chapter IV. Instead, I argue that Hegel includes extensive treatments of issues like desire and recognition in his account of self-consciousness since these are among the most "immediate" forms by means of which consciousness becomes the object of its own knowing.

Situating self-consciousness within the epistemological project of the book as a whole also helps us to see why recognition emerges within Hegel's account. While commentators often stress the importance of being recognized by others, in the account that I offer, Hegel's primary focus is on the

---

[9] *PhG* 109/¶178.
[10] See Hegel's "Introduction," where he distinguishes being in-itself, being for-itself, and being in-and-for-itself, where grasp of the latter is the ultimate aim of the science of experience. *PhG* 59/¶85.

way in which the activity of "recognizing" might be a source of knowledge, in particular knowledge of oneself. I show how the demand for recognition emerges from the specific failure of desire as a source of self-knowledge. In this account, the primary significance of recognition lies in its contribution to self-knowledge, so that we ought to understand the core idea in Hegel's treatment, that of "recognizing" (*Anerkennen*) as a form of "knowing," of relating to an object. I show that this interpretation provides the key to understanding the elements of the "pure concept of recognition" (§1.3).

Finally, I argue that we can make sense of the famous accounts of the struggle to the death, and of lordship and bondage by understanding these as the "experience" of the shape of self-consciousness that aims to know its object by immediately recognizing it. By understanding the act of recognizing (and not the condition of being recognized) as the primary source of knowledge, we can see why Hegel thinks that the bondsman, the recognizing self-consciousness, is the source of genuine insight into the character of self-consciousness, rather than the lord, who is recognized. In particular, the bondsman learns that the fundamental character of self-consciousness is "absolute negativity," the condition of not being bound by any particular determinacy, the ability to transcend any determinacy by negating it. At the same time, the self-knowledge that the bondsman wins is incomplete because the relation of recognition is not *reciprocal*, and so falls short of the requirements of the "pure concept of recognition" (§1.4). Instead of presenting Hegel's *answer* to the problem of recognition (a "social theory of self-consciousness"), chapter IV instead presents the two primary questions that will drive his account of recognition in the remainder of the text: First, under what conditions is genuinely reciprocal recognition among subjects possible? Second, how can I recognize and be recognized by another when my most basic character as a self-conscious being is nothing positive, but instead "pure negativity"? The chapter concludes with an examination of the way that chapter IVB, "The Freedom of Self-Consciousness," explores the challenge that this basic characteristic of self-conscious beings poses for self-understanding and the achievement of relations of recognition (§1.5).

1.1   Hegel's Project and the Structure of Consciousness

According to the work's "Introduction," the principal object of Hegel's *Phenomenology of Spirit* is "cognition" (*Erkennen*), or "knowing" (*Wissen*).[11] Hegel's aim is to demonstrate that "cognition of the absolute" or science

---

[11] See, e.g., *PhG* 53/¶73 and 55/¶76.

(*Wissenschaft*) is possible. This demonstration takes the form of an investigation into instances of "the appearance of knowing," or different "shapes of consciousness."[12] What distinguishes this investigation into knowing is that it does not, at the outset, identify a single specific condition or particular state as knowing, or as what knowledge is "in itself." Instead, it examines a range of different "shapes of consciousness," each of which is differentiated by a distinct claim to knowledge. Such shapes are an appropriate object of investigation because, for Hegel, consciousness always involves a determinate form of "knowing." Hegel's aim is to investigate a plurality of conscious relations to an object, each of which counts as a form of knowing. On this understanding, consciousness always involves two distinct but related acts: First, it involves an act of "distinguishing" itself (*unterscheiden*) from something that it takes to be "being in itself" (*an sich Sein*), something "existing outside of [its] relation" to consciousness, which Hegel also glosses as the "truth" (*Wahrheit*).[13] Second, it involves an activity of "relating" (*Beziehen*) to this truth, this being. Hegel identifies this activity of relating broadly as "knowing" (*Wissen*). Any particular "shape of consciousness" will involve these two elements, namely an "object" (*Gegenstand*) from which consciousness distinguishes itself, and a "concept" (*Begriff*) through which it establishes a determinate relation to that object.[14] There will therefore be as many and diverse "shapes of consciousness" as there are diverse conceptions of what an object is, and of the determinate ways in which we relate to – "know" – those objects.

However, Hegel's aim in the work is not simply to catalog or describe these different shapes of consciousness. Instead, he believes that the investigation into these "appearances of knowing" can actually bring us to "the truth of knowing" (*die Wahrheit des Wissens*), what knowing is "in itself."[15] This investigation depends on the idea that consciousness involves not only the initial acts of distinguishing itself from and relating itself to an object, but also the further action of "testing" to see whether the object that it takes to be true really corresponds to the concept by means of which it claims to know it. This activity of "testing" shows that consciousness is always, in a sense, double: "Consciousness is, on the one hand, consciousness of an object, but on the other hand it is consciousness of itself [*Bewußtsein seiner selbst*]; consciousness of what is for it the true, and

---

[12] *PhG* 55/¶76, 61–2/¶89.
[13] *PhG* 58/¶82.
[14] *PhG* 59/¶84.
[15] *PhG* 58–9/¶83.

consciousness of its knowing of this truth."[16] Consciousness is therefore, we might say, self-critical, engaged in the scrutiny of its own claims to know. So there is importantly a sense in which all conscious experience of objects is, we might say, reflexive or, as Hegel says "consciousness of itself": Object-consciousness engages in the self-critical project of testing its own claims to know. However, it is equally important to note that Hegel stops short of calling this "consciousness of itself" (*Bewußtsein seiner selbst*) "self-consciousness" (*Selbstbewußtsein*). It is an important question *why* he does not simply identify these, and this question will bear importantly on our understanding of what he takes "self-consciousness" itself to be.

For our more immediate purpose of understanding Hegel's approach in the text, however, this self-critical character of consciousness is important because it indicates that consciousness is sensitive to the ways in which its concepts fall short of their stated aim of corresponding to the object. In each case, Hegel argues that the determinate relation to the object, the determinate form of knowing under investigation, *does* disclose something about the object. However, he also argues that these forms of (merely) appearing knowing are not on their own complete and perfect, and that each specific shape of consciousness actually *fails* in its endeavor to know the truth. Consciousness attributes these failures to its "concepts" of the object, realizing that what it took to be the object, "being in itself," was really only a way in which the object was "for it," not as it is in itself.

Skepticism, therefore, plays a prominent role in Hegel's account of these "shapes of consciousness" – he calls their sequence "the way of *doubt*" – since the self-critical character of consciousness consistently raises doubt about the specific claims of each shape to grasp its object.[17] More importantly, since each shape of consciousness is essentially constituted by the determinate forms of object and concept that distinguish it, Hegel's investigation is equally the "way of despair," "the conscious insight into the untruth of appearing knowing, for which what is the most real is rather what is in truth the unrealized concept."[18]

Of course, this investigation into the failure of specific shapes of consciousness to know the truth could not on its own show us anything about the "truth" of knowing. While these shapes of consciousness will experience their failures as occasions for "despair," the same need not be true for "us," we who study these shapes with a view to grasping what knowing

---

[16] *PhG* 59/¶85.
[17] *PhG* 56/¶78.
[18] *PhG* 56/¶78.

is. Instead of experiencing these failures as ones of complete loss, of the simple denial or complete negation of a claim to know, we look instead for ways in which that failure amounts to a "determinate negation" of that claim, to the specific way in which concept and object failed to correspond.[19] Hegel describes a "*dialectical* movement" that *we* find when consciousness learns that what it took to be "being in itself" was really only an in itself "*for it*," that what it took to be the object proved really to be just an aspect of its concept of the object.[20] This movement is dialectical since Hegel holds that we can correct the shortcomings of this attempt to know the truth by attempting to relate to the object in a way that overcomes the deficiency in the previous shape. But this alteration in knowing – in the relation to the object – also entails an alteration in the object itself – in what consciousness distinguishes from itself. The modification of knowing, then, also gives rise to a new object: "*In so far as a new true object emerges* from it, this *dialectical* movement, which consciousness performs on itself, equally on its knowing and its object, is properly that which is called *experience* [Erfahrung]."[21]

The process of experience that Hegel presents in *Phenomenology* is a *generative* one. We find in the literature a range of different accounts of the character of the transitions from one shape of consciousness to the next and different conceptions of the sort of necessity that governs that process. Following the helpful account that Robert Stern offers,[22] these range from transcendental accounts, according to which subsequent shapes of consciousness are the necessary conditions for the prior shapes,[23] to Forster's account, which aims to secure the exhaustiveness of Hegel's treatment of the different shapes of consciousness by showing that the transitions between the different shapes involve minimal alterations made to correct specific contradictions rising within the earlier shapes.[24] By contrast, I think we ought to take seriously the terminology in terms of which Hegel treats these transitions, and that terminology suggests that subsequent shapes of consciousness are actually *generated*, they newly grow, within the experience process: Hegel calls this process that of the "movement and becoming" (*Bewegung und Werden*) of shapes of consciousness, in which we find the generation and emergence (*Entstehung*)

---

[19] *PhG* 57/¶79.
[20] *PhG* 60/¶86, 85–86/¶85.
[21] *PhG* 60/¶86. Italics in original.
[22] Stern 2002, 27–29.
[23] See, for example, C. Taylor 1972 and Pippin 1989 for two prominent examples.
[24] See Forster 1998, 186ff.

of a new object, so that the process as a whole is that of the formation or culture (*Bildung*) of consciousness.[25] Neither the transcendental nor the minimal alteration accounts of these transitions can make sense of the generative role of the process of experience. Conditions are neither generated by nor emerge from what they condition. And the minimal alteration account cannot make sense of the novelty of the new shapes of consciousness that emerge within the process of experience. To be sure, the suggestion that experience is generative may sound far-fetched or too metaphysically ambitious. However, as Karen Ng observes in considering these same passages, the ultimate commitment from which these notions stem is the claim that the negative – in this case, the disparity between object and concept that emerges through the process of experience – is the source of the movements that Hegel traces throughout both *Phenomenology* and *Logic*.[26]

In *Phenomenology*, this dynamic, dialectical process, experience, is the proper object of *our* inquiry. It is what connects the different "shapes of consciousness" that Hegel investigates within the text. That is, our task is to see how the specific failure of one shape of consciousness gives rise to a new shape of consciousness. What consciousness takes to be a fixed "object," we instead know merely to be a "moment," a partial element that has emerged within this specific shape of consciousness. Or for us, the object of consciousness is not merely a being, but an "essence," "the reflection of consciousness within itself."[27] Our investigation is *"science"* because it aims to track the *necessary* relations between these shapes, their movement, and becoming.[28] While, within a given "shape" of consciousness, the failure to know will be experienced as "despair," as the complete loss of itself, *for us*, that failure is rather the source from which a new shape of consciousness emerges.

It is important that this process of experience, of dialectical progress by the way of doubt and despair, is one that *we* (and not the given shapes of consciousness which we examine) find. While Hegel does stress that a given shape of consciousness will acknowledge its failure to know – it will experience the loss of itself – he equally stresses that the correction of its relation to the object and the generation and emergence of a new object along with it happens "behind the back" of the shape

---

[25] *PhG* 61/¶87, 56/¶78.
[26] See Ng 2020, 98–100, especially.
[27] *PhG* 60/¶86.
[28] *PhG* 61/¶88, 62/¶87.

of consciousness under examination.[29] Rather, it is we who grasp the "necessity" of this process of emergence, not the shape of consciousness we observe. Understanding this important aspect of the transition of one shape of consciousness to another is important for understanding the sense in which the text tracks the *Bildung*, the formation of consciousness itself.[30] The process by means of which one shape of consciousness emerges from another is one that is *for us*, not for the shape of consciousness itself.[31]

Consider as an example the first dialectical transition in the text, that from "sense-certainty" to "perception."[32] Sense-certainty designates its object – that which it distinguishes from itself as what is "true" – as "this," the complete, singular domain of what can be known through the senses. Its knowing – the way in which it relates to this object – is supposed to be an "immediate" one, specifically an immediate certainty of being undifferentiated from the object it knows.[33] However, sense-certainty learns that it is incapable of grasping its object, the "this," in its singularity, and that the this is not an immediate object, but rather something mediated, a "universal" whose "simplicity" comes from "mediation," the fact that it is *not* any one being.[34] Likewise, it learns that the "I" too is a universal, mediated by its negative relations to any particular determinacy, and not a simple, immediate form of certainty.[35] In short, what sense-certainty learns is that its object, what is true for it, which it had taken to be a singular, immediate object, is in fact a universal, mediated by its negative relation to particulars. What it had taken to be something existing in itself, a being, turns out rather to be the way in which that being is *for it*, actually constituted by its way of knowing the object. This "essence"

---

[29] *PhG* 61/¶87. Robert Stern suggests that it is consciousness itself that effects the transition from its initial shape to a subsequent one so that, for example, it is consciousness that corrects the one-sidedness of its knowing in sense-certainty with the adoption of another one-sided conception of knowing, perception. Stern 2002, 28–29. However, I find little evidence that Hegel thinks that it is *consciousness* that effects this change, instead insisting that it is our work to find the emergence of a new object within the process of experience.

[30] See *PhG* 56/¶78.

[31] I here follow Siep 2000, 77–78: "In its self-testing, consciousness knows nothing of the dialectic of the concept. It therefore also does not know to what extent the new standard is bound up with the old, or to what extent the new shape is an 'inversion of consciousness'... That the new object is a 'dialectical' synthesis of moments of the 'old' ontology and factical knowing, is not clear for the testing consciousness, but is an 'addition' of the philosopher considering it."

[32] Siep too considers this transition to be one in which we "find again the methodological descriptions of the Introduction." Siep 2000, 85.

[33] *PhG* 63/¶91.

[34] *PhG* 65/¶96.

[35] *PhG* 66/¶102.

is, within the experience of sense-certainty, what Hegel calls a "mediated universal." This realization is the *loss* of sense-certainty, since sense-certainty, as a shape of consciousness, is constituted by its commitment to the truth – that it is something singular and immediate – and by its determinate concept of that truth – that it can know this singular object by means of simple certainty.

Perception, however, takes up what *we* see emerges as the truth of sense-certainty, the new object generated by the experience process, namely that the "essence," the way in which the object proved to be merely for sense-certainty, is a mediated universal. This mediated universal is posited as the proper object of perception. However, perception is defined by a fundamentally different stance toward this object than that of sense-certainty, namely the more active stance of "perception" (*Wahrnehmung*) or "taking to be true."[36] At the same time, the object, as it is for perception, is not the simple "this" or "I" of sense-certainty. As we have seen, Hegel claims in the "Introduction" that changes in knowing, in the way in which a shape of consciousness relates to its object, equally entail alterations in the object, that which consciousness distinguishes from itself. That is, perception is not simply a more adequate way of grasping the "this" or the "I." Instead, what it "takes to be true" is something essentially new, namely a mediated universal that it "distinguishes" from itself as such, or a "thing with many properties."[37] In a sense, this object is the same as that which emerged through the course of the experience of sense-certainty, namely a "mediated universal." However, things are clearly not identical with "this" or "I." How are we therefore to make sense of the idea that there is a continuity, indeed a "necessity" even in this simple transition?

The relevant textual evidence points to a relatively weak account of dialectical transition, according to which it is not the shape of consciousness under consideration that both grasps and corrects the limitation inherent to its particular form of knowing, but rather "we" readers, engaged in the project of phenomenology: As Hegel stresses in the "Introduction," it is "we" who grasp the necessary connections between the shapes of consciousness, the "emergence" of a new object and form of knowing from the failure of the previous shape. In this account, the development from sense-certainty to perception does not take place *for* self-certainty, but only for us. In short, it is we who identify the mediated universal that emerges

---

[36] *PhG* 71/¶111.
[37] *PhG* 71/¶112.

as the essence in the experience of sense-certainty with the new object of perception.[38]

I have taken the time to explain an initial transition within the text since I believe that grasping its structure helps make sense of some of the more obviously controversial transitions in Hegel's account of self-consciousness, most notably that from desire to recognition. However, I also believe that we find a similar structure in Hegel's account of the genesis of self-consciousness itself. And it is to that account that I would like immediately to turn.

1.2 Self-Consciousness and Desire

Interpreters have struggled to make sense of the transition from consciousness to self-consciousness.[39] Part of the difficulty stems from the seemingly great thematic shifts that we find between chapters I–III and chapter IV. Many interpreters gloss these shifts in terms of a contrast between the "theoretical" orientation and concern of "consciousness" and the "practical" concerns of "self-consciousness," the account of which famously dwells on, among other things, desire, life, satisfaction, and ultimately recognition, struggle, lordship and bondage, and labor. Another part of the difficulty stems from the accelerated pace with which Hegel introduces these new terms he will use to make sense of self-consciousness.

We find a variety of responses to the puzzling shift from consciousness to self-consciousness. In accounting for the central argument of chapter IV, some (Kojève, for example) simply ignore the first three chapters, and present an account of the key argument of the text that does not depend essentially on the treatment of "Consciousness." Others argue that attempts to find continuity in the transition from consciousness to self-consciousness all fail, disavowing the suggestion that we need to see self-consciousness as developing out of consciousness. Instead, interpreters like Jenkins see Hegel as, as it were, starting anew, offering an account of desire

---

[38] By contrast, we might try to account for this transition as one of self-conscious development on the behalf of the shape of consciousness that is under observation. This thesis would help us to make sense of the continuity of the development from one shape of consciousness to the next that Hegel stresses. Indeed, in this connection, he holds that "the wealth of sense knowledge [*sinnlichen Wissens*] belongs to perception." *PhG* 72/¶112. However, this self-conscious development account depends on an idea of "formation" that is particularly strong, since sense-certainty itself would have to learn not only that its attempt to grasp the singular immediately *failed*, but that the truth that it really aimed to grasp is not an immediate this, but rather a mediated universal, a thing. But there is no textual evidence to suggest that this is how Hegel thinks we ought to grasp this transition.

[39] For a helpful account of some of the difficulties, see Pippin 1993.

anchored in a newly introduced claim about "the kinds of things that we all are – a claim about rational, sentient beings."[40]

However, the cost of pursuing these strategies for our understanding of the work as a whole is great. As we have seen, Hegel contends that the unique contribution of a *phenomenology* of spirit lies in its "scientific" presentation of the different "shapes" of consciousness that it considers. That scientific character stems specifically from the necessary dialectical links between shapes that Hegel claims this approach makes manifest. In failing to account for the relation between consciousness and self-consciousness, these interpreters, therefore, undermine one of the key commitments of Hegel's phenomenology.

By contrast, what Jenkins calls "contextual" accounts aim to save that commitment by tracing the emergence of self-consciousness out of consciousness. Pippin presents a prominent example of this contextual approach. According to Pippin, the continuity in the text stems from the fact that chapter IV presents "a further elaboration of the possibility of intentional consciousness."[41]

For our purposes, Pippin makes two key claims in the interpretation of chapter IV in his *Hegel on Self-Consciousness*. First, Pippin contends that Hegel is centrally concerned with investigating and understanding the role that *apperception* plays in Hegel's account of self-consciousness. Pippin takes the motivation of the account of self-consciousness to be broadly Kantian. Because, like Kant, Hegel takes conscious experience to be not simply a passive registering, but the product of an activity undertaken by the subject that is subject to normative assessment, Hegel is committed to the claim that object-consciousness must be inherently reflective or apperceptive.[42] So the primary sense in which Pippin takes Hegel to be interested in the issue of self-consciousness is also Kantian: "All consciousness is inherently, though rarely explicitly, self-conscious."[43]

Second, Pippin argues that Hegel acknowledges what Henrich calls "Fichte's original insight."[44] In Henrich's account, self-consciousness cannot be understood on the same model as object-consciousness, where "the self in question cannot be just another object of intentional awareness."

---

[40] Jenkins 2009, 105.
[41] Pippin 2011, 5n2.
[42] "I cannot be *sustaining activity*, implicitly trying to get, say, the objective temporal order right in making up my mind, without in some sense knowing I am so taking the world to be such, or without apperceptively taking it so. I am taking or construing rather than merely recording because I am also in such taking holding open the possibility that I may be taking falsely." Pippin 2011, 8–9.
[43] Pippin 2011, 9.
[44] Henrich 1982; Pippin 2011, 9.

Such conceptions of self-consciousness are flawed because they are subject to a regress problem. If knowing (or perceiving) that p requires that I know (or perceive) that p, we can always raise the question of how I know that I know that p. If I am conscious of myself in the same way that I am conscious of objects, then I shall have to posit another, higher form of self-consciousness, so that $I(a)$ know that I know that p. But of course, this will continue *ad infinitum*: I must posit another $I(b)$ who knows that $I(a)$ that I know that p. If it turns out that object-consciousness depends on self-consciousness, then the subject cannot be conscious of itself in the same way that it is conscious of objects. Fichte solves this regress problem by proposing a special intellectual intuition by means of which the I has immediate knowledge of its own positing activity precisely to ward off such a regress.[45] In place of models of self-consciousness that understand it to be a product of "observing an object," "conceptualizing an intuition," or "any immediate self-certainty or direct presence of the self to itself," Pippin holds that Hegel "treats self-consciousness as ... a practical *achievement* of some sort."[46] Pippin's account of self-consciousness is contextualist because it aims to show how the disparate and seemingly weird new subject matters that Hegel introduces in chapter IV – desire, life, recognition – fit within the work's initial aims, exploring the possibility of intentional consciousness by considering the ways in which that object-consciousness depends on a distinctive self-consciousness achieved through activity and practice.

At the same time, the claim that Hegel understands what is distinctive of self-consciousness primarily in terms of the issue of apperception is questionable. Pippin seems to ascribe to Hegel the same commitments concerning apperception that Kant holds. That is, he appeals to Kant in order to identify "self-consciousness" with apperception, and to suggest that Hegel shares some version of "Kant's famous formula" according to which "the '*I think*' must be able to accompany all of my representations."[47] The specific role that these ideas play in Kant aside, it's not clear that the issue of apperception is what distinguishes Hegel's interests and concerns at the outset of chapter IV.

In part, the difficulty stems from understanding exactly what is involved in "apperception." Consider the account of experience as "'implicitly' reflexive" that Pippin offers in *Hegel's Idealism*:

[45] Fichte *SW* I, 475–6, 463–8.
[46] Pippin 2011, 15.
[47] Pippin, 2011, 9.

Consciousness of objects is implicitly reflexive because, according to Kant, whenever I am conscious of any object, I can also be said to "apperceive" implicitly my being *thus* conscious. In any remembering, thinking, or imagining, although the object of my intending is some state of affairs or other, I am also potentially aware *as* I intend that what I am doing *is* an act of remembering, thinking, or imagining... It is not the case that the self-relation of apperception involves a representation of the self, whether of my self or of subjectivity itself. But it is the case for Kant that my implicitly "taking myself" to be perceiving, remembering, and so on is an indispensable component of *what it is* to perceive, imagine, remember, and so on.[48]

In what is I think the thinnest account of apperception on offer here, apperception is a sort of awareness of the *specific relation* in which I stand to the object, so that when I am imagining an elephant, I apperceive that my relation to the object is one of imagining, and not, say, actually seeing or smelling it.

However, we can identify more robust accounts of apperception that involve, in addition to (1) awareness of the specific relation in which I stand to the object, (2) an awareness of my own *activity* in instituting that relation (for example, an awareness of the active character of my imagining, thinking, or perceiving the object, in contrast to a merely passive picture of these intentional relations), and (3) an awareness that it is *my* spontaneous activity that institutes that relation (an awareness that *I* am the imaginer, thinker, or perceiver). Of course, there's much more that we might say about the relation between these ideas for Kant, but this distinction should help us to clarify what is distinctive of self-consciousness in Hegel's account.

Instead of being a distinctive feature of "self-consciousness," in Hegel's account, "consciousness" is always already (at least implicitly) apperceptive in the first sense. Recall that (as we saw in §1.1), for Hegel, object-consciousness always requires two separate acts: the act of distinguishing an object from consciousness, and then relating itself to that object. That relation, which Hegel calls "knowing," is always a determinate sort of relation – it is, for example, "perceiving" or "understanding" – and consciousness is (or always can be) conscious of the distinctive character of that relation. This is what Hegel means when he says that consciousness is also always "consciousness of itself" (*Bewußtsein seiner selbst*) because it is "consciousness of its knowing [of the truth]."[49] If by "apperception" we mean awareness of the specific relation at work in a given shape of intentional

[48] Pippin 1989, 21.
[49] *PhG* 59/¶85.

consciousness – in Pippin's terms, an awareness of the determinate character of my relation to the object, an awareness "that what I am doing *is* an act of remembering, thinking, or imagining" – then apperception cannot be distinctive of self-consciousness for Hegel. Instead, the apperceptive character of consciousness is built into Hegel's account of consciousness as such. At the same time, it is important that, in the "Introduction," Hegel does not call this "consciousness of itself" "self-consciousness," a term that he reserves for the discussion of chapter IV.[50]

However, we also find the other two aspects of more robust accounts of apperception in the earlier account of consciousness. As we have seen, consciousness knows its own *active* role in object-relations beginning at least with perception (*Wahrnehmung*), an intentional relation in which the activity of "taking-to-be-true" is explicit for consciousness.[51] And as we have also seen, the role of the "I" in intentional consciousness emerges within the experience of sense-certainty.[52] So, in none of these accounts is apperception something unique to the standpoint of self-consciousness.

If the principal distinguishing feature of self-consciousness is therefore not apperception, what is it? The account of self-consciousness is supposed to be the "presentation" (*Auseinanderlegung*) of "*what consciousness knows when it knows itself.*"[53] Indeed, if we attend to the ways in which self-consciousness emerges within the text in chapter III, we find that the central issue is not one of apperception, but rather of *self-knowledge*. We can better understand the role of self-knowledge in Hegel's account of self-consciousness by considering how the latter emerges within the account of "Force and the understanding" that immediately precedes it.

As a shape of consciousness, understanding distinguished from itself a domain of forces that it was prompted to regard as a "super-sensible" world that transcends the sensible and that it knows by means of understanding, specifically by grasping a set of laws that govern the relations of those forces. However, the understanding learns that its object – the super-sensible – is not really separate from the immediate domain of the sensible, and that it instead includes the latter within itself. In short, it learns that its object is really "*infinity*" or "difference as *inner* [difference],

[50] Outside of the "Preface," the term "*Selbstbewußtsein*" appears for the first time in Hegel's account of the understanding's activity of "explaining." *PhG* 100–1/¶163.

[51] "... I hold it be as it is in truth, and instead of knowing it immediately, *I take it to be true* [nehme ich wahr]." *PhG* 70/¶110.

[52] *PhG* 66ff/¶¶100ff.

[53] *PhG* 102/¶165.

or difference *in itself.*[54] As such, when it knows its object, it is really not grasping a being that is fundamentally different from itself. Instead, the understanding's knowing takes the form of "*explaining*," whose criterion for success does not depend most fundamentally on the character of the understanding's purported object, but rather on the understanding itself: "There is so much self-satisfaction in explaining, because in explaining, consciousness is, so to speak, in immediate dialogue with itself, and so only enjoys itself; though it seems to be concerned with something other, in fact it only has to do with itself."[55] But that means that, in explanation, consciousness really has *itself* for its object "*as that which it is,* so consciousness is *self-consciousness* [*Selbstbewußtsein*]."[56]

To be sure, there are a variety of ways in which we might take this identification of "infinity" with "self-consciousness." For example, when Hegel claims that, as "self-consciousness," "*I differentiate myself from myself,* and *therein it is immediately for me that what I differentiate from myself is not different,*"[57] we might take him to be endorsing the idealist conclusion that it is possible for consciousness to experience "beings" as distinct from itself (as it has in chapters I–III) only through the activity of self-consciousness. Indeed, elements of Hegel's account here certainly *do* recall Kant's claims about the role of self-consciousness in the Transcendental Deduction: "The *necessary progress* from the prior shapes of consciousness, whose truth was a thing, something other than [consciousness] itself, expresses this: that not only is consciousness of things possible only for a self-consciousness, but that this [the idea that consciousness of things is possible only for a self-consciousness] alone is the truth of these prior shapes."[58]

At the same time, Hegel only explicitly articulates the claim of idealism, that the activity of self-consciousness is constitutive of the experience of objects, in his account of reason, "the certainty of consciousness of being all reality."[59] By contrast, the implications of the specific claims that Hegel makes at the conclusion of chapter III are rather modest. Indeed, even though he does explicitly state here that "the truth" of the prior shapes of consciousness lies in the claim that "consciousness of things is possible only for self-consciousness," he also stresses that this truth has emerged "only

---

[54] *PhG* 99/¶160.
[55] *PhG* 101/¶163.
[56] *PhG* 100/¶163.
[57] *PhG* 102/¶164.
[58] *PhG* 102/¶164.
[59] *PhG* 133/¶233.

for us, and not for consciousness," and that "Self-consciousness has come to be *for itself*, but not yet *as unity* with consciousness in general."[60] It is again only the standpoint of reason that considers these two standpoints – object-consciousness and self-consciousness – together. Accounts like those of Pippin and John McDowell ascribe to chapter IV much higher argumentative aspirations than it is able to bear.[61]

In the transition from consciousness to self-consciousness, Hegel is therefore not investigating the role that the activity of self-consciousness plays in all conscious experience, but is instead considering the ways in which consciousness can emerge within the domain of intentional relations as an object itself, something which it distinguishes from itself with the aim of knowing it. That is, Hegel is arguing that consciousness emerges as an object for itself in the course of its experience of those objects that it differentiates from itself. As with any other object that emerges in the course of the experience set out in *Phenomenology*, consciousness attempts to know it by establishing a determinate relation to it. Indeed, in his account of self-consciousness, Hegel stresses that the primary question is not about the role that self-consciousness plays in conditioning object-consciousness, but rather, again, that of how consciousness can know itself at all, or *"what consciousness knows when it knows itself."*[62] That is, his aim is to articulate how consciousness comes to have itself for its object, how it comes to know itself.

Of course, one reason that readers might be inclined to resist this more modest self-knowledge interpretation of chapter IV stems from the conviction that Hegel acknowledges the "original insight" that Henrich ascribes to Fichte and the regress problems that it aims to avoid. As we have seen, it is central to Pippin's interpretation that Hegel not only grasps this important insight, but that it is among the primary drivers of his treatment of self-consciousness. It is of the utmost importance for understanding Hegel's conception of self-consciousness in *Phenomenology* to see that he does not appeal to any form of immediate self-knowledge as adequate

---

[60] *PhG* 102/¶164.
[61] As I argue in §1.3, chapter IV considers self-consciousness only as "independent," and so capable only of a "negative" relation to objects. It is unreasonable to expect that this purely negative attitude can make the sort of contribution to an account of the subjective conditions for objective cognition that Pippin 2011 and McDowell 2009a seek to find there. As Hegel will show in chapter V, cognition of objects presupposes a "positive relation" to the world that self-consciousness's claim to independence undermines. Likewise, the implicit aim of self-consciousness, knowledge of what self-consciousness is in truth, is itself only achieved through this "positive relation" to the world.
[62] *PhG* 102/¶165.

to make sense of self-consciousness, as Fichte, in one account, does,[63] and
he does not simply identify self-consciousness with any synthetic subjective activity. At the same time, he does argue that self-consciousness is different in kind from and not reducible to object-consciousness. However,
he specifies the difference between these not by appeal to a criterion drawn
from my own immediate awareness of myself or of my acts, but rather by
means of an essential difference of what I shall call *structure*.

We can best understand what is distinctive of this structure by contrasting it with the structure of "consciousness." As we have seen (in §1.1), Hegel
identifies consciousness in terms of the two acts of distinguishing itself from
an object, and then relating itself to that object through a determinate form
of knowing. Self-consciousness is distinct in having, as Hegel says, a "double-object."[64] On the one hand, it includes the "object" of consciousness,
which consciousness identified as separate from itself. But, in addition, self-
consciousness is that form of consciousness that ultimately has "itself" as
its object. Hegel identifies these distinct objects in terms of two moments,
which suggests their dynamic interconnection: "With this first moment,
self-consciousness is *consciousness*, and for it the entire expanse of the sensible world is preserved; but it is preserved only as related to the second
moment, the unity of self-consciousness with itself; and so [this world]
is for it a continued existence [*Bestehen*], which is only as *appearance*, or
which is a difference [*Unterschied*] that has no being."[65] In particular, Hegel
stresses that, as self-consciousness, this first object has the specific character
of being *merely* an appearance, in contrast to "itself" which takes it to be the
"true essence": "Consciousness has as self-consciousness a doubled object,
the one, the immediate object of sense-certainty and perception, which
however is *for it* marked with the *character of the negative*, and the second,
namely *itself* [sich selbst], which is the true essence, and is present initially
only in opposition to the first."[66] Instead of identifying self-consciousness as
a form of immediate self-knowledge or self-awareness, Hegel instead identifies it in terms of a specific structure, namely that of a self-relation that is
established through a relation to an object taken to be separate from it.

---

[63] Fichte's position here is complex. On the one hand, he does appeal to intellectual intuition in
order to establish how the I can immediately know its own activities, and he also acknowledges that
this intellectual intuition comprises a condition for self-consciousness. However, by contrast, in
Grundlage des Naturrechts, he stresses the need for a real-philosophy, which considers the application of concepts to objects, to establish the conditions for self-consciousness.
[64] *PhG* 104/¶167.
[65] *PhG* 104/¶167.
[66] *PhG* 104/¶167.

Self-consciousness is therefore clearly more complex than the "consciousness of itself" that always belongs to consciousness. Since, I have been arguing, such "consciousness of itself" is a consciousness of one's own determinate form of knowing, or apperception, it is therefore a mistake to simply *identify* apperception and what Hegel calls self-consciousness. Moreover, seeing self-consciousness as a distinctive structure shows not only that self-consciousness, for Hegel, is not any form of immediate awareness either of "mental states" or "acts" of consciousness, but is rather, at the most basic level, mediated by and so dependent on relations to objects that consciousness distinguishes from itself.

On the interpretive level, this account helps us to deal with some particularly thorny issues. First, it shows why Hegel thinks that self-consciousness emerges from the experience of consciousness, since it is precisely this structure, this "shape" of consciousness whose object is now "doubled" that emerged at the conclusion of chapter III. "Explaining," is just a way in which consciousness achieves unity with itself, but it does so only by means of a relation to objects that it takes to be other than itself. The primary difference between "explaining" and "self-consciousness" lies in what is taken to be "essential" from both standpoints. The realization that "explaining" is simply consciousness "in immediate dialogue with itself" proves a *disappointment* because it takes itself to be "concerned with something other," but, in explaining, "in fact it has only to do with itself."[67] That is, explaining takes the object to be essential, but experiences disappointment because it learns that explaining ultimately concerns itself. By contrast, in self-consciousness, this "unity of self-consciousness with itself" becomes "essential."[68] It is no longer experienced as a disappointment, but rather as the "truth" or "essence" of self-consciousness as a self-standing shape.

However, second, and, perhaps, more importantly, it also explains why Hegel makes the rather startling claim that "Self-consciousness is *desire* in general."[69] It is this assertion that is central to the accounts offered by so many interpreters. Indeed, we have seen that making sense of it is the primary task of Pippin and Jenkins, to name but two.[70] If we understand self-consciousness primarily as a distinctive structure, then we need not take Hegel's appeals to desire to mark any fundamental shift from "theoretical" concerns to "practical" ones.

---

[67] *PhG* 101/¶163.
[68] *PhG* 104/¶167.
[69] *PhG* 104/¶167.
[70] This claim is the point of departure and central concern of Pippin 2011.

Instead, Hegel introduces desire as part of the account of consciousness's "knowing of itself." That is, he is interested in the sense in which desire can be a source of self-knowledge, of self-consciousness's "unity with itself" that results from overcoming its "opposition" to an object that it takes to be different from itself. Indeed, Hegel identifies desire as the initial shape of self-consciousness – the initial determinate relation to an object, whose aim is ultimately the achievement of knowledge of itself – just because, like "sense-certainty," desire seems to involve the least mediated form that this self-relation through objects can take.[71] That is, desire (at least the sort of desire Hegel considers here) involves treating the object of desire only as something that is not consciousness itself, and its own relation to that object is the simple one of "negating" it, of consuming and destroying it.[72] If desire is the initial form that self-consciousness's knowing of itself assumes, it also entails a determinate criterion of the truth. That criterion is simply "satisfaction" (*Befriedigung*).[73] Desire presents a paradigm instance of the sense in which self-consciousness understood now as a structure – of the relation to itself achieved through a relation to objects – is always objectively mediated. Instead of being an immediate awareness or presence of the subject to itself, self-consciousness is a distinctive achievement that depends essentially on a relation to another, in the case of desire, to an object that it consumes in the course of perpetuating life. Likewise, instead of being a merely subjective condition, desire is a specific way of *relating* to oneself via objects distinct from one. On this score, Hegel's view is (perhaps surprisingly) close to Adorno's "materialist" conception of the subject's relation to itself.[74]

We, therefore, need not understand Hegel's assertion that "Self-consciousness is *desire* in general" to entail a fundamental transformation

---

[71] I here follow Pippin 2011, 19: "In a way that is typical of his procedure, [Hegel] tries to begin with the most theoretically thin or simple form of the required self-relation…"

[72] *PhG* 107–8/¶175. I do not devote significant attention here to the intervening discussions of life and species, since these simply provide the basis for the account of desire.

[73] *PhG* 107/¶175. However, we must at the same time acknowledge the limited role that "satisfaction" plays as a criterion for truth. Satisfaction remains bound to this specific shape of consciousness, and does not come to assume a greater role as a general criterion for truth in other shapes of consciousness. In contrast to Pippin's account, the one offered here does not see desire as central to all subsequent stages in Hegel's argument, or see theoretical concerns subsumed under practical ones.

[74] "Consciousness is a function of the living subject, its concept formed according to this image. This image cannot be exorcized from its proper meaning. The objection that the empirical moment of subjectivity is thereby mixed with the transcendental or essential moment is a weak one. Without any relation to an empirical consciousness, that of the living I, there would be no transcendental or spiritual consciousness. Analogous considerations do not apply to the genesis of objects. Mediation of the object: that it may not be statically, dogmatically hypostasized, but is only known in interdependence with subjectivity; mediation of the subject: that it would be literally nothing without the moment of objectivity." Adorno 1970, 186–7.

in the account, or a belief about the role that desires play in shaping our projects of knowing. Instead, the claim is more like a "speculative sentence," whose partial character is demonstrated through the course of the experience of self-consciousness. That experience is most directly relevant for our present purposes for understanding the roots of the idea of "recognition" in the text.

1.3 The Pure Concept of Recognition

Accounts of the role of recognition in *Phenomenology* remain in important ways indebted to the influential interpretation of Alexandre Kojève. In Kojève's account, recognition is the source of a sort of satisfaction that is unique to human beings, distinguishing us from animals, addressing a fundamental human desire, the "desire for 'recognition'."[75] The idea of a desire for recognition is ubiquitous in accounts of Hegel,[76] so that accounting for the possibility of successful recognition means identifying the conditions under which it might be satisfied. Leaving aside the fact that Kojève ignores chapters I–III, the appeal to a desire for recognition fits well with the "contextualist" accounts that we've considered already. In such accounts, Hegel aims to present a picture of how what is uniquely human emerges from a more natural situation where individuals are driven by (self-serving) desires. Honneth argues that among Hegel's aims in his earlier Jena writings is to take the "thought-model of a social struggle" that we find in Machiavelli and Hobbes and to apply it to "an entirely altered theoretical context," in order to make possible "the foundation of a philosophy of society."[77] Readings like Kojève's strengthen this suggestion of a link to early modern pictures of the state of nature like those that we find in Hobbes.

Robert Brandom's interpretation of the rise of recognition in the text fits squarely within this interpretive tradition. First, Brandom holds that Hegel's aim is to present an account of how distinctively human selves emerge from a natural condition that we share with animals.[78] This commitment tracks

---

[75] Kojève 1980, 7.
[76] In addition to Brandom's account on which I focus later, see, for example, Pinkard 1994, 52; Pippin 2011, 77ff; Bernstein 2015, 178ff.
[77] Honneth 1992, 20–1.
[78] "Making the step from the erotic awareness of animal denizens of the realm of Nature to the conceptual consciousness of knowers and agents who live and move and have their being in the normative realm of Spirit – creatures who have achieved the status of *selves* or *subjects* – requires the advent of self-consciousness." Brandom 2007, 134–135. One significant flaw in Brandom's account is that it does not acknowledge desire as a form of self-consciousness, but rather as a step toward it. I cite here the text of Brandom's 2007 essay, though that account appears again, without significant alteration, in Brandom 2019, chapter 8.

Kojève's view that chapter IV follows the emergence of a distinctively "human" reality out of a merely natural and animal one.[79] Second, Brandom holds that self-consciousness – which he glosses as a sort of "self-recognition" – is the ultimate aim of Hegel's account of recognition and that it consists of a reflexive self-relation that is possible only through the recognition of others.[80] Kojève, too, holds that desire alone is not yet self-consciousness, so that it is only with the shift from desire to recognition that we find the achievement of self-consciousness.[81] Third, for Brandom, too, a "desire for recognition" motivates this movement from mere animality to full selfhood,[82] so that recognition is so important because it satisfies a primitive and essential desire.[83] In general, Brandom takes Hegel to have shown "how *recognition* develops out of and can be made intelligible in terms of *desire*."[84]

It is difficult to overstate the role that Kojève has played in informing subsequent interpretations of the text. In part, this influence is direct, so that interpreters draw specific ideas from his interpretation, even if those ideas may not play any significant role (or any role at all!) in Hegel's text. In greater part, however, this influence is indirect. While the central commitments of Brandom's account derive in a fairly straightforward way from Kojève's, the latter's reading is so pervasive that interpreters often don't acknowledge the need to provide textual evidence for its central claims, for example, evidence that Hegel appeals to a desire for recognition in chapter IV. It is true that we owe much to Kojève for showing us just how rich with possibility are the thirty-odd paragraphs with which Hegel's account of self-consciousness begins.[85] However, in spite of the frequency with which we encounter interpretive commitments like Brandom's in the literature, I would like here to argue that this interpretation is fundamentally flawed since it depends on ideas that are alien to Hegel's text, and, by

[79] Kojève 1980, 4–5.
[80] "I cannot be properly self-conscious (recognize myself) except in the context of a recognition structure that is *reciprocal*: insofar as I am recognized by those I recognize." Brandom 2007, 137. "This is *self*-consciousness, or having a self-conception, in a double-sense. First, it is a matter of a consciousness of something *as* a self: treating it as having practical significance. Second, it is an *application* of that conception *to oneself*." Brandom 2007, 147.
[81] "In other words, all human, anthropogenic Desire – the Desire that generates Self-Consciousness, the human reality – is, finally, a function of the desire for 'recognition.'" Kojève 1980, 7.
[82] Brandom 2007, 139.
[83] This claim about the "desire for recognition" is pervasive. See also Butler 2004, 31–32; Bernstein 2015, 178f.
[84] Brandom 2007, 143.
[85] To be sure, even interpreters like Marx draw much from the accounts of recognition, lordship and bondage, and labor that we find in chapter IV. However, Kojève's lectures have proven to be a touchstone for recent interpreters of very diverse stripes and interests.

consequence, it misconstrues the basic aim of Hegel's account of recognition. I argue that we can correct these shortcomings by situating the introduction of recognition within the structural account of self-consciousness that I've defended in §1.2, and by identifying the ultimate aim of recognition as a sort of self-knowledge, rather than as self-consciousness.

The first significant problem with these interpretations is that they overstate the role that desire plays within Hegel's account of recognition. In Brandom's account, it is only recognition, and not desire itself, that ultimately establishes self-consciousness. However, if this is the case, it is unclear why Hegel would identify desire as itself a form of self-consciousness, as we have seen he famously and explicitly does in stating that self-consciousness "is *desire* in general." On a related note, and perhaps even more importantly, it is not clear that Hegel treats self-consciousness as the sort of accomplishment that interpreters like Brandom believe he does. That is, in Brandom's account, we only become self-conscious through the recognition of others, so that the "shape" of consciousness that Hegel considers in the text only becomes an instance of self-consciousness at the conclusion. However, there are reasons for questioning this sort of treatment. Consider a parallel with perception, a shape of object-consciousness. While there are determinate limitations to perception, it does not fail to be a form of consciousness. Instead, it simply gives us inadequate knowledge of its purported object. Considered along these lines, it makes more sense to treat desire as itself a form of self-consciousness – embodying the double-object structure that characterizes self-consciousness more generally – and, in a similar way, to hold simply that it provides incomplete knowledge of its ultimate object, consciousness itself. In short, interpreters have generally neglected the fact that Hegel's primary concern in his accounts of desire and recognition is consciousness's "knowledge of itself" and that it is in the achievement of this knowledge that the different shapes of self-consciousness fall short.

If we accept that desire is itself already an instance of self-consciousness, then it becomes likewise easier to see that recognition does not depend directly on desire in the way that Brandom holds it does when he says that seeking recognition is a product of a "desire for recognition." It is of the utmost importance to see that, in *Phenomenology*, Hegel never appeals to or asserts the existence of such a desire or claims that one exists in us by nature, in spite of the ubiquity of this idea in Hegel scholarship.[86] It is entirely unfortunate that interpreters have tried to read into the

---

[86] For critical accounts of the desire for recognition reading, see the helpful summary in Farneth 2017, 56; see also Gadamer 1976, 62; and Redding 1996, 121.

Phenomenology account of recognition a "state of nature" picture. To be sure, what Hegel calls the "pure concept of recognition" (*der reine Begriff des Anerkennens*)[87] does emerge out of the specific failure of desire to prove to be a complete or adequate source of self-knowledge. However, we can read Hegel's account here as one in which the truth of desire is *aufgehoben* in the "movement of recognition" – its truth is retained, but it is itself canceled and transfigured when its specific failure is corrected – rather than becoming the desire for a specific object, namely recognition. In short, instead of seeing this movement as ultimately motivated by a desire for recognition, we should instead see recognition as the "determinate negation" of desire.[88]

What is that specific failure of desire? Hegel's account of self-consciousness begins with desire because, as Pippin argues, desire is "the most theoretically thin or simple form" of the sort of self-relation that comprises self-consciousness.[89] However, Pippin stresses that this form is "theoretically thin or simple" because it "considers the mere sentiment of self that a living being has in *keeping itself alive*, where *keeping itself alive* reflects this minimal reflective *attentiveness to self*." By contrast, I'd like to identify another sense in which Hegel's account of desire is theoretically thin. That is, the question that animates the account in chapter IV is whether we can make sense of self-consciousness *without* appeal to any enduring being external to self-consciousness. Or the broad aim is to attempt to account for self-consciousness as "independent" (*selbständig*), not grounded in or requiring explanation by appeal to anything that is not self-consciousness itself. This commitment to the independence of self-consciousness is one of the reasons why Hegel's account begins with desire. If self-consciousness is to be independent, then it cannot depend on any *positive* relation to an object. Rather, its relation to otherness must be negative in a double sense: It must hold that otherness is nothing in itself, and it bears out this commitment by embodying a negative attitude to the object, and it is capable only of negating the object.

Given these limitations, it would be unreasonable to expect the account in chapter IV to present an account of Hegel's conception of the way in which positive objective knowledge is possible, in particular since he

---

[87] *PhG* 110/¶185.
[88] Stern's account of the range of interpretive issues for making sense of the emergence of recognition and its relation to desire is characteristically helpful. See Stern 2002, 75–83. My account is closest to the one that he attributes to Shklar 1976, 28. I present some arguments against Stern's own account in what follows.
[89] Pippin 2011, 19.

believes that such knowledge requires a different, and nonnegative attitude toward objectivity that we properly find only from the standpoint of
"reason":

> Because self-consciousness is now reason, its hitherto negative relation to
> being-other reverts to a positive one. Up to now, being-other had only to do
> with self-consciousness's independence and freedom, to save and preserve
> itself for itself at the cost of the *world* or its proper actuality, which both
> appeared to self-consciousness as the negative of its own essence. But as
> reason, certain of itself, it has received rest in relation to them, and can bear
> them; for it is certain of itself as all reality; or that all actuality is nothing
> other than it; its thinking is immediately actuality; it therefore relates to
> them as idealism.[90]

Consequently, if we are interested in tracing the development of the positive account of the role of apperception in objective cognition in the text,
we ought to seek that account in Hegel's treatment of reason, and not in
the very limited confines of the discussion of self-consciousness.[91]

By contrast, I am arguing that the account of self-consciousness concerns
the issue of self-knowledge. As we have seen, Hegel is interested in the way
in which desire constitutes an immediate realization of the structure of self-
consciousness. It entails a determinate relation to objects that is ultimately
oriented toward consciousness itself: Desire embodies the claim that while
objects are not me, they are nonetheless essentially there *for* me, so that
consciousness itself is their ultimate "truth." The determinate relation to this
truth consists of the activity of negating objects by consuming them, demonstrating that they are really nothing in themselves. The criterion of success
for this claim of knowledge is "satisfaction." However, the experience of this
shape of desiring consciousness is one that demonstrates the independence
of the object, *not* its dependence on an independent consciousness:

> Desire and the certainty of itself [that it attains] in its satisfaction is con-
> ditioned by the sublation of this other [the object]; this other must be in
> order for this sublation to be. Self-consciousness can therefore not sublate
> it through its negative relation; for that reason it reproduces [the object],
> and so the desire. The essence of desire is in fact something other than self-
> consciousness; and through this experience, this truth has emerged for it.[92]

In this account, the experience of desire, therefore, demonstrates that
consciousness's initial conception of itself is false: Instead of being the

[90] *PhG* 132/¶232.
[91] On the different aims and contributions of these two discussions, see Klotz 2008.
[92] *PhG* 107–8/¶175.

independent ground of dependent objects, desire demonstrates an equal
dependence on the objects that consciousness distinguishes from itself.
This failure is dialectical in the specific sense that Hegel identified in the
"Introduction": "The satisfaction of desire is, therefore, the reflection of
self-consciousness in itself," or its realization that what it took to be true –
the "in-itself" – is really simply consciousness's knowing of that truth.

At the same time, the experience of desire is generative, it gives rise
to a new object and a new determinate relation to that object. The new
object that would secure self-consciousness's claim to independence is one
that, unlike "satisfaction," would not depend on self-consciousness's own
activity of negation: "On account of the independence of the object, [self-
consciousness] can attain satisfaction only by carrying out the negation of
it; but the object must carry out this negation in itself, and so must be for
the other what it is in itself."[93] The new object is one that would not depend
on consumption by consciousness to demonstrate that consciousness is its
truth, but would instead "negate itself." At the conclusion of the dialectic of
desire, Hegel identifies this self-negating object in two ways. First, he identifies it in terms of "nature": "This universal independent nature, in which
negation is as absolute, is the species as such."[94] Presumably his idea is that
"negation is absolute" in the species, since the fate of each of its members
is their destruction, even though the species itself remains "independent."

However, he also identifies this new object as "self-consciousness"
itself. At this stage, the sense in which self-consciousness is capable of
"negating itself" is left open, though we shall see that Hegel thinks that
negativity is essential to self-consciousness and to self-conscious beings.
If we grant this capacity for self-negation to self-consciousness, then it
should be clear why Hegel states that "*Self-consciousness achieves its satisfaction only in another self-consciousness*"[95] and why we now find, for
the first time "A *self-consciousness* exists *for a self-consciousness.*"[96] That is,
what would really satisfy self-consciousness's desire – what would bear
out its claim to independence – is an object that "negated itself." Since,
as we shall see, the act of recognizing entails a sort of "self-negation,"
specifically of holding one's desires in check, there is a sense in which
what self-consciousness desires is recognition. However, *for it*, its desire
is not for recognition, but rather for any object that, by "negating itself"

[93] *PhG* 108/¶175.
[94] *PhG* 108/¶175.
[95] *PhG* 108/¶175.
[96] *PhG* 108/¶177.

could secure its self-knowledge.[97] Rather, it is only *we* who see that recognition is what would really satisfy self-consciousness, and there is no reason to think either that Hegel ascribes a "desire for recognition" to self-consciousness or that desire continues to play anything but a contrasting role in the subsequent account of recognition.[98]

With the emergence of this new "object" for consciousness, one that is self-negating, "self-consciousness," there also emerges a new form of knowing that corresponds to it. Hegel calls this form of knowing "recognition" (*Anerkennen*). It is common for interpreters to posit recognition as the aim of the shape of self-consciousness under consideration. And I shall argue that there is an important sense in which being recognized by another is constitutive of the "truth" for self-consciousness. However, Hegel is equally, if not more, interested in understanding the activity of recognizing as the source of the "knowledge of itself" that is at issue for self-consciousness. If we consider the "pure concept of recognition," we see that Hegel treats recognition primarily as a "deed" or "act" (*Tun*).[99] Indeed, it also bears note that, in *Phenomenology of Spirit*, Hegel uses the infinitive "*Anerkennen*" for "recognition," and not "*Anerkennung*," which suggests his focus is on recognition as an activity rather than as the independent result of an activity.[100] We can understand the specific sort of deed

[97] Consider a parallel case. Imagine that I am afflicted with severe back pain. Imagine also that a medicine exists – call it "Pain-Away" – that would cure me of the cause of my back pain and so eliminate my symptoms. There may be a sense in which I have a desire for "Pain-Away," since I want something that will eliminate my back pain and "Pain-Away" will do this. But this is the sort of desire that an observer might ascribe to me. I myself don't know that "Pain-Away" is what would satisfy my desire. For me, my desire makes no reference at all to "Pain-Away." Likewise, *for us*, it is clear that recognition is ultimately what would be the "object" that secures the self-knowledge that consciousness here seeks. However, *for consciousness*, there is no such articulate conception of the object of its desire. In this connection, see Stekeler-Weithofer's distinction between a "desire" and a "wish." Stekeler-Weithofer 2008, 216–217.

[98] And if we leave desire behind in this way, there is also no reason to see "satisfaction" as the criterion for success in the project of self-knowledge, since that criterion is bound to the specific form of knowing that is desire. Compare the role of satisfaction in Pippin 1989. I therefore also disagree with Stern's account of the roots of the struggle for recognition. In my reading, Stern ascribes too determinate a knowledge to the shape of consciousness under consideration, such that it could appropriately construe its aim as recognition. As I will show in §1.4, one of the significant features of Hegel's account is that this shape of self-consciousness has no adequate means for understanding the other whom it encounters. And that lack entails that it could also have no determinate conception of the recognition that it expects from the other. See Ferrarin 2019, 44 on the poverty of this initial shape of self-consciousness.

[99] *PhG* 110/¶182.

[100] Compare Markell 2003, 23ff. The substantive "*Anerkennung*" appears only once in the text of the Jena *Phenomenology* (*PhG* 248/¶456), and in *Philosophie des Geistes* it appears only in *Zusätze* (*TW* 10, 221–2/§432Z). Honneth's phrase "*Kampf um Anerkennung*" (1992) does not appear in the Jena *Phenomenology*, but only in the later work, and there again only in *Zusätze* (*TW* 10, 226/§436Z, 221/§432Z).

that "recognizing" comprises by considering its emergence from desire. That is, it is an activity of "self-negation," of holding oneself in check in light of some consideration of the other.[101]

As a shape of self-consciousness, this recognizing consciousness has a "double-object." The object that it aims ultimately to know is, as we have seen, itself. But just as desire produced satisfaction only through the consumption of an object separate from it, recognizing can be a source of self-knowledge only by means of a relation to another self-consciousness. So, for Hegel, the "first object" of recognition is another self-conscious being.[102] This point is a significant one since, as Ikäheimo and Laitinen have argued, both "recognition" and "*anerkennen*" can have multiple senses.[103] While, as we shall see, Hegel will on a very few occasions identify the object of recognition as a "law" or a norm, it is other self-conscious beings who are the primary objects of the sort of recognition that is his central concern in *Phenomenology*. Recognition, for Hegel, therefore, consists of an action of self-negation that establishes a determinate relation to another self-conscious being.

On its own, it is unclear how such an action could be a source of self-knowledge.[104] As we have seen, what distinguishes self-consciousness is its "double-object" structure, where the relation to an object that is other than consciousness ultimately contributes to the establishment of

[101] See Honneth 2008, 87. Of course, Honneth treats this self-negation as essentially identical with Kant's notion of respect, which involves the "demolition" or negation of self-love in favor of some moral consideration of another person. While Hegel will ultimately argue for the superiority of a moral idea of recognition, we do not find such explicitly moral ideas in chapter IV.

[102] By consequence, we should reject Brandom's claim that self-consciousness is a kind of self-recognition (Brandom 2007, 137), McDowell's allegorical interpretation of chapter IV (McDowell 2009a), Stekeler-Weithofer's "*intrapersonal self-relation*" interpretation (Stekeler-Weithofer 2008, 225; see also the lengthier account in Stekeler-Weithofer 2014, 1, 663–719, especially 676), and Cobben's "metaphorical" mind-body relation account (Cobben 2009, 42) on the grounds that recognition essentially involves, for Hegel, a relation to another self-consciousness. If, according to the distinction that Kelly 1972 draws, Kojève's interpretation neglects the subjective and psychological dimension of Hegel's account, these others devote insufficient attention to its essential social dimension.

[103] Ikäheimo and Laitinen 2007, 34. Stekeler-Weithofer introduces another sense of recognition, the "recognition of a tradition" (*Anerkennung einer Tradition*), though I do not believe that this sort of recognition requires a distinct category. See Stekeler-Weithofer 2008, 227.

[104] Ferrarin 2019, 36 rightly rejects accounts like Brandom's according to which recognition constitutes self-consciousness. However, he takes this conclusion to entail a rejection of any social ontology of the self. (37f) That conclusion need not follow. Instead, we can say that self-consciousness exists in-itself prior to recognition, but that it is only through establishing relations of reciprocal recognition that self-consciousness exists in-and-for-itself, where the latter is a condition of self-knowledge dependent on specific intersubjective relations that partly constitute it. On the link between recognition and self-consciousness existing in-and-for-itself, see *PhG* 109/¶178. On the distinction between the in-itself, for-itself, and in-and-for-itself in Hegel's account of self-consciousness, see Redding 2008, 95–97.

a self-relation. However, it is not yet obvious how the act of recognizing on its own could contribute to such a self-relation. Hegel finds the source of that self-relation by considering what is distinctive about the object of recognition, namely that it is another consciousness. As such, it is just as capable of the activity of self-negation as the first consciousness is, and so is equally capable of relating to that first consciousness by means of the determinate act of recognizing. In recognizing the first consciousness, this second consciousness, therefore, makes an essential contribution to the establishment of the structure that we have seen is constitutive of self-consciousness. That is, each achieves the ultimate self-relation constitutive of self-consciousness only through the like activity of the other. Recognition comprises a shape of self-consciousness only when the activity of recognizing is *reciprocal*: "They *recognize* themselves as *reciprocally* recognizing one another."[105]

To be sure, being recognized by the other is essential to the sort of self-knowledge that is Hegel's ultimate concern here. However, it is easy to understate the role that the activity of recognizing plays in contributing to the sort of self-knowledge that recognition is supposed to produce. The failure to acknowledge the importance of the activity of recognizing to Hegel's account contributes in part to the unfortunate interpretive tendency to overstate the importance of independence within Hegel's theory of recognition. That is, if recognition does not simply consist of the passive condition of being-recognized, but instead constitutes a shape of self-consciousness only insofar as both parties reciprocally engage in the activity of recognizing, then it should be clear that I am never really recognized as "independent." Instead, one of the general claims that Hegel aims to advance is that self-consciousness is never *simply* independent.[106] Even desire, the stance that was supposed to bear out the claim to independence in the most direct way, ultimately shows itself to be utterly dependent on its object. In general, as we have seen, what distinguishes self-consciousness is its double-object structure. For Hegel, then, object-relation and so object-dependence is an essential feature of any shape of self-consciousness. Likewise, whatever independence we can ascribe to self-consciousness will depend on the acknowledgment of this constitutive dependence, and so will be necessarily relative. Indeed, it is the failure

---

[105] *PhG* 110/¶184. This account addresses the question that Dahlstrom 2013 raises as to why recognition must be reciprocal for Hegel: It is only if the other recognizes me as I recognize them that either of us can be said to be a "self-consciousness."

[106] On this issue, see Redding 2005.

to acknowledge this essential dependence that initially undermines the achievement of relations of genuine reciprocal recognition.

Before turning to Hegel's account of that failure, one more point regarding Brandom's interpretation of chapter IV bears noting. On the interpretation that I have been offering here, Hegel's account of the "pure concept of recognition" is particularly sparse. It does articulate the essential task of recognition within the text: Recognition is important because of its contribution to our knowledge of ourselves as self-conscious beings. Likewise, it clarifies what sort of thing recognition itself is: It is an activity of self-negation undertaken in light of consideration of another self-conscious being. Finally, it shows why recognition is essentially reciprocal: The activity of recognizing contributes to self-knowledge only if it is complemented by the like activity of another self-conscious being who is, as Hegel will say, fundamentally the "equal" of the first self-conscious being. At the same time, it should be clear just how much this pure concept of recognition leaves open. Which specific activities of "self-negation" will actually contribute to the achievement of recognition? What further ideas about the basic character of the parties to recognition – beyond their being "self-conscious" beings – are necessary for securing these relations of reciprocity?

There is an interpretive tendency, again visible in Brandom's account, to try to anticipate Hegel's responses to these questions by depending on richer conceptions of what it means to be a self-conscious being. For example, Brandom's account ultimately depends on ideas like "accountability," "responsibility," "social substance," "selfhood," and "authority" that appear nowhere in these early parts of chapter IV.[107] As Paul Redding has argued, these aspects of Brandom's treatment should worry us since they seem to involve an excessively legalistic – we might even say bureaucratic – conception of the meaning and significance of recognition.[108] Such accounts should raise significant interpretive red flags, since they run the same risk as noncontextualist accounts do, that is, they threaten to undermine the claims about the necessity of the progression that we find within the text, and so likewise undermine the rigor of Hegel's philosophical argument, which doesn't simply aim to present an accidental collection of observations, but instead to constitute a science of the experience

[107] In this connection, see also Brandom 2019, chapter 9. These ideas predominate in Pippin 2011. We find a similar flaw in Honneth's moral account of the argument of chapter IV. Even if recognition requires checking my desires in light of the consideration of another, Hegel does not endorse the basically Kantian account of respect on which Honneth draws to interpret chapter IV. See Honneth 2008.

[108] Redding 2007.

of consciousness. While chapter IV makes essential contributions to our understanding of the role and character of recognition within the text, the remainder of this study is premised on the claim that it is only by considering specific, subsequent developments in the text that we can sufficiently grasp Hegel's account of the conditions for securing relations of genuinely reciprocal recognition.

Indeed, when we consider the immediate "experience" of this shape of self-consciousness, we do not find reciprocity, but instead, a relation of "one-sided" recognition. Instead of the realization of the pure concept of recognition, we find, in Hegel's famous account of "lordship and bondage," its determinate negation.

1.4 One-Sided Recognition and the Negativity of the Subject

That the initial attempt to secure relations of reciprocal intersubjective recognition fails is famously evident in Hegel's account of "lordship and bondage." The "struggle to the death" between two self-conscious beings, each seeking the assertion of their own independence, is resolved in a relation of recognition that is "one-sided and unequal" (*einseitiges und ungleiches*) and not "reciprocal" (*gegenseitig*).[109] The primary question for interpreters is *why* we do not initially find the full realization of the pure concept of recognition, but instead only its partial realization in a relationship where one self-consciousness counts as nothing but a thing. My aim in what follows is to suggest that the specific causes of this initial failure of recognition lie in the absence of the conditions for genuine reciprocity. In particular, what the two self-conscious beings lack is a conception of what Hegel calls their "essence" as self-consciousness. Consequently, they are unable appropriately to conceive of not only the other whom they might recognize, but also themselves. In the absence of that self-understanding, reciprocal recognition is impossible.[110]

The first point that should be noted in considering the causes of this initial failure of recognition is the fact that Hegel thinks that it is *possible*

[109] *PhG* 113/¶191.
[110] We find significant attention to the epistemic conditions for the achievement of recognition in recent literature on Fichte and his relation to Hegel. See Clarke 2014, and Gottlieb 2016. In stressing the centrality of self-understanding, I am contesting the importance of the issue of authority in chapter IVA. Ultimately, Hegel does endorse a view of knowing that appeals to discourse and language for the achievement of recognition. However, we do not find that achievement in chapter IVA, and construing it in terms of the basic dynamic of chapter IVA can lead to a skewed understanding of the role of struggle. As we shall see in Chapter 5, the conditions for discursive agreement are not the same as those of the resolution of a violent struggle to the death.

for recognition to be "one-sided."[111] This possibility raises two significant questions: First, if recognition is, according to its pure concept, essentially reciprocal, *how* is one-sided recognition possible? Second, *why* do we find relations of one-sided recognition emerge at this stage? What is the impediment preventing the two self-consciousnesses from recognizing one another reciprocally? In general, the core challenge that Hegel identifies stems from the basic stance that self-consciousness adopts toward otherness, a stance that is fundamentally *negative*.[112]

With regard to the first question, if recognition is, according to its pure concept, essentially reciprocal, it is certainly surprising that Hegel thinks that it is possible for a relation of recognition to be "one-sided" in this way. To be sure, Hegel must count the recognition of the lord by the bondsman as deficient in some sense, but it is not clear how this relation could be *only* deficient, and not, instead, simply fail to be a relation of recognition at all, if recognition is essentially reciprocal.

Clarifying the sense in which this relation can still be one of recognition, therefore, requires attention to the idea of *reciprocity* on which Hegel's view of recognition depends. As we have seen, for Hegel an individual recognizes another through the performance of specific "deeds." While it remains an open question in chapter IV which specific deeds are constitutive of recognition, the "pure concept of recognition" seems to impose some requirements on them. Specifically, recognition requires that each agent "does what it does *only* insofar as the other does the same."[113] By this standard, a relation of recognition will be reciprocal when two agents (in the formalization that I offer in what follows, I call them "a" and "b") perform the same deed, "R".

Of course, more than just common activity is required to ensure that the resulting relation will be *reciprocal*, since not every situation in which two agents perform the same deed is one of reciprocity. You and I might both walk down the academic mall today, but it doesn't make sense to say that we've done so "reciprocally." Instead, Hegel insists that reciprocity requires not simply acting in a similar way, but also treating oneself and the other in the same way. This entails first that for a relation to be one of

---

[111] Some recognition theorists deny this possibility. See, for example, Ikäheimo and Laitinen 2007, 38.
    Neuhouser argues that all relations of recognition must be reciprocal, but not all are equal. This account is puzzling since it would seem natural for Hegel to *contrast* what is reciprocal (*gegenseitig*) with what is one-sided (*einseitig*). Compare Neuhouser 2009, 49.

[112] As I stress at the outset of Chapter 2, ; the relevant contrast here is with "Reason," which adopts a positive stance toward otherness, finding itself in it.

[113] *PhG* 110/¶182.

reciprocity, each "requires" (*fodert*) the other to behave in the same way that they do.[114] To this extent, the relevant reciprocity is what we would call a *normative* idea, since it involves the application of certain standards to one's own deeds and those of others, and since it is possible for the other or for me to *fail* to meet those standards.

In addition to simply acting a certain way and requiring that the other does too, reciprocity requires specific actions done to oneself and to the other. So, reciprocity requires that the deeds one performs in relation to the other be the same as the deeds that one performs in relation to one-self. To appropriate the terminology introduced by Michael Thompson, recognition relations involve an "intrinsically relational" form of norma-tivity, and they require expression in specifically "dikaiological" judg-ments, in distinction from the more general class of deontic judgments.[115] Consequently, their formalization requires two-place predicates, one reflexive, and one establishing a relation to the other: aRa and aRb.

And finally, in order for these deeds to be undertaken reciprocally, the established relations must be *reversible*, so that, however I relate to the other, the other ought to be able to relate to me in the same way.

But now reciprocal recognition will depend on the satisfaction of at least four specific requirements for the deeds of the related parties.

RR1: If I treat the other in a certain way, they must treat themselves in the same way: If aRb, then bRb.

RR2: I require that the other treats themselves a certain way only if I treat them that way: bRb only if aRb.

RR3: If I treat the other in a certain way, then I must treat myself in the same way: If aRb, then aRa.

RR4: Finally, if the other treats themselves a certain way, then they must treat me the same way: If bRb, then bRa.

This formalization may seem a tedious exercise, but it can help us make sense of the way in which we can find a relation of recognition among indi-viduals that is, nonetheless, not reciprocal. Indeed, if we consider Hegel's account of the relation between the lord and the bondsman, we find that RR1 and RR2 are satisfied, but not RR3 and RR4. That is, Hegel claims

[114] *PhG* 110/¶182.
[115] Thompson 2004. I explain this terminology more fully in §2.2. These characteristics of the "pure concept of recognition" provide robust textual reasons for rejecting accounts of self-consciousness that involve the idea of intra-subjective relations of recognition, as Brandom's does explicitly ("I cannot be properly self-conscious [recognize myself]…" Brandom 2007, 137) and as McDowell's does implicitly.

that the bondsman treats themselves in the same way that the lord treats them, namely as a thing: The bondsman "sublates themselves as being-for-itself and thereby it does to itself what the first [the lord] does to it."[116] So the relation between lord and bondsman satisfies RR1. Likewise, since the bondsman lacks genuine agency of their own, and instead only does what the lord requires of them, Hegel says that "the deed of the second is the proper deed of the first; for, what the bondsman does is properly the deed of the lord."[117] The bondsman is permitted to act for themselves only if the lord has permitted them to act in that way. So RR2 is satisfied.

However, Hegel argues that genuine reciprocity requires, in addition, that I treat myself the way that I treat the other, and the other is justified in treating me how they treat themselves.[118] But these conditions are not satisfied in the relation of lord and bondsman. That is, the lord does not perform the same deeds as the lord requires of the bondsman, so it is not the case that the lord "does themselves, what they require of the other."[119] And so RR3 is not satisfied. And finally, the lord does not permit the bondsman to treat the lord as the bondsman treats themselves, namely as a thing. So is RR4 also not satisfied. The relation of recognition between the lord and bondsman institutes the *inequality* (*Ungleichheit*) of the parties,[120] while reciprocal recognition yields relations of *equality* (*Gleichheit*) among self-conscious beings.[121]

Of course, instead of fully reciprocal recognition, we find in the relation of lord and bondsman merely one-sided recognition, in which the lord is in a condition of "being-recognized" (*Anerkanntsein*) while the bondsman recognizes the lord without being recognized themselves. The absence of reciprocity, however, constitutes a unique configuration of self-consciousness that limits its capacity to be a source of self-knowledge.

Up to now, Hegel's claim has been that recognition can be a source of self-knowledge only insofar as it is a shape of self-consciousness that embodies its distinctive structure, that is, only insofar as it is a shape of consciousness in which a conscious being's self-relation is ultimately mediated by its relation to an object that is "other" than itself. And he

---

[116] *PhG* 113/¶191.
[117] *PhG* 113/¶191.
[118] As Hegel puts the point: "But for proper recognition is lacking the moment that what the lord does to the other, he also does against himself, and what the bondsman does to himself, he also does to the other." *PhG* 113/¶191.
[119] *PhG* 110/¶182.
[120] *PhG* 110/¶185.
[121] I will consider this institution of equality extensively in the remainder of this study. To anticipate, see *PhG* 362/¶671.

has claimed that the relevant shape of self-consciousness is one in which a conscious being *recognizes* that mediating object as itself another conscious being, who relates to the first conscious being by also *recognizing* it. The "struggle to the death" and the resulting relation of lord and bondsman indicates the *necessity* that relations of recognition be reciprocal in order to be sources of self-knowledge. In the absence of reciprocity, either one's relations to other conscious beings yield no self-knowledge – the position of the lord – or that self-knowledge is achieved not through relations to conscious others, but only through things – the position of the bondsman.

While we do not find a relation of reciprocal recognition in chapter IV, Hegel does argue that the bondsman's experience makes a positive contribution to the sort of "knowledge of itself" that is his broad concern in chapter IV. Identifying the key elements of this experience is important both for understanding *why* the relation between lord and bondsman cannot be reciprocal, but also for grasping a deep challenge to the possibility of genuine recognition among individuals.

The primary reason why the initial encounter between two self-conscious beings does not result in a relation of reciprocal recognition is that the two parties lack an appropriate conception of what it means to be a self-conscious being – the epistemic conditions for the achievement of reciprocal recognition are lacking. That is, the two self-conscious beings who become the lord and bondsman initially understand only themselves, and not the other, to be a "being-for-itself" or an "I." That is, their conception of the "I" is exclusive, and depends on grasping any object – including one another – as merely the "negative" of themselves. In turn, each understands only itself to be independent, continuing to hold that the world of objective nature is merely dependent on and only there for it. However, "being-recognized" (*Anerkanntsein*) as independent requires, in Hegel's account, an experience that undermines this strict opposition between I and other, and between independence and dependence: "It must intuit [*anschauen*] its being-other as pure being-for-itself or as absolute negation."[122] Put otherwise, what is missing is an experience whose object both is and is understood to be another self-conscious being.[123]

---

[122] *PhG* 112/¶186.

[123] The ultimate root of the struggle is therefore the attempt to assert one's own independence. That attempt entails the requirement of "negating" the other. But since the action of the first self-consciousness is equally the action of the second, it just is the first's staking its own life. We need not hold that either party to the struggle is explicitly seeking recognition, or asserting itself as a subject. Compare Stern 2002, 75–83.

Hegel argues that the lord does not enjoy this sort of experience. Instead, the lord's experience is simply a modified form of the experience of desire. Like the experience of desire, the lord ultimately comes to a sense of themselves as independent through the experience of pleasure that they derive from the consumption of the object. Unlike the merely desiring consciousness, the lord need not actively "negate" the object for it to become a source of pleasure, since the lord can depend on the labor of the bondsman to do this.[124] At the same time, the lord doesn't really experience themselves as independent, since they really are dependent on the bondsman, even if they don't acknowledge this dependence. So the lord's attempt to validate their initial "self-certainty" that they are independent is actually a failure, since the "truth" of the lord's condition is really dependence.

By contrast, Hegel does argue that the bondsman's experience provides a genuine source of self-knowledge, even if this self-knowledge is not secured through being-recognized. It is not accidental that the bondsman is the party to the relationship who engages in the activity of recognizing, which I've argued is the characteristic shape of knowing under consideration here. Like the lord, the bondsman stakes their life, trying to demonstrate their independence from their merely natural existence. However, unlike the lord, the bondsman experiences the "fear of death,"[125] and, in the face of this fear, capitulates, establishing the relation between lord and bondsman. The experience of the fear of death, however, is unique in character. It is, according to Hegel, an experience of "anxiety" or "dread" (*Angst*). As Heidegger will do over a century later, Hegel argues that *Angst* is distinct in not simply being a fear of any determinate object (it is not "for the sake of this or that, [occurring at] this or that moment"), but rather a felt response to a threat to "its entire essential being [*Wesen*]." Through the experience of *Angst*, the bondsman "was inwardly dissolved, was shaken throughout in itself, and everything fixed trembled in it." This experience of the fear of death is, according to Hegel an experience of "pure negativity" or "absolute negativity," the negation of anything and everything fixed and determinate.

At the same time, Hegel argues that the bondsman's experience of the fear of death, of *Angst*, is at the same time an experience of itself as a self-conscious being: "This pure universal movement, the absolute becoming-fluid of everything existent is, however, the simple essence of self-consciousness, absolute negativity, *pure being-for-itself*, that is in this

[124] *PhG* 113/¶190.
[125] *PhG* 114/¶194.

consciousness."[126] That is, death and "the essence of self-consciousness" are both "absolute negativity." Like death, "the essence of self-consciousness" or "pure being-for-itself" both entail the capacity to negate by transcending any particular determinacy. This transcendent capacity is grounded in our very constitution as conscious beings, since Hegel has argued from the outset of the "Introduction" that consciousness consists of the capacity to distinguish objects from itself. The very character of the I consists of being that for which any object might be, but in being, itself, not any one of those objects. To this extent, "the essence of self-consciousness" is "absolute negativity," the characteristic of *not* being any particular determination or being.

The experience of death, therefore, is an experience of the very essence of self-consciousness. As Bristow has argued, the assertion of the importance of the "independence" of self-consciousness is one of the primary features that distinguish *Phenomenology* from the prior Jena writings.[127] However, it should be clear that Hegel thinks that this "independence" is a tenuous one. And this tenuousness derives from the way in which we can come to experience it as something "*actual*" (wirklich).[128] That is, if the essence of self-consciousness consists fundamentally of "absolute negativity" then it is not immediately clear how it can become something actual, something real and existent, or how it can acquire a positive standing. Indeed, for the bondsman, this absolute negativity takes positive shape, but only in necessarily incomplete forms. Through the activity of labor, the bondsman "works off" (*arbeitet … hinweg*) their "dependence on natural existence."[129] However, this activity is incapable of asserting the independence of self-consciousness, since it depends on nature for its realization. Likewise, the bondsman does come to an "intuition of its independent being *as itself*" in the independent thing on which they work.[130] This formative activity contributes to the bondsman's development of a determinate "ability" (*Geschicklichkeit*) to labor in a specific way, which in turn is the source of a distinctive "*sense of oneself*" (eigner Sinn) or "*self-will*" (Eigensinn).[131] However, the power that a mere ability lends us is different to a great degree from the sort of "absolute negativity" that constitutes the essence of

---

[126] *PhG* 114/¶194.
[127] Bristow 2007, 189.
[128] *PhG* 114/¶194.
[129] *PhG* 114/¶194.
[130] *PhG* 115/¶195.
[131] *PhG* 115–6/¶196

self-consciousness, since the latter is supposed to be able to comprehend *any* determinacy, and not simply this or that particular domain of objects.

We do not find fully reciprocal recognition in the relation of lord and bondsman, then, because neither of the participants in the struggle to the death knows that the "essence of self-consciousness" is "absolute negativity," and so is different in kind from the basic character of the determinate objects that we encounter in experience. Conceiving of the other as a self-conscious being, therefore, requires understanding them as "absolute negativity," which entails, in turn, that they cannot be understood in the way that other given objects are.

However, this discovery of the essence of self-consciousness also poses a challenge for *any* account of successful recognition. Such recognition is, Hegel has been arguing, necessary for intersubjective relations to be a source of full self-knowledge. And this entails that, while the bondsman's experience yields an essential intuition of "the essence of self-consciousness," that essence alone is distinct from what I have been calling the *structure* of self-consciousness. It should be clear that the resolution of the dialectic of lord and bondsman has not produced the sort of intersubjective relation that Hegel presented in his sketch of the "pure concept of recognition." If recognition is a relation among self-conscious beings, and self-conscious beings are, at base, nothing positive or determinate but "absolute negativity," it is unclear what deeds would be adequate for bringing about such recognition. How can I really recognize *you* if what you (ultimately and essentially) *are* is nothing positive?

This challenge is a deep one for recognition theory. It finds partial expression in an apparent tension between the requirements of recognition and those of autonomy. As Charles Taylor has identified, when the agent of recognition has only "a confining or demeaning or contemptible" conception of the other, the resulting "Nonrecognition or misrecognition can inflict harm, can be a form of oppression, imprisoning someone in a false, distorted, and reduced mode of being."[132] The worry that Hegel's argument about the essence of self-consciousness raises is that *no* conception of the other or their "identity" will *ever* be adequate to secure relations of recognition, since it will always be an imposition from without, and will always require conceiving the other in terms of a determinacy that it is possible for them to negate, of binding them to an identity that they may just as well disavow. How is recognition, much less reciprocal recognition, actually possible for beings whose very fundamental essence is not to be anything determinate?[133]

[132] C. Taylor 1994, 25.
[133] This challenge will be familiar to readers of Sartre.

In part, Hegel's answer to this question will depend on an idea of self-definition. As Brandom puts the idea, "Essentially self-conscious creatures are (partially) self-*constituting* creatures."[134] In this account, what I am, and so how you go about recognizing me, will depend on how I take myself to be. For example, if I take myself to be the lord, the independent being, then you can recognize me only if your deeds take account of this fact. However, equally important challenges for the theory of recognition stem from adopting this position. As we have seen, recognition is, according to its pure concept, "reciprocal," and reciprocity entails that the way that I take myself to be bears on the way that I take you to be, and vice versa. So this self-constitution must be subject to the conditions for reciprocity if relations of intersubjective recognition are to be possible. But the demands of reciprocity seem to impose limitations on me that are, in principle, at odds with the idea that I am "absolute negativity," since the way I take myself to be seems now to depend on how you take yourself to be.

In light of these challenges, the argument that Hegel aims to offer in the remainder of the text is particularly ambitious. That is, he aims to argue that relations of recognition do not constitute impediments to the full realization of the essence of self-consciousness, but are instead absolutely necessary for it. Moreover, he will argue that it is only when they stand in such relations that it is possible for individuals to have the sort of self-knowledge that is the ultimate aim of his account of self-consciousness.

1.5 Self-Negation and the Emergence of Sociality

At the conclusion of chapter IVA of *Phenomenology*, the account of recognition finds itself at a significant impasse. On the one hand, Hegel has suggested that recognition comprises an important source of self-knowledge. On the other hand, he has shown that the conditions required for the achievement of a recognition adequate to its pure concept, genuinely reciprocal recognition, are absent when we consider only self-conscious beings in their existence as distinct individuals. While such beings can learn something significant about themselves – that their "essence" is "pure negativity" – that fact presents its own challenge for the achievement of recognition: What conception of the other whom I aim to recognize can be adequate to grasp that fact about them?

Hegel presents the way around this impasse by introducing the idea of what I shall call sociality into the text in chapter IVB, "The Freedom

---

[134] Brandom 2007, 128.

of Self-Consciousness." It might come as a surprise that we find this idea emerge in this context, since the "shapes" of self-consciousness that Hegel considers there – Stoicism, Skepticism, and the unhappy consciousness – are, at least initially, not intersubjective relations at all, but rather, like the relation between the bondsman and the thing, essentially "individual" ones. However, the argument that Hegel presents in the chapter is significant, since it aims to demonstrate that the fact that self-conscious beings are essentially "absolute negativity" necessarily generates ideas and norms that are "social" in the sense that they can serve as possible mediators of intersubjective relationships. Instead of being fundamentally opposed to the possibility of reciprocal recognition, the absolute negativity of self-consciousness rather serves to establish the social terms that make it possible.

In this discussion, and throughout what follows, I shall use "social" and "sociality" in a specific sense. A relationship will count as "social" if it is mediated by norms and standards that can be shared among individuals. While sociality and recognition are therefore similar in that they both involve relations between self-conscious beings, they are distinct in the following way. Recognition is a specific intersubjective relation that is essentially reciprocal, and its ultimate object is another self-conscious being. By contrast, in sociality, the stress is rather on the norms or rules that I acknowledge, and that others might acknowledge too. We can appreciate the distinctiveness of these ideas by pointing out that some forms of sociality will render recognition impossible: If the norm that I acknowledge demeans or negates you, it will undermine the possibility of achieving a relation of recognition with you. At the same time, Hegel will argue that some social relations are essential to the achievement of recognition, since acknowledging the correct norms will be necessary to mediate intersubjective relations.

The two shapes of consciousness that follow Hegel's account of lordship and bondage, stoicism and skepticism, embody a conception of the individual as independent to the extent that they engage in the activity of thinking. Stoicism attempts to demonstrate its independence by subjecting the world to a "criterion" that it finds in its own thinking.[135] In contrast to the stoic's aloof stance in relation to the world, the skeptic realizes the

---

[135] Stoicism beings together what was separated in the relation between the lord and bondsman, the independence of the lord and the bondsman's labor. And that unity of "being-for-itself" and "object" is what Hegel calls "thinking." *PhG* 116/¶197. At the same time, Hegel argues that the stoic's position is untenable, since the "criterion" on the basis of which they claim to judge – "rationality" or "the self-sameness of thinking" – is empty and without content. *PhG* 118/¶200. By consequence, the stoic must give up there merely "abstract" freedom and come to have "the actual experience of what freedom of thought is." *PhG* 119/¶202.

freedom of thinking by demonstrating the "complete inessentiality and lack of independence of [what is] other" to self-consciousness.[136] Unlike that of the stoic, the skeptic's freedom is one that is engaged with the concrete world of experience in demonstrating the nullity of that world.

Hegel characterizes both of these configurations of the freedom of self-consciousness in terms of the issue that emerged within the struggle to the death, the negativity of self-consciousness. While stoicism is "the incomplete negation of being-other," skepticism is "its absolute negation."[137] This negativity is central to the skeptic: "The negativity of the free self-consciousness comes to be in the manifold configuration of the life [of the skeptic] a real negativity."[138] So the experience of stoicism and skepticism continues the account of what self-consciousness is by considering the way in which the "absolute negativity" of self-consciousness comes to be something that self-conscious beings experience and try to make sense of.

That experience is significant in a number of ways. First, the experience of the skeptic shows that negativity is not merely abstract, but rather the "*dialectical movement*"[139] that structured the experience of object-consciousness. And, moreover, the skeptic experiences that dialectical movement not as an event that merely befalls it (it is not something to which it must "surrender" [*preisgeben*]), but rather as "a moment of self-consciousness," and so as itself.[140] The skeptic experiences their own freedom in deliberately enacting the negativity that comprises the essence of self-consciousness.

And the skeptic's experience demonstrates the challenges inherent in the project of enacting that negativity, in "realizing" it in a "life" that one could actually live. Specifically, Hegel argues that the skeptic is obliged to equivocate about what they really are. They claim an independence in relation to the world, so that every form of being-other is inessential, and their own freedom in relation to it is what is essential. However, they bear out that independence only through the negativity of thought, which requires engagement with the worldly objects that they deem inessential and null. What the skeptic needs is a means for unifying these two aspects of their way of life into a coherent self-understanding.

In my account of lordship and bondage, I stressed the way in which the negativity of self-consciousness presents a challenge to the

---

[136] *PhG* 119/¶202.
[137] *PhG* 118–9/¶201.
[138] *PhG* 119/¶202.
[139] *PhG* 119/¶203.
[140] *PhG* 119–20/¶203.

achievement of recognition. However, Hegel's account of skepticism points to the way in which it threatens the possibility of a coherent self-understanding. Hegel brings these two issues together in his account of "the unhappy consciousness." The unhappy consciousness itself unifies the two "thoughts" that comprise skepticism, that of an unchangeable essence, and a changeable existence. It takes its task to be that of overcoming its internal division (it experiences itself as "*entzweit*")[141] by annulling its inessential existence and freeing itself from it, to become what it is essentially.[142] This shape of self-consciousness is significant for the account that I am reconstructing here since the activity of *recognizing* plays such an important role within it.

That is, through the course of the development of the three shapes of the unhappy consciousness that Hegel presents in the text – that of the "pure consciousness" of devotion,[143] that of the "actual" consciousness of desire and labor,[144] and the self-negating, ascetic consciousness that has experienced itself as actual[145] – recognizing comes to comprise the primary means through which self-consciousness relates to its object, its unchangeable essence.[146] In the second shape of the unhappy consciousness, it is the activity of "giving thanks" (*Danken*) through which the laboring self-consciousness achieves a relation to its unchangeable essence, an activity that Hegel characterizes as one of recognizing: "Its *thanking* [Danken] [...], in which it recognizes the other extreme as the essence, and sublates itself, is itself *its own deed*, which offsets the deed of the other, and sets in opposition to the self-sacrificing benevolent act an *equal* deed."[147] This act of giving thanks, however, is incomplete, since the thanking consciousness still experiences itself as a singular being separate from its essence within that action.

---

[141] *PhG* 122/¶207.

[142] *PhG* 124/¶213.

[143] *PhG* 124–6/¶¶215–217.

[144] *PhG* 126–128/¶¶218–222.

[145] *PhG* 128–131/¶¶223–230.

[146] The first unhappy consciousness, that of devotion, seeks to be recognized through its devotional rituals: "Present here is the inner movement of the *pure* mind [*Gemüt*] which *feels* itself, but painfully as division [*Entzweiung*]; the movement of infinite *longing* [Sehnsucht], which has the certainty that its essence is a pure mind, pure *thinking* which *thinks* itself *as singularity*; that, because it thinks of its object as pure singularity, is known and recognized by it." *PhG* 125/¶217. However, it construes its object and its essence as an unattainable "beyond." By consequence, while it seeks recognition, it does not itself engage in the activity of recognizing. The achievement of becoming what it is requires, instead, a new conception of its essence, not as an unattainable beyond, but as an "actuality," and of its relation to that actuality.

[147] *PhG* 128/¶222.

By contrast, in the third shape of the unhappy consciousness, the ascetic consciousness,[148] the activity of recognizing gives rise to a positive significance. Because it must experience itself as an individual, separate from its essence, in its own deeds, the ascetic consciousness takes as its aim a sort of self-negation, the elimination of its own singularity. In Hegel's portrayal, this act of self-negation does bring about a sort of unity with the unchangeable essence, though that unity is achieved only through a "medium" or "mediator" (*Mitte*), a "conscious being" (*ein bewußtes Wesen*).[149] Importantly, Hegel does not treat the relation to this mediator as one of recognition. Instead, he holds that the mediator's actions are necessary for the ascetic consciousness to achieve the sought-after unity with its essence. In its act of self-obliteration (*Vertilgung*), the ascetic consciousness

> frees itself from its deed and pleasure as *its own*; it repels from itself as the extreme existing-*for-itself* the essence of its *willing*, and throws off onto the medium or the servant [*Diener*] the ownness [*Eigenheit*] and freedom of decision, and so the *guilt* [Schuld] for its deeds. This mediator, standing in immediate relation to the unchangeable essence, serves with their *counsel* concerning what is *right*. Because the action is a following of an alien decision, it ceases, considered from the side of the deed or *willing*, to be its own.[150]

This action of the ascetic consciousness is significant for our purposes because Hegel characterizes it as an act of recognizing that is generative. First, in contrasting the ascetic's self-negation with the act of thanking, Hegel suggests that it comprises an act of outward and actual recognizing: "It can prove the renunciation of itself alone through this *actual* sacrifice; for it is only in it that the *deception* which lies in the *inner* recognizing of thanking through the heart, sentiment, and mind disappears, a recognizing which passes on [*abwälzt*] all the power of being-for-itself from itself, and ascribes it to a gift from above."[151] In contrast to the merely *inner* recognizing of labor and desire, in which the individual retains their "ownness" (*Eigenheit*), the ascetic's self-negation and acceptance of the counsel of the "medium" or "servant" amounts to an outward and actual act of recognizing. Of course, Hegel never suggests that the act of recognizing has as its object the mediator. Instead, it is the essential, unchangeable self-consciousness that is the proper object of this recognizing. And that act of

---

[148] I follow Siep in identifying this moment of the unhappy consciousness as ascetic. Siep 2000, 116.
[149] *PhG* 130/¶227.
[150] *PhG* 130/¶228.
[151] *PhG* 130/¶229.

recognizing transforms the relation that the ascetic consciousness bears to that essential self-consciousness.[152]

The second significant feature of this act of recognizing is that it is generative:

> This sacrifice of the inessential extreme is not simply a one-sided deed, but contained the deed of the other in itself. For the surrender of its own will [*eignen Willens*] is only negative in one aspect, but it is, according *to its concept* or *in itself*, equally positive, that is, it is the positing of the will as the will *of an other*, and determines the will not as a singular but as a universal will.[153]

Because it comprises an act that is actual,[154] and not merely inner, the self-negation of the recognizing consciousness takes on a positive significance and generates a new "universal will." This development is of great significance for Hegel's account of recognition in the text, since the new universal will that is "posited" through the act of recognizing comprises what I've already identified as a form of *sociality*. In contrasting the singular will that the ascetic consciousness gives up with the universal will that its self-sacrifice generates, Hegel points to the possibility of *shared* norms and standards that might constrain individuals' actions. As we shall see in the next chapter, Hegel construes the idea of "ethical life" in part in terms of this idea of a shared universal that is generated through the "self-negating" acts of individuals.[155]

However, the line of thinking that Hegel sets out here also highlights the implications of construing the essence of self-conscious beings as

---

[152] Siep, I think, goes too far in identifying the relation between the individual consciousness and the universal consciousness as one of "reciprocal recognition." Siep 2000, 116. That is, Hegel nowhere suggests that the universal consciousness in turn recognizes (or even *could* recognize) the individual. Instead of instantiating the structure of reciprocal recognition, the relation between the individual consciousness and the universal will is instead a paradigmatic instance of what I shall call norm recognition (which can be shared among individuals), not the intersubjective recognition that Hegel suggests can be genuinely reciprocal.

[153] *PhG* 131/¶230.

[154] Hegel describes the distinctive "act" or "deed" of the ascetic consciousness in the following way: "This *unity* of the objective and of being-for-itself lies in the *concept* of the act, and it thus comes to be for consciousness as the essence and *object*. But because this unity is not for it the concept of its act, it does not come to be an object *for it* immediately and through itself. Instead, it allows this still broken certainty to be expressed by the mediating servant, that its unhappiness is only *in itself* the inverted act, that is, the act that is self-satisfying, or blessed pleasure; its impoverished act is equally *in itself* the inverted, that is, absolute act; according to its concept, the act is an act in general only as the act of an individual... But in this object, in which for it its act and being are as this *singular* consciousness, being and act *in itself*, the idea [*Vorstellung*] of *reason* has come to be for it, the certainty of consciousness, of being, in its singularity, *in itself* absolute or of being all reality." *PhG* 131/¶230.

[155] See especially *PhG* 194–5/¶351.

"absolute negativity." I have raised the worry that it is unclear how that conception of self-consciousness could generate a positive conception of the other whom I might recognize. In chapter IVB, Hegel presented an argument about how such self-conscious beings come to be obliged to think of themselves as a result of the experience of trying to live a life in light of that self-conception. He has argued that the only way that individuals can make sense of that experience is to understand that negativity to be generative or productive when it is directed toward themselves. Specifically, Hegel is arguing that the act of recognizing, which, we've seen (in §1.3) consists of a kind of "self-negation," generates forms of sociality, shapes of a "universal will," that can mediate relations between self-conscious beings.

To be sure, the ascetic understands themselves to be doing something quite different. That is, their aim is the simple negation of themselves in their individuality. However, Hegel's argument is that that act of self-negation *cannot help but be* productive. It too embodies the structure of the "dialectical movement" that the skeptic first discovered. And Hegel's claim is that the negativity that drives that dialectical movement generates something positive. While the ascetic does not aim to generate universal norms and standards that can mediate social relationships, Hegel wants to show that the attempt to enact ascetic ideals will necessarily shape the activity of the ascetic in ways that are in principle shareable with others. And since their self-sacrifice is a real and actual act, the ascetic really *does* "negate themselves," shape their actions and life, in light of the consideration of an other. It is the act of *recognizing* that gives rise to a new kind of reality, social reality.

CHAPTER 2

Sociality

I have been arguing that Hegel appeals to recognition to address an issue about self-knowledge: Recognition names a structure of self-consciousness in which I come to know myself by means of my relation to another self-conscious being. However, we saw that this self-knowledge was difficult to achieve, since it required a relation between self-conscious beings that is *reciprocal*. When, like the "lord" in Hegel's account, I am recognized by another, without in turn recognizing them, my purported claim to be independent is really false, since it actually depends on, but does not acknowledge, its relation to the other. Instead, we saw that Hegel believes that it is the "bondsman," the self-conscious being who recognizes the other without being recognized, who comes to a more adequate conception of themselves: They know that they are not independent, but they do learn through experience something about the basic character of self-consciousness, namely that it is "absolute negativity."

When the dynamic of recognition reemerges in the Jena *Phenomenology* in Hegel's account of "Reason," specifically in the introduction to chapter VB, "The Actualization of Rational Self-Consciousness Through Itself," this issue of self-knowledge is central. In contrast to "self-consciousness," which sustains a "negative" relation to otherness, "reason" generally is a shape of consciousness that aims to find itself in otherness, in particular by finding what is other than it to have the basic character of itself, rationality and comprehensibility. The central challenge that reason faces in coming to know self-conscious beings lies in the fact that they are capable of *action*.[1] Knowledge of self-conscious beings, therefore, requires a stance that can come to terms with their "self-productive" character, with the

---

[1] The initial stance that reason takes, "observation," is largely adequate to the task of comprehending the rest of the natural world. But it proves inadequate to comprehending the basic character of self-conscious beings, since they are always capable of realizing themselves in ways that can exceed what is given to observation at any moment.

78

ways in which self-conscious beings actualize *themselves* through their own agency.

It is in the context of explaining this notion of self-actualization that Hegel both introduces the idea of *ethical life* and *re*introduces the idea of recognition:

> If we take up the goal [which is] the *concept* of what has already emerged for us, namely recognized self-consciousness [*das anerkannte Selbstbewußtsein*] that has certainty of itself and its truth in the other free self-consciousness in its reality, or if we raise this still inner spirit up to the substance that has already blossomed into its existence, [we find that] this concept grows into the concept of *the domain of ethical life* [das Reich der Sittlichkeit].[2]

So Hegel's argument is that self-knowledge requires a relation of reciprocal recognition, and that we find the "reality" and "existence" of reciprocal recognition, recognition adequate to its "pure concept," only in the "domain of ethical life": It is only when self-conscious subjects share a common set of customs and laws, a shared set of practical *norms*, that a relation of reciprocal recognition is possible among them. That is, what I'll designate "reciprocal intersubjective recognition" depends on what I'll call "mutual norm recognition."

So far, this claim might seem uncontroversial, given a now-prominent account of Hegel's concept of recognition that we find exemplified in the work of readers like Honneth and Pippin. Both share the common interpretive strategy of seeking to link the early Jena *Phenomenology* account of recognition to the mature account of freedom that we find in *Philosophy of Right*. In that work, Hegel appeals to ethical life as part of a theory of freedom, so that I can be free – specifically, I can enjoy what Neuhouser and Honneth have called "social freedom"[3] – only insofar as I participate in a shared form of ethical life. Theorists of social freedom, such as Honneth, and interpreters of Hegel, such as Pippin, have both argued that the primary importance of recognition in this theory of ethical life lies in the contribution that it makes to the achievement of a free life: I can be free only if I am recognized by others as such.

However, we can raise significant questions about whether this account of the relation between recognition and ethical life is appropriate to *Phenomenology of Spirit*. First, while it is clear that Hegel's *Philosophy of Right* aims to present a systematic account of the objective conditions for

---

[2] *PhG* 194/¶349.
[3] See Neuhouser 2000, Honneth 2001 and 2011.

the realization of freedom, freedom does not obviously play the same programmatic role in the earlier *Phenomenology of Spirit*.[4] With respect to the issue of recognition, we have already seen that Hegel's initial interest in recognition stems from a concern not about the freedom of the will and the objective conditions for its realization, but rather about *self-knowledge*.

Second, both Honneth and Pippin stress the role of *institutions* in Hegel's theory of recognition. And this approach is certainly appropriate to *Philosophy of Right*, given the centrality of specific institutions to Hegel's theory of ethical life in that text.[5] However, it is less obvious that the defense of a specific set of institutions plays the same role in the early Jena *Phenomenology*. Indeed, one of the reasons that readers often present for arguing for the incompleteness of the argument of that book is the absence of an institutional theory of the sort that we find in *Philosophy of Right*. When Siep turns to address this issue, he instead seeks the institutional conditions for the achievement of recognition in Hegel's other Jena-era texts on practical philosophy.[6] By contrast, I shall argue that the absence of a theory of determinate institutions is not a fault of the Jena *Phenomenology* account, but instead an aspect of the distinctive account of recognition that Hegel offers there. In particular, I shall argue (in §§4.5 and 5.4) that one of Hegel's primary concerns with the idea of recognition in *Phenomenology of Spirit* lies in accounting for the possibility of profound moral transformation, a project that stands at odds with an effort to spell out a specific set of concrete institutions. Hegel's focus in *Phenomenology* lies on the more general normative level of customs and laws, rather than on the details of the character of specific institutions of the kind he considers in *Philosophy of Right* and elsewhere in the early Jena writings.

I begin by presenting an account of exactly what Hegel takes "ethical life" to be in *Phenomenology* by drawing out some useful links to Jaeggi's concepts of a "social practice" and "form of life." I stress in particular Hegel's argument that ethical life must be understood as a configuration of "spirit" to be understood rightly, and I draw out some of the implications

---

[4] Of course, freedom does play a significant role at many points in *Phenomenology*, and I consider several of those in the course of my account of the relation between recognition and the self. However, Hegel does not consistently approach the issues of recognition and selfhood in terms of a single, overarching concept, *Freiheit*, as he arguably does in the mature system as a whole, and as he certainly does with respect to the freedom of the will in *Philosophy of Right*. Instead, we find a plurality of conceptions of freedom – "independence," "the freedom of self-consciousness," "absolute freedom," moral autonomy, and "autarchy" – each playing a prominent role at different points. I am grateful to an anonymous reader for the request for clarification on this point.
[5] See *GW* 14, 1, 137/§144.
[6] Siep 2014, chapter 4.

of this contention for understanding his social theory more broadly. (§2.1) Having set out the basic elements of his idea of ethical life, I then consider his argument for why reciprocal recognition would depend on shared forms of norm-governed social life. In this connection, I stress two features of his account: first, that customs and laws, and the practices that they ground, can provide the dominant terms for individuals' self-understanding, and second, that they can establish the equality among individuals that is necessary for the achievement of reciprocity in their relations. (§2.2)

At the same time, I also argue that Hegel initially only holds that it is *possible* for ethical life to contribute to these sorts of relations. Of course, it is equally possible for forms of social life to entrench relations of domination and control, and so secure only one-sided relations of recognition, as in the relation between lord and bondsman. However, I offer an account of chapter VI.A.a–b, "The Ethical World" and "Ethical Action," according to which Hegel is there advancing a distinctive criticism of certain forms of shared social life. (§§2.3–2.4) Specifically, he shows that it is possible for a social world to be set up so that it is impossible for *anyone* to be recognized, so that not even relations of one-sided recognition are possible. We find this condition in particular where the differentiated roles established by ethical norms are understood to be grounded in differences that are *natural*. In such social worlds, the conceptual resources are lacking for understanding the agency belonging to individuals that is necessary to produce and reproduce those worlds.

I conclude by pointing to Hegel's proposed solution to this problem, which depends on a universal conception of the *self* that is explicitly articulated within a shared way of life, and I point to some of the ways in which Hegel's account of recognition in *Phenomenology of Spirit* is distinctive. (§2.5)

2.1 Ethical Life and Hegel's Social Theory in *Phenomenology*

Before we can understand why Hegel thinks that reciprocal recognition depends on a shared form of social life, we have first to understand exactly what he means by "ethical life." It will prove instructive if we consider Hegel's account of ethical life alongside Rahel Jaeggi's accounts of "social practices" and "forms of life."

In Jaeggi's account, social practices are things that we do, that are constituted by our activities. She identifies seven primary characteristics possessed by these practices:[7]

---

[7] Jaeggi 2014, 95–102.

SP1 They typically involve a sequence of many actions;

SP2 They are repeated and habitual, and so involve forms of knowledge that are implicit and practical;

SP3 They are socially constituted, and are only possible in the context of "socially imprinted significances and as moves within institutions (in a broad sense) that are socially constituted";

SP4 They are rule-guided, and so admit correct and incorrect performances;

SP5 They have a "possibilizing" character, making possible distinctive forms of social behavior, activities, and roles;

SP6 They posit and have purposes (which can be more or less determinate, latent or explicit, and subjective or objective) in terms of which we know and individuate them; and

SP7 They have an active-passive character: While a practice in a sense "preexists" any one subject, subjects are necessary for their actualization and real existence.

Jaeggi defines the idea of a "form of life" in terms of this notion of social practices. In her account, social practices are necessarily related one to another: A given social practice might have specific presuppositions in other practices, and it might make possible implications or effects for others. For example, the social practice of "cashing a paycheque" depends on the existence of other social practices ("earning a wage") and in turn makes possible others ("buying cookies"). As "Practices are thus enmeshed with manifold other practices and institutions, in which connection they first acquire their specific function and significance," Jaeggi calls these "connections and contexts" that make possible given social practices "*forms of life*."[8]

In Jaeggi's account, many of the core characteristics of forms of life are shared with social practices. First, just as the activities within social practices become repeated and habitual, and social practices have a partially "passive" character, forms of life are characterized by a kind of "inertia" so that we experience them as "second nature."[9]

Second, forms of life themselves equally possess an active character, insofar as they are sustained through the concerted activity of their members. And this activity is rooted in the determinate sort of "normativity" or binding force possessed by forms of life, so that forms of life are made

[8] Jaeggi 2014, 103–104.
[9] Jaeggi 2014, 119–127.

what they are through specific norms.[10] As normatively constituted, forms of life:[11]

NFL1 Provide standards for assessing the appropriateness of an action;
NFL2 Prescribe actions, rather than simply providing a frame for describing them;
NFL3 Mandate that behaviors not only accord with but be led by the relevant norm;
NFL4 Necessitate action on the basis of "formations" that are "artful" (*künstlich*), that are made by human beings; and
NFL5 Provide answers to why-questions about our actions by providing justifications for them.

Jaeggi identifies a central role for "customs" (*Gebräuche*) or "ethical norms" (*sittliche Normen*) in accounting for the specific normativity of forms of life.[12] In her account, customs both define and prescribe. First, customs provide *models* of behavior, defining and making possible particular moves within a norm-governed space. Second, customs require or prescribe certain behaviors. For example, a set of customs and ethical norms govern the behavior of fathers. They give definition to what it means to be a father, identifying a range of individuals who count as fathers and determining what it is that fathers do. And, once those norms are operative, they prescribe determinate behaviors for "fathers," so that a person who is subject to their normative force but fails to fulfill them does not fail to be a father, but instead counts as a *bad* father.

Hegel's account of ethical life bears some deep similarities to Jaeggi's ideas of social practices and forms of life. In the account that Hegel offers in this text, ethical life is "the life of a people" (*das Leben eines Volks*),[13] which comprises the "substance" that underlies and supports the lives of individuals.[14] Of course, such a shared form of life will be importantly diverse, so it might initially seem unclear how we can identify the essential aspects of a people's "way of life," the determinate "substance" that supports them. Hegel identifies this life in primarily *normative* terms, namely as *law* and as *custom*: "In the *abstraction of universality*, the ethical

---

[10] Jaeggi 2014, 140–141.
[11] Jaeggi 2014, 144–148.
[12] Jaeggi 2014, 153ff, 159.
[13] Sometimes the life of a "free" people. E.g., *PhG* 196/¶354. Alznauer 2017 makes much of the latter phrase. However, I think it's a mistake to think that every social formation that Hegel wants to identify as a *sittlich* must be that of a people that is also free.
[14] *PhG* 194/¶350.

substance is only the law that is *thought* [*das* gedachte *Gesetz*], but it is equally immediately actual *self-consciousness* or it is *custom* [Sitte]."[15]

Already, then, we can see that ethical life shares with social practices and forms of life an idea of normativity. As a shared form of life, ethical life mediates relations between individuals. As we have seen (in §1.5), Hegel understands *social* forms – configurations of a "universal will" – to be products of the activities of self-conscious beings: When I "negate myself," I submit myself to a norm that can in principle be shared with others, so that it is those self-negations that *generate* patterns of action. Indeed, as we shall see shortly, Hegel is unambiguous in identifying the concrete "world" that arises through those acts of self-negation as a "work" (*Werk*).[16] So it is safe to say that he considers it to be socially constituted (SP3). Likewise, in characterizing it as "the life of a people," Hegel presents ethical life as a complex of actions and activities (SP1). Moreover, both forms of life and ethical life provide standards for assessing the appropriateness of actions on the basis of whether those actions are deemed to be necessary (SP4, NFL1, NFL 2). To the extent that ethical life appears in "actual *self-consciousness*" as "*custom*," it can take the form of an implicit, habitual knowledge (SP2). But it is also possible for ethical life to be expressed as "the law that is *thought*" as an abstract universal, so that its norms can lend explicit guidance to our actions (NFL3).

Of course, there is a range of different conceptions of social practices, of norm-governed forms of life that might fit this initial description of ethical life. However, part of Hegel's work in the text is to defend a specific conception of what ethical life is, a conception that requires us to understand ethical life as a configuration of what Hegel calls "spirit." The most prominent competitor for this *geistig* conception of ethical life is what we can call individualistic conceptions of society. Hegel considers a range of these conceptions in the remainder of chapter V, "Reason." It is common for readers to interpret chapters VB and VC as critiques of individualism. In such accounts, the primary object of Hegel's line of argument there is to present a criticism of the view according to which the rational "I" can be neatly separated from the normatively structured "ethical substance" in which the "I" acts. Interpreters of this stripe seek this critique of individualism as a precursor to the theory of ethical life that Hegel unfolds more properly in chapter VIA. While Hegel is no doubt at work in advancing such a critique, as H. S. Harris notes, in the "Reason" chapter, Hegel is

---

[15] *PhG* 194/¶349.
[16] *PhG* 239/¶438.

equally interested in considering and pointing out inadequacies in different accounts of the basic character of ethical life or "society."[17] The end
point of this criticism is the *geistig* account of ethical life that we find in
the introduction to chapter VI.

2.1.1 Ethical Life from the Standpoint of "Reason"

What are the "individualistic" conceptions of ethical life that Hegel coun-
sels us to reject? As we've seen, Hegel introduces the idea of ethical life in
his account of reason. But he also claims that we merely find the "concept"
of ethical life from the standpoint of reason, as a "goal" toward which the
latter tends.[18] But, in contrast to spirit, the standpoint of reason is one that
understands individuality to be irreducible in an important way. That is,
reason takes its own individuality to be basically *separable from* what Hegel
calls ethical life, customary norms and laws.

He considers two specific shapes that this stance might take on, corresponding to two different conceptions of reason as "practical consciousness." In the first shape, the individual understands themselves primarily in
terms of their practical purposes, which they aim to realize through action.
The social world of customs and laws is understood to be an inessential
"actuality" that provides the means for the realization of the individual's
self-given purposes.[19] In its second configuration, reason is understood in
expressive terms, where the individual's aim is not to transform the world
through the realization of its own purposes, but instead to give expression

---

[17] Harris 1995, 56.

[18] *PhG* 194/¶349, 195–196/¶¶353–354.

[19] *PhG* 196/¶¶355, 356. The starting point for this argument – "Pleasure and Necessity" – aims to demonstrate that agents need to countenance the norms and customs of the social world by considering
a practical stance that grants them no genuine standing or existence at all. In this account, the aim
that the agent sets for themselves must be specifiable in terms lacking any reference to ethical life.
While pleasure is such a purpose, its attainment is ambiguous: "Pleasure enjoyed does have the
positive significance of being self-consciousness *itself* as something that has become objective, but it
equally has the negative significance of having sublated *itself.*" *PhG* 199/¶363. While pleasure does
entail an experience of oneself as objective, it equally entails the "sublation" and negation of the
agent, since "it becomes an object not as *this individual* [self-consciousness], but rather as the *unity*
of itself with another self-consciousness, thus as a sublated individual or a *universal.*" *PhG* 199/¶362.
Instead of experiencing the fulfillment of itself, such an agent rather experiences their subjection
to an impersonal "power" that negates them, an inhuman "necessity" to which they are subject. By
consequence, reason is obliged to acknowledge the importance of those "universals" that mediate
its relations to other self-conscious agents, or to countenance a positive role for the customs and
laws that structure the ethical. Or, in Harris's helpful formulation: "What we are observing is the
evolution of the concept of *society* in the mind of the individual who begins by regarding it as simply
irrelevant." Harris 1995, 56.

to a more basic or essential characteristic – first an "original nature" and then a shared "thing itself."[20] Both of these configurations of reason are committed to an *instrumental* conception of the social world: shared customs and laws exist primarily as means either for the achievement of the individual's self-given purposes or for the expression of an original nature or "thing itself."

Hegel rejects both of these instrumental conceptions of ethical life. In chapter VB, Hegel critiques the instrumental conception of reason on the grounds that it presupposes too strict a separation between the agent and their purposes, on the one hand, and the world in which they act and realize those purposes, on the other. In each case, he demonstrates that the attempt to insulate reason from the social world, which is necessary if we are to understand it in instrumental terms, is unsustainable. Reason learns through experience that the world cannot consistently be held to be an indifferent tool for the achievement of the rational agent's self-given aims, but is rather partially constitutive of their individuality: their goals cannot be radically opposed to existent actuality, but must in some ways fit within it in order to become actual.[21]

In chapter VC, Hegel challenges the expressive conception of reason on the grounds that it cannot defend the rigid distinction between individuality and social actuality that it posits. This conception of reason is subject to a specific dilemma concerning the meaning of individuality. If it tries to articulate content for what its individuality really is, that articulation takes the form of content that can be shared with others, in which case it loses its grip on the idea that individuality is what distinguishes me from others.[22] Alternatively, if it tries to retain that idea of the separateness of

---

[20] *PhG* 214–215/¶394.
[21] This is the ultimate conclusion of Hegel's account of "Virtue and the Way of the World." "Virtue" is committed to the opposition between its own high-minded purposes, which require the sacrifice of its individuality, and the self-interest that animates "the way of the world." However, it comes to learn that "individuality is precisely the *actualization* of what exists in itself" and that "the movement of individuality is the reality of the universal." *PhG* 213/¶391. But that entails that the "world" of the "way of the world" is not radically opposed to rational individuality. Instead, when it acts, that individuality gives *expression* to the universality that is merely implicit in that world: "*The hustle and bustle* [das Tun und Treiben] *of individuality* is therefore *an end in itself*; it is the *use of its powers, the play of its expressions* [Äußerungen] that gives life to what would otherwise be a dead in-itself; the in-itself is not an un-executed, existence-less, and abstract universal, but it is itself immediately this present and actuality of the process of individuality." *PhG* 214/¶393.
[22] This is one of the main lessons of the discussion of the "thing itself": When I claim to express this in my actions, what I express is equally something in which everyone can take an interest and find as their own, which means that I lose what I take to individuate me in relation to them. For the conclusion of this argument, see *PhG* 226–227/¶416.

individuality, it must sacrifice any positive content for the meaning of individuality.[23]

Instead of thinking of individuality as imprinting its own self-given purposes on the world, or giving expression to an independently given shared "thing," Hegel argues that we ought to reject reason's picture of individual and world as basically separate, and to construe them instead as mutually dependent.[24] This relation of mutual dependence is essential to what he calls "spirit."

2.1.2   *Ethical Life from the Standpoint of "Spirit"*

When he introduces the idea of spirit near the outset of chapter VI, Hegel claims that spirit is "the *self* [*das* Selbst] of actual consciousness, which confronts [the objective actual *world*], or, better, which confronts itself as the objective actual *world*, which has equally lost for the self all significance of being something alien, just as the self has lost all significance of a being-for-self divided from it, of being dependent or independent."[25] Understanding subject and substance to be dynamically related in this way fundamentally transforms both.[26] First, the ethical substance is acknowledged to be "the

---

[23] Hegel argues that the only criterion that is completely internal to rational individuality, which does not depend on the shared "spiritual essence," the social world, is noncontradiction. However, Hegel argues that this criterion is too "formal," that it cannot by itself demonstrate that we should regard any particular norm to be more rational than its opposite, and so to be the sort of norm to which I might give expression in my actions. This is, of course, the upshot of Hegel's account of "Law-giving Reason" and "Reason as Testing Laws," which are often treated as criticisms of Kant's categorical imperative. However, it is important to note that the immediate context for this critique is a consideration of the rationality not simply of abstract norms, but rather, since these are determinations of an "ethical substance," of forms of the world. *PhG* 229/¶419. For the accusation of "formalism," see *PhG* 231–232/¶¶425–426. Gillian Rose has argued that Hegel's critique of Kant and post-Kantian idealists applies equally to the positions of the significant figures in the development of social theory, Durkheim and Weber, on the grounds that they are essentially neo-Kantian accounts of social institutions and meanings. In Rose's account, Hegel's theory of ethical life takes the place of Kant's attempted "justification of moral judgments," whose analogue she finds in the transcendental accounts of the "validity" of social facts or values in Weber and Durkheim. Rose 1981, 45. Rose's approach to *Phenomenology of Spirit* is unfortunately limited by her assumption of an essential continuity in Hegel's understanding of ethical life between the Jena writings and the mature systematic works. Moreover, her claim that "Hegel's philosophy has no social import if the absolute cannot be thought" (204) is far too strong. As I show here, we can make sense of the social significance of his concept of "spirit" without depending on a specific account of what "absolute" spirit is.

[24] Discussing Hegel's mature view, Bykova helpfully identifies the relation between individuals and social practices as one of "reciprocal implication": "Hegel holds that individuals and social and communal institutions are mutually interdependent; neither exists or has its character without the other." Bykova 2019, 182. Of course, I have been suggesting that the *Phenomenology* account of the "world" of spirit need not take the form of a specific theory of institutions.

[25] *PhG* 238–239/¶438.

[26] See Alznauer's helpful account of self-consciousness and world as comprising a "feedback loop." 2017, 136.

universal, self-same, remaining essence – it is the unmoved and simple
[*unaufgelöste*] *ground* and *point of departure of the deeds of all* – and their
purpose and *aim* as the thought *in-itself* of all self-consciousness." Second,
"This substance is equally the universal *work* [Werk], that engenders itself
through the *deed* of each and all as their unity and equality, for it is the
being-for-self, the self, the deed." Instead of construing the social domain
to be an indifferent "actuality," a mere tool for the achievement of my
purposes or the expression of myself, when we understand it as spirit, this
objective aspect of ethical life takes on the significance of being a normatively structured *world*. And, at the same time, instead of understanding
the self-conscious agent as the independent source of self-given aims, we
find them assuming a position *within* that world, realizing the purposes
implicit in it.

Both of these aspects of ethical life were present when Hegel introduced
that idea in chapter VB. What Hegel now identifies as the substantial
"world" of consciousness, the objective ground of its life and activities, he
there explained in terms of the "form of thinghood" or "objectivity" of
the ethical world. Likewise, what he now identifies as the work-character
of the ethical world, its being a product of the activity of self-conscious
agents, he there explained as the form of "self-consciousness" possessed by
ethical life.

Given these concrete characteristics of ethical life – the objectivity of its
customs and laws, and its production through the activity of self-conscious
agents – it is important to note that Hegel acknowledges the *material* conditions for the existence of the social world.[27] First, instead of construing
norms and laws in the abstract, as reason does, we need to understand
them as having the "form of thinghood," as the forms of specific material
practices. Second, instead of understanding the world-producing agency
to be the abstract activity of a transcendental subject, we ought to understand it as the self-conscious activity of embodied agents possessing determinate "gifts, capacities, and powers."[28]

This commitment to a kind of materialism entails a novel understanding of the character of the subjectivity or self-consciousness that relates
to or "knows" ethical practices. In contrast to the external conception of
the relation between knower and practice to which reason was committed, spirit involves understanding self-consciousness as embedded within

---

[27] This too marks a link to Jaeggi: "[F]orms of life are *equally material and spiritual formations*." Jaeggi
2014, 121.
[28] *PhG* 210/¶385, 213/¶392.

the ethical world. This self-consciousness is the agency that animates and sustains the ethical world, which makes it "*actual* and *living*." But equally, for it, the ethical world is not "alien" and separate from it, but instead its proper "purpose" and "essence." In this account, the ethical world supplies the concrete contents in terms of which the individual understands themselves and their own activity. Instead of construing themselves as the author and inventor of their purposes, they see those purposes as given to them from within the ethical world. To be sure, their own agency is essential for sustaining and actualizing those purposes – they are the collective "work" of self-conscious subjects – but they draw them from the horizon supplied by the world. So as "spirit," self-consciousness is not thought of as radically separate from or external to the ethical world, but is instead understood as the "moment" in which its substantiality is "dissolved."[29] While we might be inclined to stress the fact that this dissolution seems to give self-consciousness a sort of power over the ethical substance, Hegel equally stresses the opposite point, one that is consistent with the argument of chapter IV, which showed that self-consciousness must be understood as "absolute negativity": Self-consciousness has no positive content outside of the "dissolution" and negation *of* the substance, which constitutes its essential "ground."

Understood as "spirit," we can identify a number of other characteristics shared between Hegel's conception of ethical life and Jaeggi's ideas of social practice and customs. First, Hegel holds that ethical life has a "possibilizing" character similar to Jaeggi's idea of a social practice: Both uniquely make possible – constitute – distinctive forms of social behavior, activities, and roles. (SP5) On this score, Hegel would agree with Jaeggi's characterization of social practices in terms of Rawls's idea of practice rules, which both define and prescribe certain actions.[30] Second, Hegel too identifies ethical life primarily in terms of determinate "purposes" that individuals pursue in their actions. (SP6) Of course, instead of those purposes being original to reason and opposed to or expressed in ethical life,

[29] While Habermas countenances the idea of norm recognition in the idea of "normatively structured action," he holds that one of the criteria for the rationality of a social world lies in whether its norms accord with the "interests" of the agents within it. So for Habermas, there are substantive criteria lying within the agents themselves to which we can appeal in assessing the rationality of the social world. (Habermas 1981, 1, 133–134) By contrast, in stressing that the role of self-consciousness is that of negation and dissolution, there are no *positive* criteria inherent in agents according to which the social world's rationality can be assessed. Instead, Hegel will argue that criteria for criticism emerge only through the "experience" of self-consciousness within the social world, in particular through their experience of breakdowns and contradictions in the norms structuring that world.
[30] See Rawls 1955, 24ff.

Hegel thinks that we can identify them as being rooted instead within given shapes of ethical life.

Third, as did social practices in Jaeggi's account, ethical life, to Hegel, has an active-passive character: While the social world preexists my engagement with it, it nonetheless requires self-conscious agency for its continued existence and actualization. (SP7) And, as we have seen, he thinks that what gives guidance to my actions when I act in accordance with ethical norms is a formation that is "artful" (*künstlich* [Jaeggi]), a "work" (*Werk* [Hegel]), that is constituted through human agency. (NFL4)

Finally, Hegel reintroduces the idea of ethical life at the conclusion of chapter VC in order to address reason's concern about the justification of actions. (NFL5) Within ethical life, actions are justified by appeal to the customs and laws that structure the normative world itself:

> The ethical disposition [*sittliche Gesinnung*] consists of insisting unmovedly on what is right, abstaining from all movement, testing, and reduction of it. A deposit is entrusted to me; *it is* the property of another, and I recognize it *because it is so* and hold myself unwaveringly in this relation... Something is right not because I do not find it contradictory, but it is right because it is right. That something *is* the property of another is *fundamental* [*liegt* zum Grunde]... Whether this or that opposed determination is what is right is determined *in and for itself*.[31]

This might seem a limited account of justification. But it does provide a certain sort of answer to why-questions asked about our actions.[32]

2.2 Ethical Life and Recognition

I have drawn on Jaeggi's account of social practices and the normativity of forms of life to explain some of the central features of Hegel's idea of "ethical life" in *Phenomenology of Spirit*. Having established this idea, we are now in a position to understand why Hegel would appeal to ethical life in the course of explaining the conditions for the realization of relations of intersubjective *recognition*.

However, before we turn to this account, it is important to note that, with the idea of ethical life and of ethical norms, we will have to distinguish two different kinds of recognition – what I will call *norm recognition* and *intersubjective recognition*.

---

[31] *PhG* 236–237/¶436.
[32] As we shall see when we consider the argument of chapter VIA.a–b in §§2.3–2.4, Hegel acknowledges that this sort of justification is fundamentally limited.

It should be clear that *intersubjective* recognition is Hegel's primary concern in the text, the recognition of another self-consciousness that we've been considering since §1.3 In intersubjective recognition, *what* I recognize is another subject or self-conscious being. The *object* of intersubjective recognition, another self-conscious being, is clearly distinct from that of *norm* recognition.[33] In *norm* recognition, the primary object of my recognition is itself a norm, for instance, the laws and customs of ethical life.[34]

While Hegel primarily reserves the term *"Anerkennen"* and its cognates for cases of intersubjective recognition, he periodically uses it in contexts where the object of recognition is instead a norm. For example, Hegel identifies the relation of the individual to the "laws" or differentiated "masses" (*Massen*) of ethical life as one of immediate recognition: "These laws or masses of the ethical substance are immediately recognized [*unmittelbar anerkannt*]."[35] Like intersubjective recognition, the recognition of a shared norm too requires a kind of "self-negation." As we have seen in §1.5, Hegel argues that the achievement of the sort of "universal" or common will that ethical life presupposes depends on the "sacrifice" and negation of merely "individual" wills.[36] Finally, there is a sense in which norm recognition too can be "mutual." Whenever you and I recognize the same norm

---

[33] The term "norm recognition" does not appear in Hegel's text. Instead, he relies on the concrete forms that norms assume (laws, customs), and stresses the embedded ness of individuals within a shared world with which they identify, and establishes the standards of propriety that shape their expectations of how others ought to act.

[34] As Ikäheimo and Laitinen argue, the term "recognition" is itself ambiguous. They distinguish between three different phenomena which, they claim, may all be "called 'recognition'": the *identification* of anything, the *acknowledgement* of normative entities, and the *recognition* of persons. See Ikäheimo and Laitinen 2007, 34. Hegel does not use the term "*anerkennen*" for the first form of recognition. Instead, he uses "*wiedererkennen*" in the contexts in which Ikäheimo and Laitinen's "identification" would be relevant. We find a notable example in his account of the way in which I can experience myself expressed in a work of art: "The universal need for art is therefore that of reason [*das Vernünftige*], that the human being has raised the inner and outer world to a spiritual consciousness as an object, in which they recognize their own self [*sein eigenes Selbst wiedererkennt*]." Hegel, *TW* 13, 51. It may be the case that Antigone's distinctive recognition ("*Because we suffer, we recognize* [anerkennen] *that we have erred*," *PhG* 256/¶470) requires a fourth sense for the term, which refers to the explicit self-conscious knowledge that this or that is the case.

[35] *PhG* 229/¶420. The recognition of the ethical law is "immediate" not requiring justification by appeal to some prior "principle": "A deposit is entrusted to me; it *is* the property of another, and I recognize this *because it is so*, and maintain myself unflinchingly in this relation." *PhG* 236/¶436. While intersubjective relations are prominent in his account of justification, the primary sense of recognition (*Anerkennung*) that we find in Habermas's discourse ethics is the recognition of principles and laws. Relations of recognition are reciprocal (*reziproke*) simply when everyone recognizes the same general norms. See Habermas 1983, 98.

[36] See especially *PhG* 131/¶230. For the importance of this development for the achievement of recognition see Siep 1998, 116–117. However, I also argue that Siep underplays the extent to which a universal consciousness is merely a necessary and not a sufficient condition for the achievement of relations of reciprocal intersubjective recognition.

as binding on both of our actions – when we both constrain our actions, "negate ourselves," in accordance with the rules of a game, for example – we mutually recognize that norm.

Distinguishing these forms of recognition is important not only because it enables us to clarify the specific kind of recognition that is Hegel's primary interest in the text – *reciprocal intersubjective recognition* – but also because it helps us to understand why Hegel believes that *reciprocal intersubjective recognition* depends on *mutual norm recognition*.[37] And, in particular, we need to consider why Hegel would argue that the specific norms that make possible reciprocal intersubjective recognition are "ethical" norms, understood in terms of Hegel's concept of spirit.

We can begin to pursue that issue by recalling that, according to its "pure concept," recognition is essentially *normative*, in that when you and I recognize one another, each of us "requires" (*fodert*) that the other act in a specific way. And reciprocal recognition demands relations of recognition be reversible, that is, that each treats the other as they treat themselves and that they treat themselves as they treat the other. Even if normativity is built into the "pure concept" of recognition, the claim that the specific norms that govern it take "ethical" form, that is, the form of laws and customs, is more robust.

"Spirit" is what links the idea of ethical life and the achievement of recognition. Hegel holds that ethical life constitutes a "spiritual unity." Ethical life is:

> [T]he spiritual *unity* of individuals' essence in their independent *actuality*; an implicitly universal self-consciousness that is actual in an other consciousness so that this has complete independence, or is a thing for it, and that it is equally conscious of *unity* with it, and is in this unity with the objective being first self-consciousness.[38]

According to its concept, spirit is the "absolute substance which in the complete freedom and independence of its opposites, namely different self-consciousnesses existing for themselves, is their unity; *I* that is *We*, and *We* that is *I*."[39] Ethical life embodies the *intersubjective* structure that

---

[37] It is unfortunately common for commentators to equivocate in their use of the term "recognition," sometimes using it to refer to intersubjective recognition, sometimes to norm recognition. For example, on the same page of his text, Hyppolite both the claim that "two self-consciousnesses … fail to recognize one another," and that "self-consciousness … recognizes the rights of the real." Hyppolite 1974, 358.

[38] *PhG* 194/¶349.

[39] *PhG* 107/¶177.

Hegel ascribes to spirit insofar as it establishes relevant *horizontal* relations between self-conscious agents. However, these intersubjective relations depend on the right sorts of *vertical* relations between self-conscious agents and ethical norms and laws.[40]

We are in a position to see the first reason why Hegel links ethical life with the achievement of recognition. Ethical life embodies an analogous structure to spirit, one in which independent terms comprise a unity that still preserves significant aspects of their independence. In ethical normativity, only one of the related elements is a self-consciousness, but it finds itself in objective form – that of a "thing" – in ethical norms, and in customs and laws. I am not identical with customs and laws, but I can nonetheless experience them as *mine*, and as informing my own self-understanding. This achievement of "spiritual unity," in which I experience myself in objective laws and customs, is significant because of the content that it provides to my experience of myself. When I experience those objective laws and customs as mine, and, just as importantly, make my actions accord with the demands that they entail – to use the language of chapter V, when I "negate myself" in accordance with their requirements – I acquire at the same time a "positive" sense and understanding of myself.[41] One of the grounds for Hegel's appeal to the idea of "ethical life" lies in the idea that being a part of "the life of a people," in the sense of a normatively governed way of life, can provide the terms within which I understand myself, in which my actions and existence acquire meaning and significance: "The laws express what each individual *is* and *does*."[42]

There is an important – if limited – sense in which this achieved "spiritual unity" with the customs and laws structuring a given way of life comprises a part of Hegel's idea of recognition. Specifically, as I've suggested, Hegel sometimes identifies this act of submitting to customs and laws as an act of recognition, namely norm recognition. And this distinctive sort of norm recognition plays an important role in his account of *intersubjective* recognition. But it cannot alone bring about intersubjective recognition for the simple reason that, in norm recognition, only one party to that relationship – me – is a self-conscious being. I can recognize the norm, but it cannot recognize me, so my relationship to the norm cannot be

---

[40] I draw the horizontal-vertical distinction from Ikäheimo 2014.
[41] There is extensive literature on the connection between spirit and the content of self-understanding. See, for a start, Bykova 2009.
[42] *PhG* 195/¶351.

reciprocal in the way that Hegel thinks that intersubjective recognition ultimately is.[43]

However, there is a second, more robust contribution that ethical life makes to the achievement of recognition: Hegel holds that shared customs and norms make possible relations of *reciprocity* between individuals. The achievement of this reciprocity depends on what Hegel calls the unique "power" (*Macht*) belonging to "the people as a whole," the way in which it transforms the pursuit of individual deeds and purposes into a shared, universal "work." Taking labor as his example, Hegel makes the (Smithian) point that laboring to satisfy my own needs can come to satisfy the needs of others, for example, when I produce a surplus of a good, and exchange that surplus with another who needs it for a good that I in turn need. However, he suggests that this "unconscious" activity is not simply limited to the satisfaction of natural needs. Instead, it also contributes to the generation of what he calls the "world," the whole of the norm-governed activities characteristic of a given people.

It is this "power" that converts individual deeds into a shared universal "work," which contributes most directly to the achievement of relations of reciprocity:

> Here there is nothing that would not be reciprocal [*gegenseitig*], nothing in which the independence of the individual in the dissolution of its being-for-self, in the *negation* of itself does not give itself a *positive* significance, of being-for-itself. This unity of being for other or of making oneself a thing, and of being-for-self, this universal substance speaks its *universal language* in the laws and customs of a people; but this unchangeable essence is nothing other than the expression of their singular individuality which seems to be opposed; the laws express what every individual *is* and *does*; the individual knows them only as its *universal* objective thinghood, but equally as *individualized* in its own individuality and in that of its fellow-citizens.[44]

We have already seen Hegel claim that when I recognize a set of customs and laws, I thereby acquire a sense of what I am. However, he is now making a second point, namely that because the customs and laws are universal, when *everyone* recognizes those customs and laws, when they

[43] This insight should place a new stress at least on our understanding of the role that institutions can play in the achievement of recognition. Consider the role that "the state" might play in a theory of recognition. "The state" cannot recognize me – though its officials and my fellow citizens can – so absent a specific account of the sorts of *specific intersubjective* relationships that life in a rational state might establish, it does not make sense to treat the relationship of the state to me as one of recognition, or to treat the state as an administrator of recognition. It is at best a mediator. On this issue, see Siep 2014, §V.1.

[44] *PhG* 195/¶351.

are shared, that activity creates the conditions for relations of reciprocity among individuals, conditions that were lacking in the relation between the lord and bondsman. Hegel writes:

> In the universal spirit, each therefore has not only the certainty of themselves, of finding nothing in the existing actuality but themselves; *they are as certain of others as they are of themselves*. I intuit in all the fact that they are for themselves only the [same] independent being as I am [*sie für sich selbst nur diese selbständigen Wesen sind, als Ich es bin*]; I intuit the free unity with the other in them so that this unity exists through me just as it exists through them. [I intuit] them as myself, and myself as them.[45]

The conclusion toward which Hegel is pushing should therefore be clear enough: Reciprocal intersubjective recognition not only requires the mutual recognition of a set of shared norms, but those norms must themselves be "ethical" norms that are embodied in the reciprocal relation between self-consciousness and world that Hegel calls "spirit." Why would Hegel hold that this specific conception of spirit is necessary for the achievement of reciprocal intersubjective recognition? Why could not other, non-*sittlich* norms – a universal moral law, for example – contribute to the achievement of this recognition?

We can appreciate why Hegel would appeal to this "spiritual" conception of ethical life in making sense of relations of recognition by considering the contrast that Michael Thompson draws between "monadic" forms of normativity and "intrinsically relational" or "bipolar" ones, and the parallel distinction between "monadic" conceptions of an agent and the relational concept of the "person."

Central to Thompson's view is the claim that obligations of justice are distinct from other moral obligations, in that they make essential reference to another person whom we might wrong in our actions, to whom we have some specific duty or obligation, and who can claim a right against us. Thompson argues that these relations distinguish specifically "dikaiological" judgments from the broader class of "deontic" judgments, and that it is a mistake to try to reduce those relations to others to a nonrelational idea of obligation or right. For this reason, he holds that the dikaiological judgment "You ought not to kill Sylvia" cannot be reduced to two monadic judgments "Sylvia has a right not to be killed" and "you have a duty not to kill." Instead, Thompson argues that "the practical bipolarity of a judgment" marks off a distinctive "'categorial' or 'intellectual' form":

[45] *PhG* 195/¶351. This account of *Sittlichkeit* recalls in some respects the earlier one that we find in the *System der Sittlichkeit* of 1802/1803. See *GW* 5, 325–326.

[T]hought takes a distinctive turn here, a turn which cannot simply be reduced to its taking a certain body of concrete relations, practical ones, as its theme – and still less by making reference to a special class of objects: namely, agents. Such thought has, among other things, a novel and particular relation to what it is about.[46]

To this distinctive sense of "dikaiological" normativity corresponds the distinctive notion of being a "person." Thompson argues that dikaiological relations require that the parties standing in those relations be understood to be more than mere "agents." Being an "agent" is, in his terms, a monadic conception of a subject in possession of determinate properties, such as "operates on the strength of practical reasons or thoughts or considerations."[47] In contrast to being an agent, persons are, for Thompson, essentially relational, and this in two ways. First, being a person means standing in relation to other persons: "The judgment *X is a person...* is essentially a 'de-relativization' of the prior bipolar judgment *X is a person in relation to Y...* 'Recognizing someone as a person' is registering her as a person in relation to yourself; it is the appropriation of such a proposition in the first person."[48] However, there is a second way in which Thompson thinks that "person" is a relational concept. Specifically, he holds that different "dikaiological orders" generate different "manifolds" of persons. For example, the norm-governed dikaiological order of chess gives rise to a specific class of persons – chess-players – who are distinct from those "induced" by the dikaiological order of Roman civil law – Roman citizens.[49]

Something like this relational conception of "the person" is operative in Hegel's account of "ethical life."[50] As we've seen, one of the core contributions that ethical life makes to recognition lies in the way in which the customs and laws that determine a shared "way of life" shape my own self-understanding. That is, a specific "ethical" order gives rise to a distinctive self-conception, just as, for Thompson, different dikaiological orders give rise to different manifolds of persons.

---

[46] Thompson 2004, 337.
[47] Thompson 2004, 352.
[48] Thompson 2004, 353. Thompson identifies the roots for this conception of the person in "classical jurisprudence," where "persons are defined as possible parties to a lawsuit, possible terms of legal nexuses." 352.
[49] Thompson 2004, 354–358.
[50] Though as we shall see in §3.3, Hegel identifies "the person" as a distinctive and explicit conception of "the self" in chapter VIA.c. By contrast, as we shall see in §§2.3–2.4, an explicit and determinate conception of the self is lacking in "the ethical world" that Hegel considers in chapter VIA.a–b. I shall argue that this lack animates the basic tension that undermines that world.

But in addition to providing the resources for a determinate self-conception, ethical life also generates the status under which individuals relate to one another as *equals*. When you and I both identify a determinate custom or law as our own, that norm can mediate our relation in a unique way. Hegel is interested in those particular norms that can secure relations of reciprocity, so that I treat you as I treat myself, I treat myself as I treat you, and you do the same. (We'll consider shortly the specific challenge that emerges in trying to specify what sorts of norms are like that.) It is these norms that are necessary for a specific "way of life" to embody the structure of "spirit" as Hegel has described it, and to secure relations of reciprocal intersubjective recognition. They make us equals, since they secure relations of reciprocity, and they make it possible for *me* to be recognized, since they shape my self-conception. This is the reason why Hegel thinks that we need to understand ethical life as a shape of "spirit," in terms of a mutual dependence of self-consciousness and the social world, and not as a one-sided instrumental or expressive relation (as Hegel thinks the social world is understood from the standpoint of "reason"). On the purposive conception, I experience the social world as a detachable means for the achievement of my own purposes, so that customs and laws do not themselves shape my self-understanding. Likewise, the expressive conception fails to provide any concrete and determinate content to the norms that are supposed to govern my action, robbing the relationships that those norms as supposed to govern of the shape that would be required for them to secure relations of equality and reciprocity.[51]

Of course, as I've presented it thus far, Hegel's argument no doubt itself sounds excessively formal: Reciprocal intersubjective recognition requires the mutual recognition of norms embedded in a specific shared form of life. However, all I have demonstrated so far is that Hegel believes that *some* shared forms of social life can make possible these relations. This point merits note because you are no doubt already thinking of forms of shared social life that are governed by norms that *undermine* the possibility of relations of reciprocity and equality. Indeed, we can identify at least three specific challenges that Hegel's account will need to address.

First, Hegel appeals to forms of shared social life governed by customs and laws to show us how relations of recognition are possible. However, the grounds for recognition, in his account, lie in the fact that we are self-conscious beings. So his appeals to "ethical life" might raise a concern about the *universality* of relations of recognition: If recognition is mediated

---

[51] See again *PhG* 226–227/¶416, and Pippin's account of the issue in Pippin 2004, 261ff.

by customs and norms embedded in the "life of a people," won't it be impossible for us to be recognized by others who share a different form of life? This is the worry that Thompson raises about Humean accounts of relations of justice, since they seem to limit the scope of *dikaiological* relations to those who share the same customs. Put briefly, if recognition is of self-conscious beings *simpliciter*, but ethical life is necessary to secure it, how can Hegel address this scope challenge, so that *everyone* could stand in relations of recognition, and not simply those who share a specific, parochial "way of life"?[52]

Second, Hegel has appealed to the thought that shared forms of social life can secure relations of reciprocity and equality among individuals. But what about customs and laws that *prevent* the emergence of relations of equality and reciprocity? For example, the institution of chattel slavery might be governed by a set of explicitly articulated norms that govern the behavior of those who participate in it. But those norms will not give rise to a single, shared self-understanding among all the participants: They license some to understand themselves as "masters" and others to understand themselves as "slaves." And they equally institute relations of extreme and obvious *inequality*, not relations of equality and reciprocity. Of course, Hegel is manifestly aware that customary norms can undermine the possibility of relations of equality – in his mature lectures, he suggests that most of human history is marked by the fact that the majority of individuals are made unfree by the form of social life that predominates in their age. So the question that Hegel needs to address is: Which specific customs and norms are those that make possible the equality on which reciprocal intersubjective recognition depends?

Finally, Hegel stresses the way in which customs and laws can positively shape my self-conception, so that I experience them as *mine*, informing my understanding of myself in a deep and important way. But it is equally possible for my social world to be structured in a way that makes it impossible for me to find myself in those customs and laws. So Hegel's account of ethical life equally faces a challenge arising from the condition of *alienation*, one in which I cannot draw a coherent conception of what I am from the norms that govern my social world.[53]

---

[52] Ultimately, Hegel addresses this challenge by introducing the idea of the self, a status that belongs equally to self-conscious beings. It is true that "self" is a designation belonging to individuals as participants in shared practices. But, in particular for the "moral" self, those practices are, in principle at least, not limited to this or that particular "people," but rather, as Stekeler-Weithofer suggests (2014, 1, 59), spirit consists of a common "we" from which "nothing human is alien."

[53] I consider Hegel's account of alienation (*Entfremdung*) in §3.3.

In any case, it should be clear that Hegel's early appeal to the idea of ethical life aims at identifying a *possibility* inherent in that concept, and it is a mistake to think that every actually existing configuration of customary and legal norm-governed activities will be one in which recognition is possible. Hegel makes this point in a particularly powerful way in chapter VIA.a–b, where he shows that it is possible for a normative order to exist in which *no one* is recognized.

2.3 Difference and Naturalization

Which specific norm-governed ways of life make possible relations of reciprocal recognition? The primary contribution that chapter VIA, Hegel's treatment of the world of ethical life, makes to his account of the conditions for reciprocal recognition is to establish the need for a determinate conception of the *self* to be embodied within the norms that structure the social world.

Hegel makes this argument by pursuing a *reductio* strategy: He sets out a shape of ethical life in which no such conception of the self exists, and shows that, by consequence, it is impossible for *anyone* to be recognized, much less for reciprocal intersubjective recognition to be possible. As we shall see (in §2.4) the central problem with worlds that lack such a conception of the self is that they fail to secure the conditions for their own reproduction. The core idea is that the social world implicitly depends on the agency of self-conscious subjects (it is their "work"), but the central norms of the social world need not explicitly acknowledge the work-character of the world, specifically insofar as they fail to acknowledge the role that agents play in producing and reproducing it.

However, before we can understand this argument about recognition, we need to consider what sort of social world might be structured in this way. The central problem in such social worlds stems from a flaw in their self-understanding. As we have seen, Hegel is emphatic that the ethical world is a "work," a product of the self-conscious activity of the agents whose world it is. This feature of the ethical world, that it is the product of self-conscious activity, is made explicit in Hegel's account of what follows the ethical world, what he calls the world of "culture." Hegel writes:

> But the existence [*Dasein*] of this world, like the actuality of self-consciousness, rests on this movement, that self-consciousness externalizes [*sich entäußert*] its personhood, and thus produces [*hervorbringt*] its world, and conducts itself against it as something alien, of which it must take

possession [*sich ... bemächtigen*]. But this renunciation [*Entsagung*] of its being-for-self is itself the constitution [*Erzeugung*] of actuality, and through this constitution [self-consciousness] immediately takes possession of [the world].[54]

In culture, the work-character of the world is thus explicit in two ways. First, the world itself is understood as something that is *constituted*. The suggestion that the social world is made and remade through human activity might call to mind the notion of social construction. However, in place of the idea of construction, Hegel prefers the biological idea of *Erzeugung*, literally "engendering," which I shall identify as "constitution."[55] Second, the constitution of the world is understood to depend on the activity of self-consciousness, its "externalization" or *Entäußerung*. This notion of externalization takes over from the idea that agency depends on determinate "gifts, capacities, and powers" that we saw emerge in Hegel's account of reason. However, in culture, those determinate and embodied capacities are understood to play an essential role in constituting the social world. Instead of comprising some unique characteristic of the individual, they and their development and cultivation, the *Bildung* of the individual, are rather understood as necessary elements for the production of the social world: "The movement of self-forming individuality is therefore immediately its becoming, and that of the universal objective essence, that is, the becoming of the actual world."[56]

While the work-character of the world is explicit within the world of culture, the claim that we need to understand the social world as constituted through the activity of self-conscious agents is one for which Hegel gives an argument, and we find that argument in the earlier discussion of the ethical world. This argument rests on the fact that it is possible for individuals to overlook the role that their agency plays in producing and reproducing their world. Instead, they might take the normative order to be a divine given, reflecting the natural order. We can call the error of treating an essentially social trait as though it stemmed from nature the error of *naturalization*.[57]

We find an instance of this error in the specific configuration of ethical "powers" that structure the ethical world that Hegel sets out in chapter

---

[54] *PhG* 267/¶487.
[55] Hegel reserves the notion of "construction" for understanding a procedure at play in mathematical proof. See, for example, the *Differenzschrift*, *GW* 4, 70 and *PhG* 32/¶42.
[56] *PhG* 268/¶489.
[57] In so designating the phenomenon under consideration, I follow Kukla's account of naturalization as an element of ideology. See Kukla 2000 and 2018. See also in this connection Honneth 2018, 223.

VIA. As we've seen, the idea of ethical "powers" is central to Hegel's account of the social world, since those powers constitute *objective* grounds stipulating which actions and activities accord with the norms that are *essential* within that world. Of course, there is a range of different "shapes" that the powers structuring the social world might assume. In chapter VIA, in which we find the "ethical world" of the "true spirit" of "ethical life," Hegel considers what he calls the "immediate" shape of spirit.⁵⁸ In identifying it this way, he likely has in mind a few different senses of immediacy.

First, the relation between individual and norm is understood to be immediate. That is, the laws and customs embodied in the world are supposed to oblige individuals in a way that does not call for further justification by reasons: "The ethical consciousness is essentially *immediately* directed toward the law."⁵⁹ As Hegel says, the laws and customs are "immediately recognized," so that the question of their source and bindingness does not go unanswered, simply because it is never asked.⁶⁰ We can put this point in terms familiar from Rawls: Agents within such a world can justify their particular actions ("I buried him because he is my brother"), but not the practice itself ("The unwritten and infallible right of the gods / not something of today and yesterday, but always / it lives, and no one knows, whence it appeared").⁶¹ Indeed, the form of language that predominates in the ethical world, that of the "command,"⁶² expresses this experience of members of the ethical world who find the predominant norms as immediately obliging. This first sense of immediacy makes possible a second: an immediate relation to others. When each individual takes the norms of ethical life to be immediately binding on them, they need not abstract from their own individual "outlook" to consider how they ought to behave in relation to others. Instead, at least initially, the activity of recognizing the same norms is supposed to bear with it immediate implications for how one should treat others, and how they stand in relation to oneself.⁶³

Finally, even if individuals within a form of social life eschew any attempts to locate the source of the norms governing their lives, Hegel holds that these norms must nevertheless have a determinate source. In the

⁵⁸ *PhG* 240/¶440.
⁵⁹ *PhG* 260/¶475.
⁶⁰ *PhG* 229/¶420.
⁶¹ *PhG* 236/¶436.
⁶² *PhG* 351/¶654.
⁶³ Against the need for consideration of the "outlook" (*Ansicht*) or standpoint of the individual, the norms is binding on me due to the nature of its *object*: "That something is the property of an other, this lies at *the ground.*" *PhG* 236/¶436.

first, immediate shape of spirit, they stem from *nature*, specifically from differences that are taken to be natural, most importantly sexual differences. In this social world, the burden of fulfilling its characteristic demands is distributed on the basis of differences that are taken to be natural. When Hegel reintroduces the idea of "ethical life" at the conclusion of chapter VC, he stresses the way in which customs and laws introduce determinate content into reason's abstract idea of "law": Through a shared way of life, reason's abstract idea of normativity secures a concrete, differentiated content, with which the individual nonetheless identifies immediately.[64] In the "ethical world," these powers find expression in determinate laws, the "human" and "divine" laws governing the state and the family, respectively.[65] This differentiation entails that the commands through which the ethical powers are expressed are not univocal, addressing each to the same degree and in the same way. Instead, the differentiation at the level of the ethical powers is mapped onto a differentiation at the level of the individuals who are obliged to respond to those commands. And that latter differentiation is tied to features that are natural: "[E]thical consciousness is essentially *immediately* directed to the law; in this determination of immediacy lies the fact that nature in general enters into the action of ethical life."[66] This initial shape of spirit is "unconscious" – unknowing – because it takes its world to be a merely natural given, when in fact it is actual only through the self-conscious activity of its members.

Attending to the ways in which the ethical powers acquire actuality points to an important feature of Hegel's conception of ethical life. If the social world depends for its existence on the continued recognition of its constitutive norms by human subjects, then it depends by extension on the diverse set of concrete, embodied, material activities by those same subjects. A form of social life that neglected these concrete activities would be fundamentally unstable, as it would fail to secure some of its basic existential conditions. This immediate shape of ethical life secures the essential contribution of concrete and differentiated activities by distinguishing

---

[64] "The distinction of self-consciousness from the essence is thus completely transparent. As a result, the *distinctions in the essence* itself are not contingent determinacies, but rather for the sake of the unity of the essence and self-consciousness, from which alone inequality could come, they are the masses of its own structure [*Gegliederung*], permeated by its own life, self-clear undivided spirits, flawless heavenly shapes, which maintain the undefiled innocence and unanimity of their essence in their distinctions." *PhG* 235–236/¶436.

[65] *PhG* 242/¶¶447–448, 248/¶458.

[66] *PhG* 260/¶475. See the helpful account of naturalization in Brandom 2019, 477–479.

between different sorts of norms and assigning responsibilities to individuals on the basis of differences that are understood to be natural. Interpreters rightly account for this specific configuration of spirit by relating it to features of ancient Greece, an interpretive strategy supported by Hegel's frequent allusions to and misquotations from Sophocles' *Antigone*. At the same time, it's important to note that this specific conception of the social world as ultimately rooted in nature (in particular in a nature that is understood to depend on a divine source) is one that finds expressions in a range of historical epochs.[67] Bearing in mind that we need not take this specific account of ethical life to be historically specific, exclusively characterizing only one epoch, ancient Greek treatments of the basic character of political and economic life provide particularly helpful articulations of the idea that is Hegel's primary interest in appealing to nature in this way. In particular, Hegel's picture of ethical life resembles, in important respects, the *Kallipolis* of Plato's *Republic*, since natural differences provide the principle for the division of labor necessary to support the city and the ultimate criteria on which determinate standards of justice are based.[68]

Having presented the essential elements of this specific "immediate" shape of ethical life, we are now in a position to ask what the primary object is of Hegel's critique of the "ethical world," especially as that critique bears on the issue of recognition.

2.4 Shadow Agency

In one account, the primary object of Hegel's critique of this "immediate" shape of spirit lies in the idea that it gives rise to relations of recognition that entrench relations of domination. Social constructionists often point to the importance of critique in situations where something that is really socially constructed is instead taken by agents to be a natural given. Gender theorists and feminists point to the importance of a critique of gender that follows these insights. While gender is, in their account, actually a social construct, the product of more basic social relations of domination, it is often portrayed as a natural trait, not simply rooted in social attitudes and practices that are subject to change and critique.[69] Likewise, social

---

[67] The shapes of consciousness that Hegel considers in chapter VI are "real spirits" (*PhG* 240/¶440), shapes of a "world." But they do not acquire a specifically historical character until they are taken up from the standpoint of religion, where they are understood as moments that emerge one from another in time. *PhG* 365–366/¶679.

[68] Plato, *Republic*, 370a–c, 433a–d.

[69] See, for example, the account on offer in Haslanger 2012, 7ff, 227ff.

constructionists argue that race is really a socially constructed status whose social function lies in the perpetuation of relations of domination, even though many operate with the belief that races exist by nature and essentially track natural differences among individuals.[70] In such accounts, the primary role of critique lies in the unmasking of these purportedly natural characteristics with the aim of showing them to be mere illusions without any basis in reality or to be mere pretenses for the continued domination of some over others.[71]

It is easy to imagine why these sorts of critiques would be important for recognition theorists. First, if real relations of domination render impossible the recognition of the subjugated, then pointing to any situation of domination – whether that domination is hegemonic (as is the case where it is veiled by these sorts of social constructions) or overt – will be significant for any critic interested in eliminating impediments to recognition. Given Hegel's argument that the relation of lord and bondsman renders impossible the recognition of the bondsman by the lord, such cases will clearly be significant for Hegel. Second, if the social construct is merely an illusion, but one that effectively entrenches a relation of domination, or even reinforces a false and pernicious conception of those who fall under it under the pretense that it presents an account of what those individuals are like "by nature," then it can prove an impediment to relations of recognition that, as we have seen, require an accurate conception of the other whom we recognize.[72] In both of these accounts, the problem with these forms of ideology, which present what is really a product of social activity as a natural essence or given, is that they promote the conditions in which a dominant group or individual can be recognized while making it impossible for others to be.

If we take the relation of lordship and bondage to provide the primary or sole model that *Phenomenology of Spirit* presents for social critique, then we are liable to seek a specific account of the problem that emerges in the "ethical world." In this account, only one-sided recognition, and not fully reciprocal intersubjective recognition is possible. The continued recognition of the norms that comprise the ethical world simply enforces the existing disparity between the "man" and "woman," so that only the public activity of the man – and not the private activity of the woman – makes him a candidate for recognition, just as only the lord – and not the subjugated bondsman – could be an object of recognition.

---

[70] See Haslanger 2012, 235ff; and P. Taylor 2013, 88ff.

[71] On this issue, see Honneth 2018, 223ff.

[72] Recall C. Taylor (1994, 25) on the harm that comes from nonrecognition and misrecognition.

Some interpreters have taken Hegel's argument in chapter VIA to target the role that relations of domination played in the ancient Greek world. Terry Pinkard, for example, argues that Hegel's primary criticism of the ancient Greek world was that, while it did make possible a certain sort of freedom and self-sufficiency, that freedom depended in fact on the institution of slavery. In Pinkard's account, Hegel focuses on Sophocles' *Antigone* since he believes that it presents a situation where the dominated "woman," Antigone, seeks to assert herself and her own freedom, to win "recognition," by violating the decree of the relevant "man," Creon: "As a daughter of a ruling family, she demands full recognition, which is fully at odds with the status of women in that shape of life. Her uncle, Creon, has the unlimited right to issue commands for the good of the community, and he has clearly spoken."[73] In Pinkard's account, then, the relation between the "man," active in public affairs and subject to the "human law," and the "woman," whose place is the *oikos* and whose responsibilities stem from the "divine law," presents an instance of dominating one-sided recognition.

However, in addition to lacking a basis in the text,[74] this account fails to locate the really genuine problem for recognition that Hegel aims to articulate in these passages. While relations of domination are no doubt impediments to recognition, in these passages, Hegel wants rather to point to the neglect of the role that *agency* plays in the "ethical world." In particular, he wants to show that, absent an explicit, shared conception of the self, even the sort of dominating relation of recognition on the basis of privilege or power that we found between lord and bondsman is impossible.

Hegel does suggest that limited forms of recognition *are* possible in the ethical world, especially within the family.[75] He does not hesitate to call "the *relation* of the *husband* and *wife* the *immediate* self-knowing of one consciousness in the other, and the knowing of reciprocal being-recognized [*Anerkanntsein*]."[76] At the same time, he calls this relationship

---

73 Pinkard 2017, 77. While the account in Pinkard 2017 is based primarily on Hegel's later lectures on history, Pinkard makes similar claims about recognition and ethical life in Pinkard 1994, 142–143. In general, Pinkard construes spirit as depending on mutual recognition among self-conscious subjects. See Pinkard 1994, 8. By contrast, I argue that reciprocal intersubjective recognition depends on the mutual recognition of shared norms, or we find relations of recognition among subjects only where we already find spirit.

74 Hegel nowhere claims that Antigone seeks the *recognition* of Creon or anyone else. If anything, Antigone's problem is that she is prevented from engaging in the activity of *recognizing* that is her duty, and that defines her and gives shape to her life.

75 In this connection, see Ciavatta 2009.

76 *PhG* 246–247/¶455.

of being-recognized merely *"natural"* and not "ethical" self-knowing "because it is mixed with a natural relation and with sentiment."[77] For this reason, it can only be "the *representation* and *picture* [*die* Vorstellung *und das* Bild] of spirit, but not actual spirit itself." The limitation in this case presumably stems from the pure concept of recognition that anchors the demand for reciprocity in the equality of the parties who recognize one another. By contrast, the "piety" of husband and wife in the ethical world is certainly not a relation of "equality," and it is anchored in the specific differentiated "natural" affection of the two parties, not their knowledge of the other as a self-conscious individual.

Likewise, Hegel finds a form of "recognition" (*Anerkennung*) in the familial relation between brother and sister, specifically in the sister's recognition of the brother.[78] Unlike that of husband and wife, this relation is "pure and unmixed with natural relation" or desire so that "the moment of the recognizing and recognized *individual self* may here claim its right." However, in spite of the importance of these ties for Hegel's account of the structure of the ethical world, he never calls this form of recognition *reciprocal.*[79] While he stresses that "The loss of the brother is therefore for the sister irrecoverable, and her duty to him is the highest," he does not identify similar duties toward her that would make the relation one of reciprocity. Even if this relation is not one of reciprocal recognition, Hegel does identify it as "the equipoise [*Gleichgewicht*] of blood and desire-less relation" in distinguishing it from the more natural form of recognition that we find in the relation of husband and wife.

Of course, in the context of the patriarchal ancient Greek world, these relations were certainly structured by dynamics of power. And we can equally acknowledge the centrality of the institution of slavery in the ancient world of *Antigone*. However, if we devote too much attention to these historical facts, then we are liable to overlook the unique argument about recognition that Hegel is advancing.

Indeed, it is striking that the only relations that Hegel identifies as relations of recognition in the text are those that we find *within* the *oikos*, the "private" domain of the household. This fact might surprise us, since we might expect to find relations of recognition in the domain of the state,

---

[77] *PhG* 246/¶455.

[78] *PhG* 248/¶456.

[79] I therefore disagree with Siep's (2000, 183) assertion that the relation is one of reciprocal recognition, and Stern's (2002, 137) claim that "brother and sister fully recognize each other." Likewise, nowhere does Hegel claim, *pace* Pinkard (1994, 143), that the sister enjoys any recognition from the brother.

the sphere of the "human law" – either relations of one-sided recognition in the subjection of all to the publicly acting males, or relations of reciprocal recognition in relations among those males.[80] Hegel does identify this sphere as "the self-conscious actuality" of the ethical world, and the (male) individual as the "proper, *positive* purpose of the family" who "is only *actual* and *substantial* as a citizen."[81] However, he never identifies the citizen as an object or administrator of *recognition*. Instead, the male's mortality constitutes an enduring threat to his achieved individuality. Indeed, the terms in which Hegel explains that threat point to the abiding problem with the ethical world and its significance for his understanding of recognition. That is, Hegel claims that even the citizen who acts in public remains, within the ethical world, "*something unreal*, [a] hollow shadow [Unwirkliche *marklose Schatten*]."[82] In general, in the ethical world, "self-consciousness has not yet emerged in its right as *singular individuality* [einzelne Individualität]; individuality counts in [this domain] on the one side only as *universal will*, on the other as the *blood* of the family; *this individual* [Einzelne] counts only as an *unreal shadow* [unwirkliche Schatten]."[83]

While Hegel does not spell out its meaning in any detail, the image of a "shadow" is a rich one, and it is at the heart of the challenge that this configuration of ethical life raises for the achievement of recognition. That is, Hegel wants to point to the way in which certain activities might be understood to be essential to a shared form of social life, but in which the agents of those activities are not themselves acknowledged as essential. It is helpful to consider this image of being a "shadow" with the notion of "social death" that Patterson has articulated to make sense of slavery: "Alienated from all 'rights' or claims of birth, [the slave] ceased to belong in his own right to any social order. All slaves experienced, at the very least, a secular excommunication."[84] Of course, being a "shadow" is importantly different from the status of the slave who suffers a social death. Most importantly, as we have seen, even the individual who enjoys the greatest extent of legal and political privilege in the ethical world, the "man," remains a shadow,

---

[80] Both aspects are operative in Habermas's brief account of the ancient Greek public sphere, which comprises a domain of equality for its participants, but which is premised on the domination of the members of the household (Habermas 1990, 56–57), and in that of Arendt (1958, 28ff) on which Habermas's is based.
[81] *PhG* 242/¶447, 243, 244/¶450.
[82] *PhG* 244/¶450.
[83] *PhG* 251/¶463.
[84] Patterson 1982, 5.

while the social death of the slave is the symbolic and cultural correlate of the overt domination and subjugation of the slave. In one sense, Hegel's account of the "shadow" being of even the "man" is actually the inversion of Patterson's "social death." In Patterson's account, what is denied the slave are the ties that link them to a family, what Hegel would gloss as their "blood." By contrast, Hegel is arguing that if *all* an individual is understood to be is a link in a natural chain defined essentially by ties of "blood," then the grounds of recognition are absent.

However, these differences belie some very significant similarities. First, the condition of being a "shadow" does bear in common with the notion of social death the idea that the individual does not count in the way they would have to in order to be a full agent. Second, mortality plays an important role in both cases. As Patterson stresses (acknowledging Ali Abd Elwahed), slavery emerges from conditions that would otherwise have resulted in the death of the slave, whether from war, capital punishment, exposure, or starvation.[85] The gap between the "social death" and natural death of the slave stems in part from the fact that, but for the action of their master, they would no longer exist. The prominence of the mortality of the slave, their susceptibility to finitude, is the root of the master's claim on them, and so of their becoming a "social nonperson." Similarly, as we have seen, Hegel stresses that the mortality of the "man" is what undermines their capacity for full agency: They exist only as mutable moments of a fluid movement, and their existence depends on a "power" external to them, their memorialization and its rituals. The difference, in this case, is that in the "ethical world" there is no correlate to the "master" in Patterson's account. There is no "higher" power to whom the man is subject, only a distinct ethical power. However, this incomplete social standing rooted in mortality entails that *all* of the "men" are mere shadows, incapable of full agency.

Indeed, what distinguishes Antigone's action is the fact that it is inconceivable as anything *but* the deed of a real *agent*, even though the ethical world provides no terms for making sense of it. From the standpoint of the family (represented by Antigone's sister, Ismene), it exceeds the authority granted by the divine law and the ethical power corresponding to it. From the standpoint of the state (represented by Creon), it is a capricious violation (and so one rooted in individual choice) of the human law. The roots of this problem, however, lie in the very basis of the normative order of

[85] Patterson 1982.

this social world, which contains no terms for making sense of agency. In short, the ethical world lacks a determinate conception, embodied in its central norms, of what it means to be an individual – and that lack affects not only the "woman," but also the "man."

However, this lack introduces a basic instability into the ethical world. The difficulty to which Hegel points is that the agency of self-consciousness – and not mere nature, or a mysterious divine source – is in fact necessary to sustain and reproduce the ethical world, which, we have seen, he unambiguously identifies as the "work" (*Werk*) of self-conscious individuals. Expressed in the terminology we have been considering, we can say that the existence of a normatively structured social world depends on the continuing activity of *mutual norm recognition* undertaken by agents within that world. (For example, the institution of marriage depends for its existence on the fact that agents continue to hold its norms to be binding on themselves.) However, it is possible for those agents to recognize a set of norms in a way that leaves no space for their recognition of one another, specifically when their relation to those norms is "immediate," since such recognition obscures the role of their agency in sustaining the norms. Such agents commit the error that I have identified as "naturalization": They *mistake* what is really the product of their own activity of norm recognition for a merely natural or divine order whose existence does *not* depend on their own activity. Put otherwise, it is possible for mutual norm recognition to render impossible reciprocal intersubjective recognition.

In short, the problem with this form of ethical life is that *no one* is recognized *as an individual agent*, even though the agency necessary to support the ethical world is ultimately that of self-conscious individuals. The central challenge that the ethical world raises for the problem of recognition is not that of the dialectic of lord and bondsman, where one individual is recognized but the other is not. The standoff between Antigone and Creon is not the product only of a dominating relation of power in which only one party is capable of being recognized.[86] Instead, Hegel's argument is that, in the absence of an explicit conception of what it means to be an agent, it will be impossible for *anyone* to be recognized, and that is a problem that afflicts the "man" just as much as the "woman" in the ethical world.

---

[86] That is, the primary challenge for the achievement of *recognition* within this account of ethical life does not stem from such a power imbalance, but instead from the absence of a true conception of the self. This position is perfectly compatible with holding that such imbalances can *also* be impediments to recognition (which Hegel recognizes, for example, in the account of lordship and bondage), and that they are pernicious and bad for other reasons.

The collapse of the ethical world makes this fact explicit when individuals come to see their actions as governed not by a rational or benevolent divine law, but by an opaque necessity that is indifferent to those individuals as agents.[87]

Overcoming these deficiencies will require important modifications to the structure of the social world and the relations its agents bear to it. The first challenge stems from the fact that the central norms in the ethical world address themselves to distinct individuals on the basis of purportedly natural differences. One implication of the collapse of the ethical world is that a social form that is capable *only* of addressing its normative requirements to individuals in this plural way will be fundamentally unstable. Instead, what is required is the availability of at least one mode in which the norms are addressed in a single voice, to everyone.[88] Even if the actions necessary to sustain the social world are essentially different, if every agent plays a role in sustaining that world, it must be possible for each agent's standing within the world to be acknowledged in a way that establishes their equality with others.

The second challenge stems from the model of normative authority that is operative in the ethical world. As we have seen, the form of language that predominates in the ethical world is that of "command." This feature is embodied in the relation that individuals bear toward the predominant norms in that world, namely the "immediate" relation that refrains even from seeking an account of the authority of the norms. The collapse of the ethical world indicates that, instead of requiring unmediated responsiveness to the norms construed as divine commands, a social world must make possible relations to its central norms that are self-consciously mediated either by agents' reflection and thought or by their activity. But this self-conscious mediation is incompatible with the norms taking the form of absolute commands.

2.5 Institutions and the Self

Recall that Hegel initially appealed to the idea of ethical life to secure the conditions for equality required by the pure concept of recognition. That

---

[87] See *PhG* 256–260/¶¶471–475.
[88] It is therefore not clear that the ethical world comprises what Thompson calls a "dikaiological order," if a dikaiological order is supposed to engender a uniform class of persons. The normative order of the ethical world gives rise to statuses that individuals would not enjoy outside of that world – for example, the distinctive notion of what it means to be a "sister," including the duties attendant on that status – but there is no single, shared status to which all can make a claim.

is, reciprocal intersubjective recognition depends on an equality between the parties, and ethical life was supposed to secure this equality by submitting members to a set of common norms where individuals already identified with those norms as their own. However, what we have seen is that, even if individuals within a shared social world all acknowledge the same norms, that alone is not sufficient to secure the conditions for reciprocal recognition. As I've stressed in my reading of chapter VIA.a–b, reciprocal intersubjective recognition is not only undermined by relations of domination and subjugation of the sort that we found in the relation between lordship and bondage. The failure of recognition that we find in the ethical world rather stems from the fact that there is no common *self-conception* shared by all participants in that world. Instead, the normative order addresses itself to different individuals differently, even though each plays a role as an agent in producing and reproducing it. What is required, then, is a social order that is self-conscious in the sense that there are norms explicitly acknowledging the role that each agent plays in its constitution.

I'll devote significant attention in Part II to considering what sort of normative order fits this bill. However, before we turn to that account, it is important to take stock and consider what lessons we can draw concerning the idea of recognition from Hegel's initial account of ethical life.

A prominent group of interpreters considers the ethical life theory to derive its importance from its contribution to Hegel's conception of practical reasoning. The ethical life theory might be essential for grasping the *form* of practical reasoning, as a social practice in which individuals engage with others, or the *material* of practical reason, where my reasons for acting are always rooted in my practical identity, not only as a rational being, but as the inhabitor of specific social roles. If the central question at issue is about the nature of practical reason, then we might be inclined to invoke the idea of recognition as an element of this *sittlich* conception of practical reasoning. But then we will also need something like the systematic theory of ethical life as articulated in *Philosophy of Right* to find the conditions in which genuinely reciprocal recognition is possible, since it is only as an "ethical" agent that I am genuinely recognized as a concrete agent with particular ethical ties. In these accounts, the theory of recognition that Hegel sets out in *Phenomenology of Spirit* is essentially incomplete. As we've seen, many interpreters argue that the earlier text sets out only the circumstances in which relations of recognition are generated, but not what those relations themselves are like. It is one of the major contentions of the remainder of this study that these accounts of *Phenomenology* are basically misguided. In that text, Hegel does not simply establish the conditions for the generation of relations of recognition, but presents a theory of the conditions for reciprocal intersubjective recognition itself, not simply its formation or *Bildung*.

We can begin to appreciate the distinctiveness of this account by considering the unique failure of recognition that we find in the "ethical world." The central problem is that the normative order structuring that world lacks the resources according to which individuals are understood equally as agents whose activities shape and reshape the world itself. Instead, its central norms are understood as commands (so that individuals are understood simply as executors of required and necessary demands, and not as real agents), and those commands address themselves differently to different individuals depending on their "natures" (so that none of the norms address themselves in the same way to all). To introduce the term to which Hegel appeals in addressing this shortcoming, what is lacking is a shared and universal conception of the *self*, of what it means to be an individual on whose agency the social world itself depends. As long as such a conception lacks a central place within the normative order itself, not only will that order remain fundamentally unstable, but the conditions for reciprocal intersubjective recognition – the sort of recognition that is ultimately constitutive of "spirit," the "I" that is a "We," and the "We" that is an "I," and that is necessary for self-knowledge – will be wanting.

While Hegel's concept of "the self" and its role in his theory of recognition will be my primary focus in Part II, it's important to note already one feature that is distinctive of this concept, and which we find expressed in the collapse of the ethical world. A conception of the self is universal, in the sense that it is shared equally among members of the social world, applying in the same way to all agents, irrespective of natural differences among them. To this extent, it is distinct from other sorts of *sittlich* statuses and roles. Those statuses and roles apply to different individuals differently, depending on a variety of factors. Again, role differentiation is essential to the sustainability of any social form. For example, it's important that not everyone possesses the status of being a philosophy professor, since if everyone had the obligations attendant on that status, a number of other valuable forms of social labor would remain undone. However, one of the main arguments in Hegel's account of the collapse of the ethical world is that, in addition to the plurality of ethical statuses, *some* universal and shared status is necessary within the social world and, in being universal and shared, that status is importantly different from other *sittlich* self-conceptions.

A second feature distinguishes the idea of the self from such *sittlich* self-conceptions. This is the fact that selfhood is a normative *status* that is made explicit within the normative order itself. The ethical world depended on the agency of individuals, but the norms constitutive of it did not acknowledge or clarify what an individual itself is. By contrast, the idea of the self is, in the account that Hegel develops, one that is contained within the normative order itself in the sense that it is acknowledged explicitly within the laws and customs of the social world. As a normative status and not simply a natural description, it is *deontic* in character. Being a self means having a certain standing in relation to others, a standing that is already the source of reasons binding on oneself and others. Of course, a normative order could be structured so that it picks out which beings *count* as selves by appealing to features that are (at least taken to be) natural, for example, the capacity for rationality. However, being a "self" is, in Hegel's account, distinct from being a "rational being" in that the former is explicitly and automatically a normative conception, a determination of "spirit."

Before setting out the elements of the concept of the self, we can already see an important distinctive feature of the account of recognition that we find in *Phenomenology of Spirit*. I have suggested that that account is self-standing and complete, and does not require supplementation by the philosophy of objective spirit that Hegel articulates in *Philosophy of Right*. But so far, the claim that recognition depends on a shared normative status does not seem to be obviously different from Pippin's argument that I am recognized only if I am recognized as an agent, and where agency itself is a sort of normative status rather than a natural property possessed simply by each and every individual, independent of their engagement in a normatively structured social world.[89] In addition, Pippin holds that the most central role of recognition in Hegel's theory lies in its contribution not to an achieved form of self-awareness, but rather to a condition of "true individuality," which Pippin interprets in terms of the idea of freedom.[90] Pippin therefore both identifies the centrality of the question of what a subject really is to Hegel's theory of recognition, and stresses the idea that "true individuality" is a normative achievement.

However, in what follows, I hope to show that idea of the "self" is importantly distinct from Pippin's conception of an "agent." Before turning to

---

[89] Pippin 2008.
[90] "A *true individual* is a *free* subject and recognition relations function in a complex way as conditions for that possibility." Pippin 2000, 156.

the details of that account, I would like to point to two specific features of Pippin's view that themselves pose problems. First, Pippin's view is weaker as an *interpretation* of the text. The central terms in which Pippin spells out the normative status that is a product of recognitive attitudes, "agent" and "agency," do not play a very significant role in Hegel's account of these issues in *Phenomenology*.[91] Instead, as we have seen, Hegel holds that reciprocal intersubjective recognition requires a shared conception of the *self.* Indeed, providing an adequate conception of the self is both the central challenge that structures the development of Hegel's account of spirit in chapter VI,[92] and an essential component of the account of the conditions for reciprocal intersubjective recognition. In focusing on the issue of agency, Pippin's account neglects the centrality of the role of the idea of the self.

Second, the *concept* of the self is distinct from that of an agent. For Hegel, it is not sufficient simply to say that individuals are selves. Instead, we need also to determine which specific conception of the self can both be affirmed of everyone equally and can comprehend those elements of our constitution that are necessary to support the social order itself. This fact distinguishes conceptions of the self, first, from the particular "ethical" shapes of identity that can belong to particular individuals within a form of social life, like being a "sister" or "colleague" or "citizen," since conceptions of the self are supposed to apply equally to all participants in social life. And second, it distinguishes the idea of the self from the more general and abstract idea of being an "agent," since it remains an open question which determinate conception of the self can both be affirmed equally for all, and also comprehend individuals' particularity.[93]

Of course, Hegel never denies that an adequate conception of selfhood needs to include an account of what it means to be an agent, and issues of agency are clearly important in the account that he develops in chapter VI.[94] However, the question of what it means to be an agent is narrower than

---

[91] It is true that Hegel does on occasion identify the acting individual as a "*Handelnde*," for example, at *PhG* 179/¶322, 255/¶468, 256/¶470, and 357–360/¶¶665–667. However, the framework of questions about agency of this sort seems to fit much better the mature *Philosophy of Right*, where the central questions are directly connected to these issues of agency and freedom.

[92] See especially *PhG* 341–342/¶633.

[93] When Pippin does consider the specific conceptions of the self that Hegel presents in chapter VI, he rightly identifies that they are products of attitudes of recognition – their being "being-recognized" – but he does not acknowledge their centrality as conceptions of what the self is, treating them instead as one conception of what agents are like among other "ethical" ones. See Pippin 2008, 199–200.

[94] On these issues, see especially Speight 2001.

the question of what it means to be a self.[95] The latter does not simply concern the social and institutional conditions under which freedom is possible, but is rather ontological, a question about what it is that I am.[96]

We are now again at the point where we can see the connection between recognition and self-knowledge that emerged in chapter IV. There, the basic idea was that the "truth" of self-consciousness was a sort of knowledge possessed by consciousness of itself. The activity of recognition emerged within Hegel's account in mediating relations between individuals aimed at the achievement of self-knowledge. In chapter VI, these issues return explicitly with the introduction of the idea of "the self." And again, the central concern remains the same: Hegel will argue that it is only through the recognition of others that I can achieve the status of being a self, so that knowledge of what it means to be a self – "self-knowledge" – depends essentially on recognitive relations.

[95] I have already pointed to Thompson's distinction between monadic and relational conceptions of the "person." See again Thompson 2004, 353ff.

[96] McDowell has objected to Pippin's conception of the relation between recognition and agency on the grounds that it makes agency too much dependent on actually being recognized by others as an agent. See McDowell 2009c. In one sense, my proposal here should help us to relax McDowell's worry, since it does not make the status of agency so dependent on actual recognition by others. However, in another sense, it might heighten McDowell's concern, since it does make the status of selfhood dependent on the actual recognition by others. I will return to this issue in Chapter 5.

PART II

The Self

CHAPTER 3

Equality and Alienation

The question of the nature of the self is at the heart of the account of spirit that Hegel offers in chapter VI of *Phenomenology of Spirit*. Moreover, it provides the key to understanding how relations of reciprocal intersubjective recognition are really possible. You and I can recognize one another only if we share a conception of what the self is, since it is that conception that will shape our interactions, giving them the structure of reciprocal intersubjective recognition. Successful recognition, however, requires that the conception of the self that we share is *true*, so that the conception of the self that determines how it is appropriate to treat you is one that you have reason actually to affirm of yourself, so that the resulting relation is reversible, where the conception of the self that shapes your interactions with me is one that I can also share, and affirm of myself, and so that that conception could shape similar interactions for any "you" and "I," for any beings exhibiting the structure of self-consciousness. The idea of the self, therefore, plays a central role in the elaboration of the concept of recognition that Hegel develops over the course of the whole text, most notably from chapters IV–VI.

In addition to the role that it plays in mediating relations of intersubjective recognition, the idea of the self that Hegel presents and defends in the text is social in a second sense. The idea of the self is a determination of spirit. In *Phenomenology*, spirit refers to the relation of reciprocal dependence between self-conscious beings and their social world. "The self" (*das Selbst*) is the distinctive designation that applies to self-conscious beings *qua* participants in a social world. On the one hand, it is selves who animate and sustain the world, demonstrating its "work"-character, by enacting its constitutive customs and laws. Likewise, the world is the "*ground* and *point of departure*" for the deeds of the self, providing its "*purpose* and *aim*," its intelligible intrinsic being.[1] Hegel holds that there are

---

[1] *PhG* 238/¶438.

different "worlds" of spirit, distinguished by different fundamental norms that give structure to shared ways of life,[2] and he argues that new and distinct predominant conceptions of the self emerge with each distinct world. For Hegel, the self is therefore socially constituted: Different worlds give rise to distinct conceptions of what the self is, and those conceptions in turn structure the relations of self-conscious beings to their actions, and to one another.[3] My understanding of what I am will therefore depend on the determinate world in which I find myself, and the predominant conception of the self will change along with changes in the basic normative structure of the social world.[4]

Among the core arguments that Hegel aims to advance over the course of his account of "Spirit" is that we find not only different conceptions of the self as we track the emergence of different "real spirits," different "shapes of a world," but that we find genuine progress in the project of self-understanding and self-knowledge.[5] Subsequent conceptions of the self are not only distinct from earlier ones, but more true, helping us to better make sense of our experience as agents within a shared social world. The dynamic of recognition is among the core drivers of this movement toward self-knowledge, since reciprocal intersubjective recognition requires a conception of the self that I can affirm of myself, but that can equally be affirmed for everyone. And Hegel argues that identifying such a conception is a particularly fraught matter. The failure of a conception of the self to give rise to relations of reciprocal intersubjective recognition need not entail the complete rejection – the "simple negation" – of that conception. Instead, Hegel treats subsequent conceptions of the self as arising from the specific failure – the determinate negation – of a given conception of the self, and of what I shall call the "model" of recognition to which it corresponds. The idea of the self is therefore central to the account of recognition that Hegel develops and completes in chapter VI.

---

[2] *PhG* 240/¶440.
[3] Notwithstanding the differences that I highlighted in §2.5, the idea of the self therefore shares significant features with Pippin's account of what it means to be an "agent" for Hegel, where that term designates an achieved normative status, rather than a natural or metaphysical property possessed by beings of a certain kind. See Pippin 2008.
[4] I therefore agree broadly with Cobben's (2009) strategy of reading chapter VI in light of the distinctive conceptions of the self that emerge therein. At the same time, aspects of Cobben's approach are puzzling. He reads chapter IV as already addressing the question of the nature of the self, understood as the question of the relation of mind and body. But the mind-body relation is not obviously the core question at stake in chapter IV, and Hegel too does not use the same term – *das Selbst* – in chapter IV.
[5] *PhG* 240/¶440.

It therefore ought not to surprise us that, on the interpretive level, the idea of "the self" emerges as one of the core principles structuring the account of spirit that Hegel offers in chapter VI of *Phenomenology of Spirit*. Indeed, given the centrality of this distinctive concept – "the self" – that Hegel elaborates uniquely in *Phenomenology of Spirit*, it may surprise us that interpreters have generally overlooked its significance for the argument of chapter VI and for the work as a whole, and, particularly salient with respect to my interest, for the resolution to the account of recognition initiated in chapter IV.[6] There are at least three possible reasons why this concept and its centrality have proven so elusive.

First, the idea of the self emerges in the text gradually, and without Hegel flagging it at the outset as a particularly important one. Outside of the Preface (which Hegel composed only after having completed the rest of the text), the specific term, *das Selbst*, only appears for the first time late in chapter VC, in Hegel's account of "law-giving reason."[7] He does not highlight the fact that he is introducing a new and distinctive term. However, the term becomes ubiquitous in the argument of chapter VI. And, by the time Hegel reaches the conclusion of the chapter and sets out to review the development that we find within it, he does so in terms of the different conceptions of the self – personhood, absolute freedom, and conscience – that emerge within those different "worlds" of spirit.[8]

We might be inclined to dismiss the recapitulation of chapter VI that Hegel offers by appealing to the idea of the self by recalling the frenetic pace with which much of this part of the work was apparently completed.[9] Perhaps things had really gotten out of hand at this point, and Hegel was clumsily searching for a principle that could (retroactively) give shape to the story that he'd told thus far. However, notwithstanding the good evidence that we have concerning the circumstances of the text's composition, the question of whether the recapitulation is an apt one can only be decided by considering the development of the text itself.[10] And I aim to show that considering this development through the lens of the idea of the self throws valuable light onto the structure and aims of the chapter as a whole.

---

[6] There are some prominent exceptions. See again Cobben 2009, Wildt 1982, 384 and Siep 2014, 132.

[7] *PhG* 228/¶417.

[8] See *PhG* 341–342/¶633.

[9] On the circumstances of the work's composition and their relation to its structure, see Pöggeler 1961 and 1966; and Forster 1998, part IV.

[10] Given the importance of recollection (*Erinnerung*) to the project of *Phenomenology* as a whole, it may not be a big problem that these recapitulatory accounts articulate something essential about the development of its core ideas. See *PhG* 433–434/¶808.

Second, it can be challenging to identify what is actually distinctive about the idea of the self. Given the little fanfare with which Hegel introduces the idea of the self into the text, we might be inclined to dismiss the suggestion that that idea is actually a distinctive or new one, reading it simply as a gloss on the familiar conception of "self-consciousness" that we find throughout the text. However, here too the fact that Hegel does not flag this idea as a significant one at the time of its introduction cannot establish that it is not distinctive or important. I aim to demonstrate this distinctiveness by contrasting the idea of "the self," as Hegel comes to articulate it more explicitly over the course of chapter VI, with others – consciousness, self-consciousness, self-conscious reason – with which we might be inclined to elide it.

The most central distinguishing feature of the idea of the self is that it is a determination of "spirit." So far, I have explained the idea of spirit in the terms that Hegel introduces at the outset of chapter VI: "Spirit" identifies the relation of reciprocal dependence between self-conscious beings and their social world. As a determination of spirit, the self is therefore inherently social, constituted in part by the normatively structured world shared among self-conscious beings. As inseparable from the idea of a shared social world, the idea of the self is therefore distinct from "consciousness," "self-consciousness," and "reason."

Third, the idea of the self can be easily missed since determinate conceptions of the self only emerge through the course of experience. Not only does Hegel not begin his account by pointing to the centrality of the self, but he holds that a conception of the self is not given to us in advance and independent of experience. Rather, because the self is "the totality or actuality which presents itself as the truth of" a given world of spirit,[11] determinate conceptions of the self are best understood as products of practices of collective sense-making, as self-conscious beings engage in the project of understanding their social world and their place within it.

Stepping back from these specific developments to identify the general terms in which Hegel explains the idea of the self requires a particular sort of reflective work, and it is that work with which I begin here (§3.1). I next turn to consider the first two specific conceptions of the self that Hegel identifies in his account of "spirit," those of the "person" (§3.2) and "absolute freedom" (§3.3). I conclude by considering the criticisms that Hegel

---

[11] *PhG* 341/¶633. The full quotation refers specifically to the self of personhood as the truth of the "ethical world." However, I demonstrate that this is general feature of the idea of the self that Hegel defends.

develops of these conceptions of the self by considering them in relation to Stephen Darwall's conception of "recognition respect" (§3.4).

3.1 The Idea of the Self

"The self" is the designation belonging to self-conscious beings when they are understood as participants in a shared social world. This notion is at the core of the characterization of "spirit" that Hegel offers at the outset of chapter VI:

> [Spirit's] spiritual essence has already been identified as the *ethical substance*; spirit however is *the ethical actuality*. It is the *self* of actual consciousness, which confronts, or, better, which confronts itself as the objective actual *world*, which has equally lost for the self all significance of being something alien, just as the self has lost all significance of a being-for-self divided from it, of being dependent or independent. The *substance* and the universal, self-same, remaining essence – it is the unmoved and simple [*unaufgelöst*] *ground* and *point of departure* of the deeds of all – and their *purpose* and *aim*, as the thought *in itself* of all self-consciousness. This substance is equally the universal *work*, that engenders itself through the *deeds* of all and each as their unity and equality, for it is the *being-for-self*, the self, the deed. As *substance* spirit is the unwavering just *self-sameness*; but as *being-for-self* it is the dissolved [*aufgelöst*], the self-sacrificing benign [*gütig*] essence, in which each completes their own work, tears apart the universal being and takes its own part. This dissolution [*Auflösung*] and individuation of the essence is equally the *moment* of the deed and self of all; it is the movement and soul of the substance, and the effected universal essence. Precisely therein, that it is being dissolved in the self is it not the dead essence, but *actual* and *living*.[12]

I would like to begin to develop the idea of the self and articulate what is distinctive about it, by considering this passage, which we've already encountered in considering the character of Hegel's social theory, with some care. Consequently, the initial steps in my articulation of the idea of the self will recapitulate and then develop some already familiar claims.

3.1.1 *Self-consciousness and the Self*

First, Hegel identifies the self here as the moment of "being-for-self" of the unity between self-consciousness and world that comprises spirit. The sorts of beings that are selves embody the structure of self-consciousness that I identified in §1.2. What distinguishes "the self" as a particular

---

[12] *PhG* 238–239/¶432.

configuration of self-consciousness is its object, namely the normatively structured social world that it shares with other self-conscious beings. The world comprises the "first object," through whose mediation the self seeks knowledge of itself, which is the "second object."[13] While the ultimate aim of the self's world-relation is knowledge and understanding of what it is, Hegel will argue that the achievement of this self-knowledge poses a particularly strong challenge – it will not be possible in all configurations of the world, or with every determinate conception of the self.

We might already be inclined to challenge the claim that there is anything particularly distinctive of this idea of the self. It might be objected that, if "the self" simply designates self-consciousness, investigation of this social conception of the self will ultimately require some positive account of a more basic idea, namely what self-consciousness is.[14] Anticipating possible resistance to the social constitution conception of the self that Hegel defends, we can attach the name "atomization" to the set of critical tendencies that seek the real or fundamental character of the self not in social relations or in social reality, but instead solely in the individual who is designated as a self. The move to find the self solely in the basic character of self-consciousness is an instance of atomization.

Of course, I have already offered some characterization of what self-consciousness is, namely the particular structure that we see instantiated in the self-world relation. But more importantly, Hegel has argued that the attempt to consider what self-consciousness is, simply by itself, independent of determinate object-relations, including the specific world-relation distinctive of the self, is bound to yield only a negative result. And the reason for that limitation stems from the fact that self-consciousness is, at base, "absolute negativity," not itself anything positive. Consequently, Hegel will present a reason for resisting this initial move of atomization, since the attempt to understand the self exclusively as self-consciousness

---

[13] The significance of this "knowing of itself" emerges clearly and directly in *PhG* 240/¶¶440, 441.

[14] For an instance of this position that rejects the idea that the ontology of the self is a social ontology, see Ferrarin 2019, chapter 1. Ferrarin argues that the social constitution view is incoherent because it would entail that a relation constitutes its relata. This is a flaw in views like Brandom's, where it is self-consciousness that is a social achievement. By contrast, on the social constitution view of the self, there are already self-conscious beings – so as relata they are not constituted by their relation – but they can only achieve self-knowledge by establishing the rights sorts of recognitive relations with one another, where those relations are governed by a conception of the self. Ferrarin does acknowledge a central role for "the self" in Hegel's thought, but treats this concept as identical with "subjectivity" so that, for example, because it has "the potentiality of being in relation to [it]self in the development and interaction with its other," "The squirrel is a subject and has a self." Ferrarin 2019, 11, 25. This account may fit with Hegel's *Encyclopedia* position, but not that of *Phenomenology of Spirit*.

will eliminate the possibility of providing positive content to what the self is. Instead, as I showed in §1.5, he develops the ways in which the negativity characteristic of self-conscious beings is generative of social reality, namely when the individual surrenders their own singular will, making possible a universal, shared will. And Hegel looks to social reality for the terms in which such beings are ultimately capable of understanding themselves.

3.1.2 Spirit, Self, and World

The second aspect of the idea of the self that we find expressed in the passage quoted at length earlier is that the content for the idea of the self stems primarily from the way in which the self engages with its world. There are two aspects of this engagement. First, the social world provides us with the terms in which we make sense of ourselves, and of our relations with others, so the idea of the self plays an essential intersubjective role. Second, the primary means through which we engage in the world are practical, they are activities, and a conception of the self links agents to their actions in a determinate way.

First, the world supplies the self with its "*ground* and *point of departure*" and its "*purpose* and *aim*, as the thought *in-itself* of all self-consciousness [*das gedachte* Ansich *aller Selbstbewußtsein*]." That is, the self derives significant aspects of its self-understanding – what it is "in-itself" – from the world in which it engaged. I suggested in §2.2 one of the significant respects in which the world, in the form of customs and laws, can supply the materials for an individual's self-understanding.

We might be inclined to think of these norms as structuring the individual's self-understanding by providing them with a determinate role or set of ethical obligations that are distinctively theirs, and that they come to inhabit. However, we have already seen, in §§2.3–5, one reason why that form of social differentiation will be inadequate to provide the materials for a conception of the self. Such differentiation need not entail a single status that every participant in social life shares, and in the absence of such a shared status, relations of reciprocal recognition will be impossible. For a genuine conception of the self, we will instead require a form of worldly, norm-governed engagement that provides for the equality of all selves.

We also saw that Hegel appeals to social reality to provide the terms that mediate relations between individuals, by establishing expectations for how it is appropriate to treat others. A shared conception of the self, rooted in the normatively structured social world, provides the terms through which individuals understand their relations to one another. Common engagement in a shared social world is the primary means through which these relations are established.[15] So a conception of the self, first, links us to others in specific ways.

Second, this practical dimension of shared worldly engagement emerges clearly in the passage under consideration. Hegel points there to the distinctive way in which the self engages with its world, that is, practically, through its "activity" (*Tun*). As we have seen, the sort of being that the world possesses is that of a "work" (*Werk*). The shared social world exists as a product of the activity of the self, so that it is an essential being that is "*actual* and *living*," and not "dead." This point about activity – and ultimately agency – bears significantly on the condition for the achievement of self-knowledge that worldly engagement makes possible. Put most simply, active engagement is necessary to achieve that self-knowledge that depends on shared social practice rather than merely reflective theory.

While our actions are generative of the social world – they produce and reproduce it[16] – the social world also provides us with the norms that link us to our actions. The normatively structured social world bears with it its own standards for whether an action is one that I am bound or expected to perform, for whether it is something for which I am obliged to claim responsibility, or whether it actually gives expression to who I am. A conception of the self, therefore, binds the agent and their actions in determinate ways.

The idea of the self, therefore, depends on the idea of spirit. As I've developed that idea so far in relation to Hegel's social theory, spirit is the unity that explains the reciprocal dependence of self and world. A *geistig* account of social reality will therefore understand the self to be both embedded in and also constitutive of that reality. For Hegel, the idea of the self is primarily a "linking" or "binding" idea that establishes specific relations between self-conscious beings and their actions, and among self-conscious beings. Such ideas are social in the sense that they are generated through the activity of self-conscious subjects, take the form of shared norms that are binding on all the participants in a form of social life, and provide the materials for a self-understanding that can be shared among those participants.

3.1.3 Language

Given the way in which shared worldly engagement mediates relations between individuals, it should not surprise us that Hegel links spirit and

---

[15] Shared understanding requires common practical engagement in a particular form of life, just as much as it requires theoretical or reflective endorsement of a particular idea of what the self is.
[16] See again *PhG* 268/¶489.

language as consistently as he does. The most direct statement of this connection holds simply that language is "the existence of spirit [*das Dasein des Geistes*]."[17] We can account for this connection by relating it to the linking function of the idea of the self.

First, language makes individuals intelligible to one another. For Hegel, language:

> Is the *existence* [Dasein] of the pure self as self; in it, the *individuality* [*Einzelheit*] *existing for itself* of self-consciousness emerges into existence [*Existenz*], so that it is *for another*. *I* as the *pure I* otherwise does not yet exist [*ist sonst nicht* da]; in every other externalization it is sunk in an actuality and in a configuration from which it can draw itself back; it is *reflected* in itself out of its actions, as out of its physiognomic expressions [*Ausdrücke*], and leaves behind an incomplete existence in which both too much and too little always lies ensouled. But language receives it in its purity, it alone expresses *I* [*spricht* Ich *aus*] itself. This its *existence* [Dasein] is an *existence*, an objectivity, which has the I's true nature in it. *I* is *this* I - but equally *universal*; its appearance is equally immediately the externalization and disappearance of *this* I, and thereby its persisting in its universality.[18]

Language, therefore, contributes not only to the achievement of shared understanding generally, but to relations of understanding of individual agents by other individual agents. It is capable of giving direct expression to the individual's "pure self," the "*individuality existing for itself* of self-consciousness," in a universal form that can be grasped by others.

Second, language also makes intelligible the relevant link between the agent and their actions in a given social world. We find an instance of this link within the particular world of spirit that we've already encountered, the world of "ethical life": "In the world of ethical life, [...language] has the *essence* as its content, and is its form, as *law* and *command* [Gesetz *und* Befehl]."[19] Language gives expression to what is essential in a given social world. The form of language characteristic of the ethical world – law and command – implies a specific way of linking the agent to their actions. Those actions are properly theirs which are commanded or demanded of an agent by the (human or divine) law. In the ethical world, this link is particularly strong. As we have already seen, in the ethical world, the relation between agents and the shared norms comprising their world is "immediate." The actions commanded by the law are not even understood

---

[17] *PhG* 351/¶652.
[18] *PhG* 276/¶507.
[19] *PhG* 276/¶507. See also *PhG* 351/¶652: "The language of the ethical spirit is the law and simple command, and lament, which is more a tear shed over necessity."

to be obligations or duties which the individual might fulfill or neglect. Instead, those actions are understood to be simply "right": "I am in the ethical substance only because right is for me *in* and *for itself*, thus it is the *essence* of self-consciousness; self-consciousness, however, is [the] *actuality* and *existence*, [the] *self* and *will* [of the ethical substance]."[20] The predominant forms of language in the ethical world, law and command, articulate this immediate relation that is to hold in that world between the agent and their actions. The agent understands those actions to be theirs that actualize the norms that give structure to the ethical world.

Of course, if the only forms of language that can articulate the relation between the agent and their world are those of law and command, requiring, in turn, the immediate identification by the agent of those commands as their "essence," we would have good reason to reject the idea of the self that Hegel advances. If his idea of the self required that sort of identification, Hegel would seem to be committed to an entirely premodern – or we might say with Habermas, conventional – conception of the self, completely eliminating space for the sort of reflective distance from one's particular place within the social world that is characteristic of the modern, reflective – for Habermas, postconventional – stance.

However, we have already seen (in §2.4, in particular) that Hegel argues that the "ethical world" suffers from an irreparable contradiction because of its failure to give rise to an explicit idea of the self, which, again, is distinct from that of a particular ethical role or status, specifically because it must be universal, in principle sharable among all participants in social life, while no single ethical role or status possesses that characteristic. As Hegel puts this point "the actuality of the self" is "not present in the ethical world."[21] We might say that the ethical world depends on the existence of selves – they are its producers and reproducers – but there is not yet understanding or knowledge of what the self is; in Hegelese, in such a world, the self exists in itself, but not yet for itself.

3.1.4 The Self and Social Dynamics

At this point, two features of the idea of the self – perhaps controversial ones – emerge with particular prominence.

First, Hegel holds that the predominant understanding of what the self is changes over time. This idea might not surprise us, since he has argued

[20] *PhG* 237/¶436.
[21] *PhG* 264/¶482.

that "the self" is simply the concept of a self-conscious being understood as a participant in a given social world, and the social world, which he identifies primarily in terms of its predominant norms, itself changes over time. However, in chapter VI, Hegel identifies two transformations in the basic structure of the social world that are so profound that they amount not just to gradual changes within a particular world, but to the inauguration of a new "shape of a world."[22] These are the move from the ethical world to the world of "culture" (*Bildung*), and then from the world of culture to the world of morality.[23] Hegel does not simply say that *the* world changes through these transformations. Instead, each distinctive shape is the shape of *a* world. I shall work subsequently to identify the basic structural differences that distinguish these worlds as we track the different conceptions of the self that emerge in them. But we ought now to attend to the fact that the emergence of a new shape of a world will ultimately bring with it a new conception of the self.

So far, I have generally considered the *idea* of the self, that is, the idea of a self-conscious being considered a participant in a shared social world, who produces and reproduces that world through their actions, and whose relations to others and to their actions are structured and made intelligible by the form of language that predominates within that world. It should now be clear that, in addition to this more general idea of the self, we shall have to consider different and competing *conceptions* of the self, the specific ways in which agents within a given social world with its characteristic norms and linguistic forms come to understand themselves. While the idea of the self includes several elements that will be common to all of those specific modes of understanding, the particular conceptions of the self that emerge through the course of the experience of spirit – the legal "person," "absolute freedom," and "conscience" – will embody those common features in different ways. By implication, I will understand my relation to others and to my own actions differently, for example, when I understand myself to be a person or when I understand myself to be conscience.

The second feature of the idea of the self that appears with special prominence when we consider its link to the social world is the fact that

---

[22] The shapes (*Gestalten*) that Hegel considers in chapter VI "distinguish themselves from the foregoing ones because they are real spirits [*realen Geister*], proper actualities, and instead of being shapes of consciousness are shapes of a world." *PhG* 240/¶440.

[23] Brandom's (2019) account of these shifts, from a premodern to a modern world, and then from a modern to a postmodern world, captures the scope of the dynamic. However, I shall argue that he downplays the significance of the idea of the self to understanding these transformations, and that designating the world of morality as a "postmodern" world is misleading and unhelpful.

a determinate conception of the self is not immediately given with the appearance of a particular shape of the social world. We have an instance of this fact already: In the ethical world, there is no common, universal, explicitly articulated conception of the self. Instead, Hegel argues that such a conception emerges only for the first time with the collapse of the ethical world in the "condition of right" (*Rechstzustand*), in the specific form of the person. As Hegel expresses this idea in one of his recapitulations: "The totality or actuality which presents itself as the truth of the ethical world is the self of the *person*."[24] We find this dynamic repeated across the course of chapter VI. An explicit and determinate conception of the self emerges only as the "totality or actuality" or the "truth" of a given world. Up until that point, the self-understanding of agents within that world will be confused and contradictory so that proper self-knowledge, knowledge of what the self really is, will be lacking for them. The experience of spirit is, for Hegel, the experience of the gradual emergence of a conception of the self as a result of agents' efforts to make sense of their relations to their actions and to others. Even having such a conception is a specific sort of achievement, won through an effort at making sense.[25]

The terms that make possible that self-understanding will possess for those agents a sort of stability. As we have seen, Hegel holds that there are characteristic forms of language that play a prominent role in shaping that understanding. They supply something like a worldview, or a paradigm, or the "historical *a priori*" for the inhabitants of a given world. However, at significant moments those structures of intelligibility can disappear, so that new predominant terms for self-understanding emerge. And at that point, agents within a given world are obliged to give up their prior conception of the self – to acknowledge that that conception was the truth of a world that no longer exists – and to begin the task of working out anew what the self is. A determinate conception of the self that serves to make sense of the agent's relations to their own actions and to others within their particular social world therefore not only is the *goal* of the project of understanding within that world, but also (at least in the case of the ethical world and the world of culture) inaugurates the collapse of that world and the emergence of a new one.

We find the generic structure presented by the idea of the self in all of the social worlds that Hegel considers. In a sense, that idea is part of

[24] *PhG* 341/¶633.
[25] See in this connection Moyar's characterization of conscience as "a fragile achievement": "There is a sense, central to Hegel's account, in which conscience is itself a *social* practice that has developed with the advent of religious and political changes in modernity." Moyar 2011, 14.

Hegel's social theory, since it provides the model for understanding the participants in social life, as beings existing in a relation of reciprocal dependence with the social world. However, in addition to assigning it this structural role, Hegel also evokes the idea of the self to explain social dynamics. He aims to argue that among the core projects of the participants in a given social world is that of self-understanding, of articulating a determinate conception of the self in terms of which they can understand their relations to their own actions and to others. The dynamics of the social changes that Hegel considers in chapter VI are animated by the demand to achieve "consciousness of what [spirit] is immediately" so that spirit must "proceed [*fortgehen*] ... through a series of shapes to attain [*gelangen*] knowledge of itself."[26] The demand for self-knowledge is at the heart of this account of social transformation.

3.1.5 Defending the Social Constitution View

At the heart of this social constitution view of the self is the claim that the idea of the self depends on the idea of spirit. We reach this view by the same means that we reach any position within *Phenomenology of Spirit*, by tracking its emergence from prior shapes of consciousness and by attending to the ways in which contradictions develop from the attempt to enact the claims to knowledge that individuate them. There is a much longer story that one could tell that would document the significant and interesting details of that critical account, an account that would engage more closely than I have here with the various configurations of reason.[27] Instead, I would like to highlight some of the core developments that give rise to the social constitution account and clarify the ways in which it differs from some prominent social constructivist accounts of the self.

I've already suggested how the idea of the self is distinct from self-consciousness, namely the self is a specific configuration of self-consciousness, whose object is the world of spirit, the shared social world. For this reason, we can accept core aspects of the interpretation offered by Alfredo Ferrarin, but still hold that there is not only space, but a need for a conception of the self as socially constituted. For Ferrarin,

---

[26] *PhG* 240/¶440.

[27] It would focus in particular on considering conceptions of the self that understand it to be something that we can know through observation, where the self is understood biologically to be the living organism, or psychologically to be the consciousness that persists across time, or materialistically to be the thing that is the mind.

Social roles and practices, language, normative relations of recognition will never be able to constitute the peculiar relation to oneself that self-consciousness is. They do fill the I's life, give it substance and scope, but only insofar as they are experienced and willed—recognized—by an I. However, demanding that they give rise to an I and at the same time that I recognize them—that is, that the I constitute them through social interaction—is circular.[28]

I have been arguing that we find a variety of configurations of self-consciousness throughout *Phenomenology*, and many of those forms of self-consciousness are not generated through social interaction. So Ferrarin is correct to say that the I is not a product of recognition. However, self-consciousness is also not limited to the I's relation to itself. Instead, a variety of shapes of consciousness count as configurations of self-consciousness for Hegel, namely when they have the double-object structure characteristic of it. And Hegel's argument is that subsequent configurations of self-consciousness, most notably for my purposes reason and spirit, are not simply adjuncts to it, but essential configurations of it, necessary in the project of achieving self-knowledge. So "social roles and practice, language, normative relations of recognition" not only "fill the I's life, [and] give substance and scope," but they are necessary for the project of self-knowledge.[29] In what follows, I argue that we find that self-knowledge not only in the absolute knowing with which Hegel's text culminates, but in the experience of spirit too, in the engagement of self-conscious beings in their shared social world.

What, specifically, is missing from mere self-consciousness that distinguishes it from the self? We have already identified several core aspects of Hegel's answer to this question. First (§1.5), since self-consciousness is, by itself, nothing positive, but only "absolute negativity," providing a positive account of the self will require attention to the ways in which self-consciousness's activities can be generative, in particular of social reality (forms of "universal consciousness"). Second (§2.1), we have also seen that Hegel argues that we can only understand the agency of self-consciousness, the ways in which it is self-productive, by seeing it as embedded in a world,[30] and indeed a world that is essentially social, shared with others.[31]

---

[28] Ferrarin 2019, 36–37.
[29] Of course, differentiated social roles play a diminished role in my account of the conditions for reciprocal recognition and for the constitution of the self.
[30] The argument of chapter VB is that instrumental conceptions of the world, which understand social practices to exist merely for the advancement of individual purposes are incoherent.
[31] The argument of chapter VC.a is that the *Sache selbst* to which I give expression in my actions cannot coherently be understood to be only *my* thing, but is rather essentially shared with others.

"Spirit" identifies the relationship of reciprocal dependence between self-conscious beings and this world. Finally (§§2.3–5), we have also seen that Hegel argues that a positive conception of the self as a status that is shared by participants in the social world is required over and above any particular social role that individuals might occupy. These developments provide the materials for the argument for the need for the social constitution view.

At the same time, the social constitution view is distinct from other prominent constructivist views. We have already seen (in §2.5) some significant features that distinguish the account of the self that I offer here from Pippin's account of what it means to be an "agent." At the same time, we've also seen that one of the essential functions of a conception of the self is to link the agent and their actions in a determinate way.

Extending our consideration more broadly to the idea of social construction, while the social constitution view that I ascribe to Hegel bears some features in common with some social construction conceptions, his account is ultimately distinctive. Ian Hacking's taxonomy of social constructivist views is helpful in this connection. Hacking identifies distinctive "gradations of constructivist commitment," whose starting point is the observation that (0) at present that phenomenon x, in our case, the self, is taken for granted and seems inevitable. The elevating gradations of commitment expand on this basic claim in more significant ways, from the view that (1) x was actually "constructed in the course of social processes" and so is "the contingent upshot of historical events"; to the ironic attitude that (2) x "could have been quite different"; to the reformist who holds that (3) x could be modified to improve it; to the unmasker who aims to identify (4) the hidden function that x plays; to the rebellious constructivist who holds that (5) we would be better off without x; and finally to the revolutionary who (6) "moves beyond the world of ideas and tries to change the world" with respect to x.[32]

Where can we situate the social constitutivist account of the self? Many, or even most of us are committed to the idea that the existence of the self is taken for granted and seems inevitable. And Hegel does argue that determinate conceptions of the self are actually formed in the course of social processes, since his argument with respect to the ethical world is that there is no shared conception of the self common to participants in that social form. However, the ideas of contingency and alterability that emerge at gradations (1) and (2) are, in important senses, out of place in Hegel's

---

[32] Hacking 1999, 19–20.

account. From a certain perspective, we might imagine that the timeline on which an articulate conception of the self emerges in history might have been different. But from the recollective perspective of *Phenomenology of Spirit*, whose aim is to identify the relations of necessity that govern the transitions from one configuration of spirit to the next, the idea of the self is necessary in the sense that it emerges as the resolution to a contradiction that rendered the participants in a prior social form unintelligible to themselves. One of the primary reasons that I have chosen to identify Hegel's view as social constitutivist rather than social constructivist is because he sees the idea of the self as addressing a central and unavoidable challenge for us, not as an arbitrary concept overlaid onto events. It is true that this idea emerges only through engagement in shared social practices, but that fact need not be strictly opposed to the idea that it is still in some sense necessary for us. The idea of the self embodies a structural analogy to the ancient idea that the human being is a political animal, since both hold that there are distinctive and essential elements of our constitution that are only actualized and realized in specific, linguistically mediated social forms, and that these are not simply adjuncts to a self that we can understand and know independent of them, but partly constitute it.[33]

3.2   Equality and Personhood

Conceptions of the self, then, establish determinate relations of individuals to their actions and to others. They also make an essential contribution to the achievement of relations of recognition. A shared conception of the self is necessary to guide the activities of recognizing so that when I endeavor to recognize you through my actions, those activities are appropriate to the sort of being you actually are. Since recognition is essentially reciprocal for Hegel, that same conception of the self must be one that I can equally affirm of myself, so that when it guides your activities of recognizing, those activities do not express a false conception of what I am. By contrast, if I hold a false or inadequate conception of the self, or

[33] In his critique of Pippin's constructivism, Stern (2017, 102) suggests that, even if it is not explicable solely in "biological terms," the category of "person" comprises "a natural kind in the philosophical sense" that articulates "the essential nature of the individual." The social constitutivist account that I defend here can make sense of the way in which "person" is a necessary conception of what it means to be a self, but does not depend on an idea of an "essential nature" to make sense of that necessity. Of course, this social constitution would not be possible were certain things not true of us "by nature." But what matters from the standpoint of the social constitution view is how those features of our nature are taken up and shaped, not that their actualization is the realization of anything like an essential purpose or end.

one that cannot be affirmed equally of all, or lack a conception of the self completely (as is the case in the ethical world), then my activities of recognizing will be inappropriate to the sort of being you are (we might characterize these as activities of misrecognition, and Hegel will show that they give rise to a condition of alienation), or will give rise only to one-sided relations of recognition, or will fail completely to give rise to any relation of recognition at all.

The core concept linking the idea of the self to recognition is that of *Gelten* – having validity, or counting, or achieving a relevant sort of standing.[34] When I satisfy the criteria stipulated by a particular conception of the self, then it is possible for me to "count" as a self, and so to recognize and be recognized by my fellows. Thus, "counting" is the "universal actuality of the self."[35]

3.2.1 *Personhood as a Conception of the Self*

The first determinate and positive conception of the self that emerges in the text, that of the "person," indicates the role that conceptions of the self play in Hegel's recognition theory. Personhood is the conception of the self that we find within the world of the "condition of right" (*Rechtszustand*). However, appreciating the positive contribution that this conception of the self makes to the recognition theory is complicated by at least two factors. First, interpreters often consider the transition from the harmonious and beautiful ethical world to the formalistic and atomized condition of right to be one of decline and loss.[36] This interpretive stance is likely generally informed by a tendency to read the argument of *Phenomenology* through the lens of other of Hegel's texts, where the ethical world receives a more positive portrayal. Second, Hegel is ultimately critical of the idea of personhood. In fact, it is challenging to present an account of what is positive in the discussion of personhood in chapter VIA.c in distinction from the robustly critical stance that Hegel defends there. In §3.2.2, I turn to consider that criticism and its implications for Hegel's conceptions of the self and recognition. However, before considering Hegel's criticism of the person, we need to understand exactly what sort of conception of the self the person is, and how it might contribute to the achievement of relations of recognition.

---

[34] See, for example, *PhG* 260/¶476, 261–262/¶479, 267/¶¶487–488, 351/¶653, 353/¶656.
[35] *PhG* 264/¶482.
[36] For a recent account along these lines, see Hoy 2009.

The person addresses the core shortcoming that undermined the ethical world, namely the absence of a status that could be shared universally among its participants that could secure the equality necessary for reciprocal intersubjective recognition. Indeed, Hegel goes so far as to claim that "the actuality of the self" is "not present in the ethical world," but instead "has been won through its return into the person."[37]

In Hegel's account, persons are thinking beings. The logic that animates this account is the same as that which structured the development of the "freedom of self-consciousness" in chapter IVB, only in contrast to stoicism, skepticism, and the unhappy consciousness, personhood is the actualization of thought in a shared social world.[38] What makes someone a person is the same characteristic that stoicism identified as essential to self-consciousness, namely the "unity of thinking" that is possible for the "I."[39]

According to this conception of the self, thinking is what links the individual to their actions. It is by being taken up into this formal unity of thinking that a "content" comes to be one that counts as mine.[40] The paradigmatic case of this coming-to-count by being made intelligible through thinking in the "condition of right" is that through which a possession of mine comes to be my property, where something that I contingently factically possess takes on the intelligible and normative characteristic of something to which I am entitled.[41] However, Hegel suggests that such countings are not limited merely to external objects, but equally to the individual's character and deeds. The principles governing these links – to my possessions, character, or deeds – are "contingency and arbitrary will." (Zufall und Willkür) Of course, initially, Hegel does not specify whose arbitrary choice determines these links, but it's clear that at least in some cases it will be that of the individual person. In connection with my property, for example, it is my own choice that determines what is mine – I own a bag of apples because I chose to buy them, and not oranges – so that the contents that belong to me are contingent because they stem just from my arbitrary will, not from any sort of necessity. Likewise, by this standard, those actions are mine that I choose, for whatever reason, within the circumstance. As a person,

---

[37] PhG 264/¶483.
[38] PhG 261/¶478.
[39] PhG 261/¶478.
[40] PhG 262/¶479.
[41] As Hegel puts this idea in a more critical tone, "The spiritless universality of right takes up every natural mode of character and existence in itself and justifies [berechtigt] it." PhG 267/¶487.

the self is understood to possess independence (*Selbstständigkeit*), and that distinctive freedom is what links me to the particular contents with which I identify.[42]

As a conception of the self, personhood equally provides the foundation for the establishment of determinate relations with others. Hegel expresses this point in explicitly recognitive terms. As a person, "the *I* of self-consciousness ... counts as an essential being [*Wesen*] existing *in and for itself,* this *being-recognized* [Anerkanntsein] is its substantiality."[43] Specifically, when I establish what is "mine" as a person, through its incorporation into the unity of thinking, I establish a "positive actuality" on the basis of which others can recognize me: In "right," what is "mine" comes to acquire "*a recognized* and *actual validity* [Gelten]."[44] Personhood shapes my relation to others by means of the mediation of the idea of right, which acquires its determinacy through the particular identifications that individuals make. You and I respect one another as persons when we recognize one another as independent choosers and deciders.[45]

This intersubjective dimension of Hegel's idea of personhood is particularly important for understanding the positive contribution that it makes to the account of recognition that he develops in the text. What is lacking in the ethical world is an explicit and shared conception of the self that is necessary for satisfying the equality condition on which relations of reciprocal recognition depend. By contrast, in the condition of right, instead of a differentiated system modeled on organic nature, we find "an *equality* [Gleichheit] in which *all* count as *each*, as *persons.*"[46] As we have

---

[42] We find here a first link between Hegel's account of personhood and Rawls's. For Rawls, even the obligations stemming from my conception of the good are to be understood, from the standpoint of justice at least, to be self-imposed, based on my own rational choice. Rawls 1999, 181. Being a person, for both Hegel and Rawls, means being something that exists prior to and in some respect independent of their particular commitments. On this score, see Sandel 1984 and 1998.

[43] *PhG* 261/¶476.

[44] *PhG* 262/¶479.

[45] Here, then, is a second similarity to Rawls's conception of the person, since for Rawls being a person means being willing to abide by a public conception of justice that establishes determinate relations between persons. Rawls 2005, 19.

[46] *PhG* 260/¶476. These claims about equality and universality require comment. Since Hegel's model for the "condition of right" seems to be ancient Rome, it was of course *not* the case that all individuals enjoyed the equal status of personhood, from which women, noncitizens, and slaves were all excluded. See the helpful account of the historical details in Bernasconi 1989, 1701–1702. While this exclusion certainly merits critical attention and justifies scrutiny on our part in thinking through the implications of Hegel's account, I think that what matters for the prospects of the theory of recognition that Hegel develops is the fact that the conceptions of the self that he develops are affirmable, in principle, universally of human beings. Epictetus was certainly denied this status during the period of his slavery, but he was certainly a thinking being, and so by the standards of this conception of the self, ought to have counted as a person.

seen, this equality requirement stems from the pure concept of recognition, and Hegel argues that it is satisfied when all agents in a shared social world accept the same norms as binding on them. In this case, those norms stem directly from the idea of the person, and the standards governing how it is appropriate to treat them.

Hegel stresses that this conception of the self and the specific recognition that it requires are both "immediate." First, the person is the "*immediate ... self*"[47] because, even if personhood is acknowledged as a shared norm within the social world, the ground of personhood, what makes someone a person, is a characteristic that is not itself explicitly social, namely the capacity to think that belongs to the I. This characteristic is not socially constituted, but instead belongs to the individual independent of their determinate relations to others. It is a characteristic that the individual could not fail to possess, that they have irrespective of any effort on their part, and that is inalienable.[48] Personhood is what we could therefore call an atomistic conception of the self, since the ground of selfhood exists prior to and independent of social relations.

Second, recognition of the individual as a person is what Hegel calls "immediate recognition."[49] For different conceptions of the self, we can identify distinct corresponding *models* of recognition. In the model of recognition corresponding to personhood, we identify some generic, self-standing feature that individuals share – it might be the capacity for thought, dignity, rationality, or the capacity to suffer – and then hold that we recognize another when we respond to that characteristic in the appropriate way – for example, by showing respect, giving them reasons, or promoting their welfare. We can designate this particular responsive model of recognition *automatic*: Since the ground of recognition is simply whatever generic, self-standing characteristic we hold to be salient, and since individuals could not help but possess this trait, the demand that we recognize them is therefore unconditioned and automatic. Recognition is their due simply for being the sort of being they are. Moreover, this model is one species of a conception of recognition as a basically *responsive* activity, where recognition is simply a matter of responding appropriately to some particular feature of the self.

---

[47] *PhG* 264–265/¶483.
[48] Stekeler-Weithofer (2014, 2, 624ff) points out that the "person" is a concept of the self that is not dependent on any competence belonging to them, in contrast to the subsequent selves of culture and morality.
[49] *PhG* 267/¶487.

3.2.2   The Critique of Personhood

Hegel's critique of personhood as a conception of the self makes explicit why that conception is inadequate to secure relations of reciprocal recognition. The core challenge that he raises is that personhood is an atomistic conception of the self, at odds with the social constitution account that Hegel defends. We find here, again, a *reductio* argument, which aims to demonstrate the socially constituted character of the self by developing the contradictions that emerge from the attempt to enact the atomistic conception, according to which the self exists independent of and prior to social relations.

Personhood has normative implications, since respecting you as a person means treating you only in certain ways. As a norm, personhood specifies the links that ought to hold between the individual, their actions, and others, so that possessing the capacity for thought entails a justification for the content that belongs to me as a result of arbitrary choice and contingency, and so that others recognize the rights that I have to those contents. However, Hegel argues that personhood also has normative foundations, in the sense that it is a form of "universal consciousness" that emerges only when self-conscious beings treat one another as persons, which simply means constraining their own activities, "negating themselves," in accordance with it. Hegel's account of the ethical world shows that such a norm need not exist, since there can be systems of social practices that do not countenance it, even if such systems will be subject to the basic instability Hegel has identified in the ethical world. In his account of the experience of personhood, of the attempt to enact this conception of the self in social practice, Hegel demonstrates that it is possible for everyone to mutually recognize this norm of selfhood, but for that universal mutual norm recognition to be inadequate to secure relations of reciprocal intersubjective recognition.

Personhood is an atomistic conception of the self, since, as we have seen, persons are understood to exist independent of and prior to shared customs and laws. Persons are understood to be "atoms," where the self is something "brittle" (*spröde*), not soluble within the shared social substance.[50] Likewise, the ground of personhood, what makes someone a person, is equally taken to be a nonsocial characteristic, the capacity for thinking. And the "independence" (*Selbständigkeit*) that is possible for persons is itself "spiritless" (*geistlos*) because it is merely formal, and abstracts from the concrete social world that gives rise to it. Indeed, personhood

---

[50] *PhG* 260/¶476, 262/¶482, 261/¶477.

denies any role for participation in a shared social world for constituting the self.

Even though it holds that the self exists independent of the world, personhood is actually the conception of the self appropriate to a very specific social world, that of the "condition of right." In contrast to the ethical world that preceded it, in this condition of right, we no longer find an immediate unity between the individual and the unconscious social substance. The primary characteristic of the world of the condition of right is the *loss* of immediate identification with ethical customs and laws and so of a common substantiality. The "person" is the conception of the self that corresponds to this world of loss. In it, individuals are themselves understood to be "substances" and the unreflected and opaque ground of the ethical world is replaced by the self-conscious actuality of the thinking "I."[51] The self is the "actuality" or "truth" of a given social world. As the "actuality" of the lost ethical world, personhood is a "*negative* universal *self*," a conception of the self that is universal and so common to all persons, but which is understood atomistically or negatively, as a response to the loss of the "*positive* universal," the customs and laws that were shared within the ethical world.[52]

Of course, so far this account is merely diagnostic – accounting for how personhood emerges as the predominant conception of the self – but it is not yet explicitly critical. The critical dimension of Hegel's argument emerges in his account of the experience of personhood. In general, Hegel will take issue with the fact that personhood is a merely *formal* conception of the self that makes it impossible for the individual to understand, in a positive way, the specific contents with which they identify.

As we have seen, personhood is merely the formal unity of thinking which transcends any particular content. However, in isolating this formal and "*empty unity*" and treating it as the self, personhood leaves to "the substance the form of *fulfillment* [Erfüllung] and *content*," which is "allowed to go free."[53] Consequently, when I am understood as a person, the only connection between my selfhood and the determinate contents which I take to be "mine" is a contingent one:

> The actual content or *determinacy* of what is mine [*des Meinen*], whether it be an external possession or the inner wealth or poverty of spirit and character, is not contained in this empty form and does not concern it. It therefore

[51] *PhG* 260–261/¶476.
[52] *PhG* 260–261/¶476.
[53] *PhG* 262/¶479.

belongs to its own *proper power*, which is other than the formal universal, that of contingency and arbitrary choice. The consciousness of right experiences therefore in its actual counting much more the loss of its reality and its complete inessentiality, and to designate an individual a *person* is an expression of disrespect [*Verachtung*].[54]

As a mere formal unity, personhood cannot include any determinate content. Instead, this content has to belong to another power, that of contingency and arbitrary will. Since personhood is indifferent to any content, merely counting as a person comes to be a marker of "disrespect" since the status can apply equally to all. However, the implicit suggestion here is that determinate contents *matter* to individuals, which is why merely counting as a person is the source of an experience of disrespect. As a self, I am not indifferent to what makes me a determinate individual. However, as a person, I can identify this "content" – my embodied existence, my actions, my real powers – only as "mine" but not as *myself*, as a necessary element of my constitution.[55] The first criticism of the idea of personhood, then, is that it is indifferent to those determinate contents that we deem essential to the self.

We might be inclined to dismiss this criticism by pointing to the role of choice in personhood. Even if the choice at stake is that of "arbitrary will," it still seems possible to identify myself as the capacity to choose determinate contents. However, Hegel will take issue with this objection on two grounds. First, he has already suggested that personhood is not itself the capacity to choose, but rather the unity of thinking. He now observes that the capacity to choose is "another power," separate from thinking. Personhood is the norm that is the source of the requirement that these be linked. Second, and more importantly, he stresses that the powers governing the contents that come to be mine do not solely belong to me. While the arbitrary choice that links me to content might be my own, it could equally be that of others, and the content that belongs to me can equally be the result of luck. With respect to arbitrary choice, Hegel suggests that in letting the "power of content" go "free" from persons, this power will be

---

[54] *PhG* 262/¶479.
[55] We can appreciate an aspect of this criticism by considering Rawls's account of the way in which individuals' talents and abilities are treated from the standpoint of justice as fairness. Since it is arbitrary, from the moral point of view, that I enjoy this or that talent, I can make no default moral claim to my particular actions and powers. Instead, the distribution of the fruits of those actions and powers will be determined by the terms of the social contract. They therefore do not comprise me, and they only become mine by means of the assignment of benefits and burdens stemming from established principles of justice.

gathered in *one* equally spiritless point alien to them, which is in part a purely singular actuality like the brittleness of their personality, but in opposition to their empty singularity, has for them the significance of all content, and so of the real essence, and against their supposed absolute actuality, which is in itself essenceless, is the universal power and absolute actuality. This lord of the world is in this way the absolute person who concerns themselves with all existence, for whose consciousness no higher spirit exists.[56]

In failing to establish a necessary link between the self and the content with which individuals identify, these contents become subject to the influence of the arbitrary choice of others, in this case, the power of a single lord of the world. The second criticism of the idea of personhood holds that, even though asserting myself as a person is supposed to be empowering, an assertion of my "independence," this assertion actually leaves me subject to the domination of others.[57] So personhood actually fails to establish determinate links between the individual and the "content" with which they identify, the first essential dimension of a conception of the self, including their actions, since it is possible to acknowledge the rights of the person, but for that content to belong not to them, but to another.

Finally, Hegel argues that the atomism of personhood generates insurmountable boundaries between individuals, who are able to understand their relations to others only "negatively," where each excludes each. The reason for this negative relation is, again, the absence of content that can unify them, in terms of which they can jointly identify. In the condition of right, that content belongs to a power that is alien to each. They might look to this power as a source of shared identification – where the lord of the world constitutes their "relation or continuity" – but that alien power is subject to no real normative constraint (unlike the laws and customs of the ethical world), and so can, in turn, undermine and "destroy" their legal personhood (*rechtliche Persönlichkeit*).[58] So personhood fails to establish relevant positive links to others, the second essential dimension of a conception of the self.

Personhood is therefore a flawed conception of the self. Because of these flaws, relations of reciprocal intersubjective recognition are impossible when the norm governing the activities of recognition is that of personhood. While personhood does satisfy one of the criteria that is essential to

---

[56] *PhG* 262/¶480.
[57] Hegel here anticipates Marx's critique of the person, an empty legal status whose apparent universality and equality belies its contribution to domination and exploitation. Marx 1953, I, 90–91.
[58] *PhG* 263/¶481.

the achievement of recognition, the equality criterion, it fails to satisfy a second criterion, which we can, following Hegel, call the fulfillment criterion. The conception of the self that regulates the activities of recognition must be one in which individuals can find "fulfillment," one that can include the positive "contents" that they take to matter and with which they identify. Because personhood is indifferent to these contents, it cannot satisfy this second, fulfillment criterion. Recognition as a person does ascribe to the individual a certain sort of standing. But this counting is one that they experience as *alienating*:

> This *universal counting* [Gelten] of self-consciousness [as a person] is reality alienated from it [*die ihm entfremdete Realität*]. This *counting* is the universal actuality of the self, but it is immediately equally its inversion; it is the loss of its essence. The actuality of the self that was not present in the ethical world is won through its return into the *person*, and what was united in [the ethical world] now emerges developed but alienated from itself [*sich entfremdet*].[59]

When I am recognized as a person, I count, but that counting is equally the loss of my "essence," of what I take to matter about myself. What Hegel calls "alienation" (*Entfremdung*) is a condition of misrecognition. When I am recognized as a person, that recognition does take account of a significant feature of my constitution, namely that I am a being capable of thinking. But that recognition generates a condition of alienation because it fails to capture any positive content, most importantly in the form of what I take to matter about myself.

We have now a second instance of a failure of recognition that is not a failure of mutuality. In the ethical world, we found not unequal and one-sided relations of recognition – as in the relation between lord and bondsman – but rather the absence of recognition, due to the lack of a shared conception of the self. Likewise, in the condition of right, we find the emergence of the condition of alienation, where everyone recognizes the same conception of the self, and everyone enjoys the same equal status, but where genuine recognition is impossible since that conception of the self is incomplete, failing to capture what matters to individuals.[60]

---

[59] *PhG* 263–264/¶482.

[60] Critical accounts of the movement of recognition like the one that we find here show that Hegel's account of recognition is not straightforwardly or naively optimistic. Instead, Hegel is acutely aware that recognition according to predominant conceptions of the self can be alienating. On this issue of the ambivalence of recognition, in particular as that issue emerges in the work of Judith Butler, see the essays collected in Ikäheimo, Leopold, and Stahl 2021.

3.3   Culture and Alienation

Alienation is the name that Hegel gives to the condition that arises from the experience of the failure of personhood as a conception of the self. Alienation arises when the predominant conception of what it means to be a self fails to capture those elements of my constitution that are essential to my own self-understanding. Intersubjective relations are alienating when others strive to recognize me according to that incomplete and flawed conception of the self.

The distinctive social constitutive conception of the self that we find in Hegel's account of "spirit" is at the heart of his account of alienation. This means that alienation is neither simply a subjective failure to integrate different aspects of one's experience,[61] nor a failure to identify with the norms structuring the objective social world.[62] Instead, as a determination of spirit, the idea of the self is a conception of what I am as a self-conscious agent, but one engaged in and belonging to a specific objective social world.[63] Alienation arises not when I fail to integrate the world into my experience, or when I experience its norms as completely other than me. Rather, it arises when those specific norms that are supposed to concern me – the norms governing what it means to be a self – fail adequately to comprehend me.

According to this account, alienation can take at least two forms. First, it can be individual in scope. For example, when I work hard to develop an ability with a view to securing employment, but that ability is not valued in the job market, the result would be an experience of alienation. Traits that I take to be important about and constitutive of myself – my acquired abilities – do not find expression from the standpoint of the objective practices that structure the social world – in this case, the job market. However, second, Hegel is also committed to the idea that alienation can be global in scope. As the subtitle of the "Culture" (*Bildung*) chapter, "self-alienated spirit," indicates, it is possible for "spirit" – for the normatively structured social world taken as a whole, and the self-conscious agents who animate and sustain it – to be "alienated from itself."[64] We find this global condition where there is no understanding of the self available within which *any* agent could find

---

[61] For Jaeggi, alienation arises as a result of a failure of "appropriation" (*Aneignung*) arising when an individual is incapable of incorporating an element of their experience into a coherent understanding of themselves as an agent. See Jaeggi 2005.

[62] Brandom straightforwardly opposes *Sittlichkeit* and alienation, where the former is a condition of immediate identification with norms, and the latter a failure of identification. See Brandom 2019, 472ff.

[63] Moyar (2008, 150) is correct to identify that alienation has both subjective and objective components. However, he does not identify that it is the idea of the self that unifies these two aspects.

[64] *PhG* 320.

themselves "fulfilled," or no coherent, concrete self-understanding that both applies universally to all and includes those elements of my constitution about which I care. Finding such a self-understanding is the fundamental task that drives Hegel's account of "culture" in *Phenomenology*.[65]

3.3.1   The Self of Culture and Purpose-Mediated Recognition

Hegel tracks the development of a new conception of the self and a new model of recognition from the experience of alienation. He contrasts this new conception of the self with personhood, which he identifies as "the *immediate* [self], that is, the self existing in and for itself *without alienation*";[66] and he contrasts the new model of recognition with recognition as a person, which he designates "immediate recognition."[67]

In contrast to the condition of right, and indeed to the ethical world as a whole, within "culture":

> Self-consciousness is *something*, it has *reality* only insofar as it alienates itself from itself [*es sich selbst entfremdet*]; it thereby posits itself as something universal, and this universality is its counting [*Gelten*] and actuality. This *equality* [Gleichheit] with all is therefore not the equality of right, not the immediate being-recognized and counting of self-consciousness simply because *it is*; rather, the fact that it counts [*gelte*] is through the alienated mediation of making itself accord with the universal. The spiritless universality of right takes up the natural mode of the character and of existence and justifies it. But the universality that counts here is that *which has come to be* [*die* gewordne], and thereby it is *actual*. That through which the individual [*Individuum*] here has validity [*Gelten*] and actuality is *culture* [*die* Bildung].[68]

Instead of identifying the self with a characteristic or set of characteristics that everyone always already has, the experience of alienation brings with it a demand for self-alteration – which Hegel here characterizes as an activity of "alienat[ing] from itself" – so that what makes an individual a self is determined by what it *becomes* rather than what it already *is*.[69] While it is

---

[65] It seems that he also thought this condition of alienation is one that pervaded Europe from imperial Rome up to the turn of the nineteenth century.

[66] *PhG* 264–265/¶483

[67] *PhG* 267/¶487.

[68] *PhG* 267/¶¶487–488.

[69] To this extent, the verb "to alienate" need not have a pejorative connotation. If a self is something I must become, then being a self requires a process of "alienating" what is merely natural from myself. Instead of conceiving of alienation as a condition in which we are separated from an "essential nature" that always belongs to us (see Schacht 1984, 51), Hegel rather thinks that alienation demands the activity of transforming one's mere naturalness.

true that different individuals can become different things, this new conception of the self still satisfies the equality criterion – it is a status that can be ascribed equally to all – since in Hegel's account this self-alteration is undertaken with a view to specific norms that are themselves universal. The activity of self-transformation takes place with a view to a posited common "purpose" (*Zweck*) or goal, and that purpose is articulated in terms of standards that are universal.[70] In contrast to personhood, this new conception of the self includes what Hegel calls "content," since the process of becoming depends on the "determinate individuality" of the agent, their specific character, talents, abilities, and embodiment, transforming these into "essentiality," to the achievement of the common purpose. This process of transformation and becoming is what Hegel calls "culture." It is essentially social, since Hegel claims that it is identical to the process through which the social "substance," which as we have seen is itself a "work" or product of self-conscious activity, itself comes to be real or actual.[71]

This new conception of the self, which includes the "content" excluded from personhood as what is necessary for the activity of becoming and self-transformation, requires a new model of recognition. In contrast to the "immediate recognition" that we found in the condition of right, which I have called the automatic model of recognition, we can call this new model the *achievement* model of recognition, since individuals come to merit recognition – they have "validity and actuality" – only to the extent to which they draw on their capacity for self-transformation to achieve the universal purpose or goal with which the self is now identified.[72] We can identify this particular achievement model of recognition as purpose-mediated recognition, since it makes recognition dependent on the achievement of a universal purpose.

This new conception of the self and the model of recognition corresponding to it mark genuine advances in the immediate conceptions of the self and recognition that we found in the condition of right since they are oriented to addressing the challenge posed by the experience of alienation

---

[70] *PhG* 267/¶488.

[71] *PhG* 268/¶489. Siep (2000, 194) identifies *Bildung* as a "two-sided process," involving both the socialization of the individual and the actualization of spiritual order.

[72] Like chapter VB, "The actualization of rational self-consciousness through itself," Hegel is here considering a practical stance that stresses self-actualization through agency. However, the stance of reason is atomistic both in holding an instrumental attitude toward ethical life and the social world, and in attempting to draw its self-definition entirely from itself, not from others (the account of reason is not directly about recognition). By contrast, with the alienated self, the social world provides the terms for its actualization and expression, and it acquires its standing only through the recognition of others.

stemming from it. However, it is important to note that this new conception of the self and model of recognition remain largely formal. The most
prominent question that they raise is, I shall argue, the question that structures the remainder of Hegel's account of "culture": what are the shared,
universal purposes whose achievement makes the individual a self who
"counts," and so merits the recognition of others?

Answering this question will prove challenging for a number of reasons. Before we examine (in §3.3.2) the possible answers to this question
that Hegel considers in chapter VIB, we ought to note that the condition
of alienation itself complicates the effort to secure relations of genuinely
reciprocal recognition. In Hegel's account, it is "spirit" as a whole, the
unity comprehending the reciprocal dependence of the self and the shared
social world, that is alienated from itself. This alienation, in turn, generates
a series of divisions:

> The substance is in this way *spirit*, self-conscious *unity* of the self and the
> essence, but both also have the significance of alienation for one another.
> Spirit is *consciousness* of an objective actuality that is free for itself; this con-
> sciousness stands opposed to the unity of the self and essence, *actual con-*
> *sciousness* [stands opposed to] *pure consciousness*. On the one hand, actual
> self-consciousness passes over through its externalization into the actual
> world, and this world returns into it; on the other hand, this same actuality,
> in addition to the person and objectivity, is sublated; they are purely uni-
> versal. This, their alienation, is *pure consciousness*, or the *essence*. The present
> has immediately its opposition in its *beyond*, that of its thinking and being-
> thought; just as this beyond has its opposition in this world [*Diesseits*], that
> is its alienated actuality. Spirit forms [*bildet … aus*] for itself therefore not
> only *one* world, but a doubled, divided, and opposed world.[73]

The first aspect of the condition of alienation is a denigrated status for
"this world," the world of "actuality," that is, the shared social world that
agents produce and reproduce through their activity. In contrast to this
world, we find a second world, a "beyond," whose element is "thinking,"
and it is this latter world that the self of culture comes to identify as the
essential one. Alienation entails a bifurcation into a city of man and a city
of God.

Second, this bifurcation also extends to the second aspect of spirit, the
self. In conditions of alienation, the self is understood to have a dual constitution, mirroring that of the "unhappy consciousness,"[74] so that there is

[73] *PhG* 265/¶484.
[74] See *PhG* 263/¶482.

a division within the self between "actual consciousness," the self understood as agent within the world of "actuality," and "pure consciousness" or
the "pure self," which is understood to be the essence of the self, an essence
that transcends the world of social actuality, and toward which the actual
self ought to strive.

Within the world of culture, achieving recognition requires overcoming
these conditions of alienation, and the divisions that structure them. As
we have seen, the self of culture consists not simply of what the individual
always already is, but rather of what they become, how they draw on and
shape their determinate individuality to accord with a universal purpose.
In the new achievement model of recognition, recognition is dependent
on and justified by the achievement of this purpose. If that essential purpose is supposed to stem from the "pure self," then the achievement of
recognition will depend on somehow transcending the division into two
worlds, and the division within the self that corresponds to it.

It is important to note that Hegel is here offering a specific diagnosis
of an important idea about the self that finds expression in philosophical
accounts of selfhood. This is the thought that the essence of the self, what
the self really is, is something that is "pure," that is, that is not rooted in
the actual world of our experience, but whose basic character is understood
to transcend the world of experience, and the shared social world. Hegel's
diagnostic claim is that the roots of this conception of a "pure self" lie in
a social condition of alienation. When the shared social world of actuality comes to be understood as unable to provide the terms for a coherent
understanding of the self,[75] Hegel suggests that we respond by seeking that
understanding in a separate, pure domain, unaffected by the realities of the
social. The idea of a pure self is, in this account, the product of a "return
from" (*Rückkehr aus*) the "actual world," experienced now as alien to what
is essential to the self.[76]

As we track the experience of culture, we will see that Hegel supple-
ments this diagnostic claim with a critical one. That is, he will demonstrate
that this conception of the self as something "pure," as insulated from the
travails of the social, is incoherent, and so must be given up. However, we

---

[75] This global condition bears something significant in common with what Fricker calls "hermeneutic
   injustice." See Fricker 2007, chapter 7. In both cases, the terms for an adequate understanding of
   oneself are absent in the social world. Of course, they are distinct, since Fricker is interested in
   conditions of injustice, where the hermeneutic deficit is an effect of relations of power. By contrast,
   Hegel thinks this condition is a global one, and so he does not treat the absence of these hermeneutic resources as something that can be corrected primarily by altering relations of power.
[76] *PhG* 289/¶529.

will also see that, instead of rejecting purity as a characteristic of the self, he will argue that we ought to reconstrue the idea of purity so that it is understood to be the product of an activity of purification that is essentially social and worldly, rather than a condition possessed by the self *a priori* independent of its relations to others and to the world.

3.3.2   *The Critique of the Self of Culture and Overcoming Alienation*

In an important sense, the project of overcoming the condition of alienation is, for Hegel, bound up with answering the core question at the heart of his theory of recognition: What is the self? While the dynamic of recognition may seem to take a back seat in the discussion of culture, the question of the basic character of the self is a central one there. As we have seen, a determinate conception of the self emerges as the "actuality" or "truth" of a given world of spirit. The conception of the self that emerges within the world of culture is that of "absolute freedom":

> The *second self* is that of the world of culture or the self-reflected spirit of division [*sich wiedergegebene Geist der Entzweiung*] come to its truth, absolute freedom. In this self the initial immediate unity of singularity and universality is broken asunder; the universal that remains equally a pure spiritual essence, being-recognized or universal willing and knowing, is the *object* and content of the self and its universal actuality. But it does not have the form of existence [*Dasein*] free from the self; it therefore comes in this self to no fulfillment [*Erfüllung*], and no positive content, to no world.[77]

Given that, as was the case with the person, Hegel presents a famous criticism of absolute freedom – bound up with an account of the French revolutionary terror[78] – it can be challenging to unpack what is positive in this conception of the self. We can begin to clarify the idea of absolute freedom as a conception of the self by considering how it emerges from the experience of the world of culture.[79]

First, considered as absolute freedom, the self possesses a unique transcendence in relation to the shared world of "actuality" that Hegel considers in chapter VIB.I.a. The experience of culture is one that demonstrates

---

[77] *PhG* 341/¶633.
[78] The literature here is extensive, and captures well Hegel's ambivalence, an ambivalence also expressed in his account of absolute freedom. See especially Habermas 1971 and Comay 2011.
[79] Of course, the "Culture" section is the longest one in chapter VI of *Phenomenology*, and a complete account of its action would require a significantly lengthier commentary than I can offer here. Instead, I focus in particular on those developments that are central to the accounts of recognition and the self that we find there. While selective, my treatment does focus on a set of core themes and issues.

the inadequacy of the actual world to supply the terms, the shared purposes, in terms of which the individual ought to shape their own activity. Hegel begins by considering the possibility that the content for the self, its constitutive purpose, is one that stems purely from the actual world of social life, and then argues that no such purpose is to be merely "found" with which the individual can both identify, in which they can experience their own "being-for-self," and which can be affirmed equally of all.[80] Instead, the individual learns through this experience that their existence as a self is not entirely dependent on or defined by any objective determination, like wealth or power, that they merely find in the actual world of shared social life. Rather, as a being capable of judgment, they learn that they possess a distinctive independence in relation to what they judge:

> The true spirit is just this unity of what is absolutely divided, and thereby through the *free actuality* of these *selfless* extremes it comes into existence as their medium. Its existence [*Dasein*] is universal *speaking* and the destructive *judgment* which dissolves all of these moments that ought to count as the essence and actual parts of the whole, and which is equally this self-dissolving play with itself. This judging and speaking are therefore true and unconquerable while it overpowers everything; the *only really true* thing that is at work in this real world.[81]

Absolute freedom is committed to a similar claim about the individual's transcendence in relation to the world, and the movement of "culture" or "formation" is in part a movement away from determination from without and toward a sort of self-determination on the part of the individual.

The second core development that gives rise to absolute freedom is a clarification of the sense in which the self exists as something "pure." Within the world of culture, the individual is understood to be divided between an actual consciousness of the world of shared social life, and a pure consciousness or pure self, understood to comprise the essence of

---

[80] In the world of culture, the individual takes themselves to be governed by an abstract value, nobility, striving to avoid its opposite, the base. The core question that animates the account is what concrete ends can count as realizations of the noble. The individual begins with service to state power as the most likely candidate, since this purpose is one that can be shared broadly among the participants in social life. However, Hegel argues that service to state power cannot by itself be a source of recognition as an individual self, and that the individual cannot find themselves adequately affirmed – they do not find themselves "being-for-self" – as an individual in that service. *PhG* 275–276/¶¶505–506 esp. By contrast, the individual can identify with the pursuit of wealth because it is a source of pleasure, and so already contains "the moment of being-for-self." *PhG* 280/¶515. However, the pursuit of wealth also brings with it a form of reification, since the individual experiences wealth as an alien power on which they become dependent. *PhG* 280/¶515.

[81] *PhG* 283/¶520.

the self. In his account of the "struggle" between the enlightenment, the stance of "pure insight," and "superstition," the stance of "faith" opposed to insight, Hegel argues that the pure self cannot be understood simply as a thinking being. Instead, the experience of enlightenment's struggle with superstition demonstrates that the pure self is, in some sense, to be identified with "the concept," so that the self is not simply a thinking being, but one capable of comprehending and knowing.[82] And that comprehension takes the form of "the concept," the intelligible structure that makes possible insight into the truth. It is because of this identification with the concept, which it takes over from "enlightenment," that absolute freedom construes what is essential as itself a product, not something given: "Enlightenment asserts the moment of the concept, that of being a deed of *consciousness*; it asserts this *against* faith – that its absolute essence is the essence of *its* consciousness as a self, or that it is *produced* through consciousness."[83] To understand the self as absolute freedom, therefore, means identifying the self not just with the capacity to think – as was the case with personhood – but rather with the capacity to grasp the truth, with the capacity for actual insight and understanding. And it is to understand that project of grasping the truth as one in which the individual is active, so that the result is understood to be a product of the individual's activity – the key terms here are *Hervorbringen* and its cognates[84] – rather than as the acceptance of a determination that is given.

Absolute freedom is the conception of the self that grasps its own individual will as the universal will.[85] As a consequence of its identification of the self with the concept, absolute freedom embodies a specific relation between the individual and the "spiritual masses," the norm-governed practices of the social world. In the first instance, it acknowledges in an explicit way the claim, essential to "culture" as a whole, that the shared

---

[82] Hegel holds that faith is actually an attitude of thought, and is a "pure consciousness of *essence*, that is, of *the simple inner*." *PhG* 289/¶528. However, as a simple, immediate relation to essence, it is distinct from the "negativity" belonging to the "absolute concept," which makes possible a mediated relation to its objects, and so an insight into and knowledge of them. This feature distinguishes pure insight from the judging individual who emerged in the actual world of culture. Their judgment was limited and unsatisfying because it could incorporate any content, and so demonstrate their independence from that content, but without yielding actual knowledge or understanding. Consequently, its pinnacle was a stance of vanity in relation to the actual world. By contrast, pure insight aims at a grasp of the truth. Judgment can offer *assessment* of its object, but without "the concept" it lacks the ability to *grasp* it. On the contrast, see *PhG* 286/¶525.

[83] *PhG* 307/¶566.

[84] Knowledge of the productive character of the concept is central to pure insight and the enlightenment. See *PhG* 297–298/¶¶549ff.

[85] *PhG* 317/¶584.

social world is a "work," the product of the activity of self-conscious agents. That is, it holds that "its certainty of itself is the essence of all spiritual masses of the real and of the super-sensible world," so that "the world is for it simply its will."[86] As such, it acknowledges that the social world is a product of its own activities. As a result, the individual is understood to transcend the given order of the social world, so that their actions are not determined by or answerable to it. Instead, the individual identifies their own will as decisive as a result of the immediate identification between their individual will and a shared universal will.

As a conception of the self, absolute freedom is to establish determinate relations between the individual and their actions, on the one hand, and the individual and others, on the other. With respect to the former, the individual sees their actions to be direct realizations of the demands of the universal will. Hegel explains this relation primarily in negative terms. The individual does not see their actions as answerable to the norms stemming from any "particular mass" of the social world, which they instead see merely as "limitations":

> In absolute freedom, all estates [*Stände*], which are the spiritual essence, in which the whole divides itself, are destroyed; the singular consciousness that belongs to such a division, wills it and brings it about, has sublated its limitation: its purpose is the universal purpose, its language the universal law, its work the universal work.[87]

Instead, as absolute freedom, an action will count as mine to the extent that it can be seen as an expression of the universal will. And that means that my actions will not be purely individual ones, conditioned and limited by a particular part of the social whole in which I might find myself. Instead, actions will count as mine to the extent that they are not singular acts, but rather insofar as they can take the form of "laws and actions of state."[88]

Likewise, absolute freedom is to establish determinate relations among individuals. Because, as absolute freedom, the individual's will is the universal will, and the universal will is "the will of all *singular* wills as such," it is to mediate relations among individuals:

> For the will is in itself the consciousness of personhood or the consciousness of each, and as this truly actual will it ought to be as the *self*-conscious essence of all and every personhood, so that each undividedly always does

---

[86] *PhG* 317/¶584.
[87] *PhG* 318/¶585.
[88] *PhG* 318/¶587.

what all do, and what emerges as the deed of the whole is the immediate and conscious deed of *each*.[89]

Each can identify with the others to the extent that they share and realize this common universal will.

This conception of the self fits with the achievement model of recognition that, we have seen, Hegel adopts in his account of "culture." On this model, I come to count in the eyes of others, and so to merit their recognition, by virtue of my success in transforming myself in accordance with a purpose understood to be shared with others. As absolute freedom, that purpose lies in making myself accord with the universal will, which I do through the exercise of my insight into actuality, or by accepting the slogan of the enlightenment "*Be what you all are in yourselves – rational.*"[90] At the same time, this project of achieved rationality is one that is understood to be universal, to be inclusive of all, so that any individual can, in principle at least, be the object of that recognition.

Absolute freedom is, in many respects, a peculiar conception of the self, and, unlike the idea of the person, it is not obvious who actually subscribes to it.[91] Given that the experience that arises from the attempt to live out this conception of the self gives rise not to heaven on earth – its stated aim – but rather to "terror" (*Schrecken*), it should be clear that Hegel holds that absolute freedom is inadequate as a conception of the self. However, its specific inadequacy is not immediately clear.

The core problem with absolute freedom is its conception of the relation between the individual and the universal. Absolute freedom begins from two important truths. First, the individual understands themselves to be capable of insight, of grasping objective and normative realities in terms of universal laws and principles. So they are capable of identifying those universal laws and principles as their own without having to sacrifice or renounce their singular individuality. Second, absolute freedom understands that it is the actions of self-conscious beings that constitute the world, that its world is its work, and that "its object is a law given from itself and a work completed by it."[92] However, absolute freedom fails to acknowledge that that world and the shared norms that constitute it are only generated and sustained through activities shared *with others*. The individual's identification of their

---

[89] *PhG* 318/¶584.
[90] *PhG* 292/¶536.
[91] See in this connection Stern's helpful account of absolute freedom and Rousseau in Stern 2002, 157–168.
[92] *PhG* 318/¶587.

own consciousness with the universal consciousness and will is immediate so that the individual takes their own claims to know as not requiring further justification. Instead, they take any deviations from their own claims to know as the work of an illegitimate faction.

In effect, absolute freedom ends up denying the reality of the shared social world. While it correctly grasps that its world is a "spiritual reality," the product of the activities of self-conscious agents, it fails to acknowledge any claims that the world might make on it, and, to this extent, the self of the world of culture remains an atomistic self.[93] Even if it understands selfhood to be an achievement arising from the realization of a universal purpose, it understands that purpose – whether pure or worldly – to be one that is a property of the individual simply, and not as jointly constituted through the like activities of others. This denial that the world makes genuine claims on the individual robs them of any positive relation to their actions and deeds.[94] But it also undermines their claim to act on behalf of the universal, which is understood to be radically opposed to those particular worldly determinacies. Because our actions always take place within a shared and internally differentiated social world, and those differentiations will always only appear as "limitations" for absolute freedom, it is incapable of any "positive work or deed."[95] So as a conception of the self, absolute freedom fails to establish a positive relation between the individual and their deeds.

But this denial of the world also undermines the second essential dimension of a conception of the self, establishing determinate relations with others. As we have seen, Hegel invokes the idea of norm-governed practices to identify the conditions under which relations of reciprocity among individuals are possible. Absolute freedom denies that such norm-governed practices are binding on it, at least in the form of the distinct "masses" and "estates" that it claims to transcend. But in so doing, it undermines the basis for relations of real reciprocity.[96] The denial of

---

[93] This is the primary reason that the language of personhood returns in these passages: "Because of its own abstraction, [absolute freedom] divides itself into equally abstract extremes, into simply inflexible cold universality, and into the discrete hard brittleness and obstinate punctuality of actual self-consciousness." *PhG* 319–320/¶590.

[94] In Hegel's account, the primary means through which absolute freedom engages in this denial is in denying a positive role for socially differentiated roles arising from individuals' distinct estates (*Stände*). *PhG* 318–319/¶588

[95] *PhG* 319/¶589. Siep (2000, 203) articulates the tension between universal and individual in absolute freedom: "The universal will must equally be free from particular interests and individual opinions and at the same time the immediate expression of the individual will."

[96] As we shall see, it is essential to the moral worldview that the estates-based conception of the shared social world that roots obligation in particular social roles is not the only available conception of norm-governed practices.

the world is equally a denial of the conditions under which it can exist as a self. And Hegel thinks that this "destruction of the real organization" of the social world has as its consequence the real destruction of the individual:

> The sole work and deed of universal freedom is, therefore, *death*, indeed a death that has no inner complexity or fulfillment, for what is negative is the unfulfilled point of the absolutely free self; it is therefore the coldest, flattest death, no more significant than chopping a head of lettuce or a gulp of water.[97]

This experience of its proper "work" as that of "death" is absolute freedom's experience of itself as an object in which "self-consciousness experiences what it *is*. *In itself*, it is equally this *abstract self-consciousness*, which destroys all distinctions and all persistence of distinctions in itself. As this [self-consciousness] it is itself the object; the *terror* of death is the intuition of this its negative essence."[98] In one respect, this experience repeats that of the individual who would become the bondsman, who, in facing the prospect of their death, experiences their essence as a self-conscious being in objective form.[99] However, the experience of absolute freedom is different in an important respect. Specifically, absolute freedom identifies the individual with the universal consciousness and will. The individual's experience of terror at their own death modifies their conception of that universal consciousness and will: "As *pure* self-sameness of the universal will, absolute freedom, therefore, has *negation*, and so *distinction* within itself, and develops this again as *actual* distinction."[100] Or the experience of terror is the source of a demand for the mediation of the individual and universal, so that the individual does not immediately find their own claims to know to be universally true or binding simply on their own.

The form that this mediation takes lies in an affirmation of the world, and a restoration of differentiation within that world, so that "the organization of spiritual masses cultivates itself again, and the mass of individual consciousnesses is assigned to it," and so that these individuals "return to their divided and limited work, and thereby to their substantial actuality."[101]

---

[97] *PhG* 320/¶590.
[98] *PhG* 320–321/¶592.
[99] See §1.4, and *PhG* 114/¶194.
[100] *PhG* 321/¶593.
[101] *PhG* 321/¶593.

At the same time, the path forward from this acknowledgment is unclear. Hegel considers and rejects one possible course. This would be a simple return to "the ethical world and real world of culture," only "refreshed and rejuvenated" through the "fear of the lord."[102] If absolute freedom immediately identifies the individual and the universal will, this approach acknowledges their distinction by stressing that the production and reproduction of the social world is the result of the concerted activity of many individuals occupying diverse roles. However, Hegel clearly rejects this course on the grounds that it would simply repeat the experience of the worlds of ethical life and culture, ending ultimately at the same impasse. Instead, what is required is an alternative path that acknowledges that the experience of absolute freedom is, in Hegel's words, "the ultimate and most sublime" form of culture, because "In the loss that the self experiences in absolute freedom, all these determinations are lost; its negation is meaningless death, the pure terror of the negative, that has nothing positive, nothing fulfilling in itself."[103] A conception of the self has to take account of the transcendent character of self-consciousness, the capacity for the negation of any worldly determinacy.[104]

The conception of the self and model of recognition that are adequate to these demands will have to incorporate and address the deep tension that emerges from the experience of absolute freedom. On the one hand, as we've just seen, the experience of the "pure terror of the negative" entails a demand that a conception of the self acknowledge self-consciousness's transcendence, and of the radical individualization that emerges from its experience. On the other hand, that conception of the self will also need to establish the basis for equality and make possible the positive relation to others that reciprocal intersubjective recognition requires.

However, before turning (in Chapter 4) to consider the conception of the self and model of recognition that incorporate both dimensions of this tension, I would like to consider the significance of Hegel's critiques of the person and the self of culture for one prominent contemporary conception of recognition.

---

[102] PhG 322/¶594.
[103] PhG 322/¶594.
[104] So it is not obvious to me that the way forward from this point is the theory of ethical life that we find in the mature system. This is, by contrast, Pinkard's (1994, 186) account of the transition from absolute freedom: "With the experience of the Terror before it, the logic of this self-conception thereby leads to a deinstitutionalization of itself; it realizes that self-understanding in more stable institutional forms in which individuals play particular roles and have determinate duties according to those roles." The stance of morality – at least as conscience – is compatible with the existence of determinate duties. But Hegel does not present those duties as bound to a particular scheme of institutions in *Phenomenology*.

3.4 Equality, Alienation, and Recognition Respect

Specifically, I would like to consider Hegel's critique in relation to Stephen Darwall's conception of second-person recognition respect. I demonstrate that Darwall's account is vulnerable to Hegel's criticism according to which mere recognition of personhood is alienating, and I draw out some of the implications of that criticism for understanding the conception of the self and the model of recognition that make possible relations of reciprocal recognition.

Darwall's account of recognition respect is rooted in his Kantian conception of the person. In Kant's view, the individual's dignity (*Würde*) consists of their capacity to be both author and subject of universal laws, and this dignity is the proper object of our respect (*Achtung*).[105] Moreover, dignity is, for Kant, inalienable, a necessary characteristic belonging to all rational beings simply in virtue of their having a will. As Christine Korsgaard makes explicit, it is our humanity (*Menschheit*), "the capacity for the rational determination of ends in general," and not our personality (*Persönlichkeit*), "the capacity for adopting morally obligatory ends," that is the proper object of respect.[106] Put otherwise, we show respect for individuals in virtue of unchangeable and necessary facts about them – that they have a will, the capacity to adopt ends – not the concrete expression of that capacity in particular deeds and a particular character.

Darwall adopts this Kantian conception of dignity to provide a model for reciprocal recognition. In Darwall's account, we rightly ascribe dignity to others in virtue of their having what he calls second-person authority and competence, the ability to make claims and demands on others, and to be responsive to those claims in one's own actions.[107] For Darwall, as for Kant, dignity is an inalienable characteristic belonging to us in virtue of being free and rational. Rather than being a product of the attitudes of others or social practices, he holds that dignity is an "irreducibly normative" (and not a "socially constituted") characteristic, that is, in turn, a source of obligations of respect.[108] Because we possess dignity simply by virtue of our freedom and rationality, others have an obligation to show

---

[105] "Our own will, insofar as it would act only under the condition of universal law-giving [*Gesetzgebung*] ... is the proper object of respect [*Achtung*], and the dignity [*Würde*] of humanity consists of this capacity to be universally law-giving, even with the condition of likewise being subordinate to this law-giving." Kant *AA*, 4:440.

[106] Korsgaard 1996, 111.

[107] Darwall 2006, 21.

[108] Darwall 2013, 16.

respect for us, and it is this sense of respect that Darwall identifies as a form of recognition, specifically of "second-person recognition respect."[109] When an individual makes a claim on another, and the other acknowledges that claim, Darwall calls this a relation of reciprocal recognition.[110] Darwall endorses a model of recognition where every individual possesses a specific characteristic – dignity – that is the source of an obligation on the part of others to recognize them.

Darwall explicitly distinguishes this form of respect, second-person recognition respect, from two other forms of respect, and these distinctions are helpful for understanding why he thinks that we find relations of reciprocal recognition only in instances of second-person respect. First, he distinguishes this "second-person recognition respect" from "honor respect," the form of recognition that predominates in class societies in which social status constitutes the primary basis for behaviors of recognition. These are distinct since honor respect is merited in virtue of features that are socially constituted and that distinguish individuals from one another, while, as we have seen, recognition respect is based on a shared identity that is "irreducibly normative," not founded in specific social arrangements.[111] Second, he distinguishes recognition respect in general from what he calls "appraisal respect" or "esteem."[112] Like honor respect, appraisal respect is merited in virtue of features that distinguish individuals one from another, most notably the accomplishment of having an upright character or being an agent of some moral accomplishment. However, unlike honor respect, which, like recognition respect generally, "is something we broadly *do*," esteem is primarily an "attitude" that "we simply *have* toward a person," which need not be social, calling for or requiring acknowledgment and response from another.[113]

For Darwall, then, recognition respect does not have as its object features that distinguish individuals one from another. This aspect of recognition respect is clearly connected to an important feature of Darwall's conception of morality. While Darwall argues that moral obligations are ultimately based on second-personal relations, the concrete identities of the related parties are irrelevant to the foundations of morality, since every moral agent possesses

[109] Darwall 2006, 120.
[110] Darwall 2006, 39.
[111] Darwall 2013, 15. See also Darwall 2006, 143–145.
[112] He initially draws this distinction in Darwall 1977, but see also Darwall 2006, 122–126.
[113] Darwall 2013, 17. Like Darwall, Honneth aims to understand recognition in terms of the idea of respect. Unlike Darwall, he holds that recognition depends not only on actions, but also on a specific attitude, that of "value-ascription." (*Wertschätzung*) See, for example, Honneth 2003.

a dignity equal to the others. From the moral standpoint, I must be able to understand myself as "one among others."[114] Darwall holds that this equality is necessary for relations of reciprocal recognition, and it is the reason why, with the decline of societies oriented around honor, recognition cannot take as its object individual particularity, becoming "psychologized" in egalitarian societies as a mere subjective "attitude," that of esteem.[115]

In spite of the importance of specifically second-personal relations to others, Darwall's conception of the self remains *atomistic*. The morally significant feature of the self that is the object of the recognition of others is its dignity, which Darwall stresses is not socially constituted, but rather something individuals possess prior to any relation to others. It is an inalienable characteristic that I could not fail to possess, and so is like personhood in Hegel's account.[116] Likewise, corresponding to this atomistic conception of the self, Darwall presents a prominent example of a *responsive* model of recognition, indeed of a specifically *automatic* model of recognition: Since the ground of recognition is dignity, a generic, self-standing characteristic, and since you could not help but possess this trait, the demand that I recognize you is, therefore, unconditioned and automatic. Recognition is simply the appropriate response to your dignity.

As we have seen, Hegel offers a trenchant critique of personhood and the "immediate recognition" that corresponds to it. If Hegel is right, then Darwall's model of recognition and the self-conception corresponding to it will be *alienating*, since they do not include "content." Merely being recognized as a person will prove insufficient since that form of recognition neglects the positive aspects of my constitution that are essential to being a self.[117] The sort of recognition that Darwall calls second-person recognition respect, where each individual is simply "one among others," will fall short of what Hegel calls reciprocal recognition, since it is grounded in a merely partial conception of the self. Recognition respect, like recognition as a (mere) person, will give rise to experiences of *alienation*.[118]

---

[114] Darwall 2006, 102.

[115] Darwall 2013, 18.

[116] I do not claim that Hegel's conception of the person is identical to Darwall's, particularly since, for Hegel, personhood is merely a determination of right, not of morality, and he does not link it explicitly to dignity as Darwall does. However, both conceptions of the person are atomistic, and both find the source of personhood in features of the self that are inalienable and prior to society.

[117] Saunders 2016 raises a significant challenge to the very possibility of intersubjective recognition for Kant.

[118] On the connection between morality and alienation, see Railton 1984. Railton considers the possibility that moral demands and the moral point of view might effect an estrangement between the affective and rational aspects of our constitution, between individuals bound by particular interpersonal relations, and indeed from morality itself. His strategies for mitigating the alienating effects

Darwall might well respond that this critique misses the mark, by point-ing out that his primary interest is in the idea of moral obligation specifi-cally, not in articulating a complete conception of the self. Of course, he does hold that there are other sorts of attitudes that we can hold toward per-sons that are distinct from recognition respect, but he claims that these are not necessary for morality.[119] Indeed, if Darwall is right, Hegel's attempt to find a universal conception of the self shared equally by everyone is incon-sistent with the attempt to find a conception of the self that includes the positive contents that distinguish individuals from one another. After all, one of the primary reasons Darwall distinguishes recognition respect from honor, respect, and esteem is because only the former admits of full reci-procity, since it is based on a characteristic shared equally by all persons, their dignity. In this account, Hegel's attempt to articulate a conception of reciprocal recognition that does not exclude the features that distinguish individuals from one another is doomed to fail.

But the new conception of the self and model of recognition that Hegel introduces in his account of "Culture" suggest that this doom need not be certain. Within culture, selfhood is not simply a determination of the indi-vidual's "being," a property or characteristic they always already possess, but rather a product of the individual's "becoming," a condition that they come to acquire by means of a project of self-alteration undertaken with a view to a universal purpose. Likewise, we find an achievement model of recognition in the world of culture, specifically purpose-mediated recogni-tion, where recognition is not simply an automatic response to a generic property, but rather a response to the individual's success in that project of self-shaping. This new conception of the self and model of recognition provide the basis for Hegel's answer to the hypothetical Darwallian chal-lenge. Both demonstrate that the challenge is anchored in a false dichot-omy. Darwall is wrong to hold that a shared "universal" conception of the self and one that includes what differentiates individuals from one another

---

of morality bear much in common with Hegel's solution to the problem of alienation. Instead of understanding the self atomistically, he instead suggests that we consider the self as socially and historically embedded from the outset, where moral demands emerge in concert with the relations in which we thus always already find ourselves. However, his account bears more in common with the *sittlich* conception of the agent that we find in Hegel's mature practical philosophy. By con-trast, the self that we find in *Phenomenology of Spirit* is constituted through relations to others, but is not defined by particular social roles (like those of parent or husband).

[119] Esteem is a response to moral characteristics, but it would seem it is not necessary to morality, since I have obligations to others in virtue of their dignity, not in virtue of their being virtuous or morally upright themselves. Likewise, it seems possible that honor respect could track moral relations, if the society in which one lived were one that determined class distinction based on moral worth.

are mutually exclusive. Instead, understanding the self in terms of the idea of what an individual might become, instead of what they always already are, entails that our particular deeds and character are actually essential for achieving a shared, universal status. Recognition of what individuates us need not be bound up with a conception of "honor" or "esteem," but is instead an essential requirement of any universal conception of the self.[120] While Hegel does think that individuals come to merit recognition in virtue of their success in this project of self-shaping, because the standards that guide that project are "universal," such success can be the basis for a reasonable demand for equal recognition from others. So Hegel presents us with a model of recognition that incorporates *both* an equal status and what distinguishes individuals as essential elements.[121]

At the same time, the experience of culture shows that specifying the determinate conception of the self that fits these requirements presents a deep challenge. Absolute freedom, the conception of the self that is the actuality and truth of that world, makes manifest a profound tension that a conception of the self will have to address. That is the tension between the radical transcendence of the individual in relation to any positive content, and the demand for a basis for equality with others that is necessary for the achievement of relations of reciprocal recognition. Addressing this tension and showing how reciprocal recognition is possible will require important modifications to the predominant conception of the self, and the model of recognition corresponding to it. Overcoming alienation will require jettisoning the atomism that characterizes both the person and absolute freedom, and adopting a conception of the self as socially constituted. Since engagement with others is therefore necessary for being a self, the model of recognition that corresponds to social constitution conception of the self will be an achievement model of recognition. However, unlike the purpose-mediated recognition that we find in the world of culture, in this new model, recognition will not be understood merely as a response to an independent achievement of the individual, but rather as constitutive of their selfhood.

The conception of the self that resolves the tensions that emerge from the experience of absolute freedom and that makes possible relations of reciprocal recognition is the moral self, or conscience.

---

[120] In this connection see McBride's measured consideration of the expectation for esteem in McBride 2013, chapter 3.

[121] By contrast, other theorists point to the need for different forms of recognition to include these dimensions of our constitution, such as Honneth's (1992) accounts of love and solidarity, and Ikäheimo's (2007) account of love as the "axiological" dimension of recognition.

CHAPTER 4

Conscience

Darwall begins his exposition of the core ideas in *The Second Person Standpoint* with an epigraph from Rawls: "People are self-originating sources of claims."[1] In turn, he identifies "*the second-person standpoint*" as "the perspective you and I take up when we make and acknowledge claims on one another's conduct and will."[2] We have already seen an important sense in which claim-making is at the heart of Darwall's account of reciprocal recognition as acknowledging "each other's standing to demand, remonstrate, resist, charge, blame, resent, feel indignant, excuse, forgive, and so on,"[3] in short, to make claims on one another. Given the prominence of claim-making in Darwall's account, it might surprise us how small the role is that specific claims play within his account. The example on which he depends a good deal is a reasonably straightforward one, in which I make a claim on you or address a demand to you to stop stepping on my foot. Less prominent in his account are the more controversial claims that we make on and before others, on which we often expect less agreement when we make them, but which are nonetheless often central to our self-understanding. Instead of exploring the diverse claims that emerge in moral practice, Darwall's account of reciprocal recognition focuses on the sorts of authority that we must possess in order to make claims on one another in the first place.[4]

It might seem natural to hold that moral discourse – the linguistic practices through which we give expression to our convictions, agree with or contest the claims of others, and, in some cases, arrive at shared understanding or at least engage in moral repair – is secondary in importance

---

[1] Rawls 1980 cited in Darwall 2006, 3.
[2] Darwall 2006, 3.
[3] Darwall 2006, 141.
[4] As he puts it in a recent paper, "My own moral philosophizing has been steadfastly transcendental... I have been arguing that a form of value I call *second-personal authority* can be grounded in transcendental conditions or presuppositions of the address of any putatively valid claim or demand." Darwall 2021, 564.

in comparison either to moral action or to the agent's moral authority or competence. Even if moral talk sometimes has instrumental value as a means for determining what is really right to do, if it is ultimately actions that are right or wrong, moral talk might seem unnecessary, or even at times harmful. As Kurt Baier notes:

> Moral talk is often rather repugnant. Leveling moral accusations, expressing moral indignation, passing moral judgment, allotting the blame, administering moral reproof, justifying oneself, and, above all, moralizing—who can enjoy such talk? And who can like or trust those addicted to it?[5]

In *Phenomenology of Spirit*, by contrast, moral discourse is not just an essential part of morality. In addition, engaging with others in moral talk is both partly constitutive of the self and necessary for the achievement of reciprocal recognition. For Hegel, we cannot hope to bypass engagement with the concrete claims that the other makes. Consider again the case of Elizabeth Costello. Holding that she is recognized by others simply because they do not challenge her authority to issue moral claims is to overlook the depth of the rupture that she experiences when her moral understanding proves not to be shared. Even if my convictions are subject to change, I do not experience them as separable from who I am, so when I fail to secure agreement from others with respect to those convictions, that failure can give rise to an experience of estrangement that threatens the possibility of recognition.[6] By contrast, speaking with others is essential to the establishment of a shared understanding on which recognition depends.

Language, and moral language in particular, can play this role for Hegel for several reasons. First, language makes possible forms of likemindedness with others by giving expression to my subjectivity in a way that is equally available to others. As we have seen (in §3.1), language

> is the *existence* [Dasein] of the pure self as self ... [L]anguage receives [the I] in its purity, it alone expresses *I* [*spricht* Ich *aus*] itself. Thus its *existence* [Dasein] is an *existence*, an objectivity, which has the I's true nature in it. *I* is *this* I - but equally *universal*; its appearance is equally immediately the externalization and disappearance of *this* I, and thereby its persisting in its universality.[7]

[5] Baier 1958, 1.
[6] One way of putting this contrast is to say that Darwall's account of recognition is Fichtean, driven by the question of what sorts of rights or obligations can we derive as a condition for the achievement of recognition. Unlike Fichte, for whom recognition has its proper place in a doctrine of right, for Hegel, we find fully reciprocal recognition only in the domain of morality, and in particular in the sphere of conscience.
[7] *PhG* 276/¶507.

However, Hegel is also committed to a stronger claim, namely that language, particularly in the form of illocutionary speech, can actually be constitutive of the self. That is, there are certain determinate conceptions of the self whose existence depends on engagement in specific intersubjective discursive practices. Hegel introduces this thought by considering the ways in which the illocution of "naming" can actually *make* an individual into a "monarch."[8]

However, perhaps surprisingly, it is with the conception of the self as "conscience," the "third self" that emerges in the course of the experience of spirit, that this constitutive role of language is most prominent. It is by engaging in practices of moral discourse with others – acting on and giving linguistic expression to my convictions – that I am conscientious. Conscience is, for Hegel, not primarily a form of interiority – a special "voice" or "inner court" – insulated from and more original than interaction with others. By contrast, being conscientious requires not only realizing my convictions in outward actions available to others, but articulating the understanding that gives rise to them in ways that others can also understand. In short, conscience is a "social constitution" conception of the self that acknowledges that discursive interaction is not simply an adjunct to selfhood, but partially constitutive of it. And corresponding to this social constitution conception of the self, we find a new model of recognition, constitutive recognition, where the practices through which we arrive at shared understanding are understood to be constitutive of selfhood, and not simply to be responses to a trait that the individual possesses independent of that relation, as recognition is a response to dignity for Darwall. Instead of depending on a transcendental account of the conditions in the individual that make mutual address possible, Hegel's account of reciprocal recognition instead requires a pragmatics of moral discourse.[9]

I begin by identifying the emergence of morality as a shape of spirit from the world of culture, and show that we find the first explicitly social constitution conception of the self in the moral world (§4.1). I then set out the essential elements of conscience as a conception of the self (§4.2). I argue that the key to understanding the experience of conscience lies in a flawed conception of moral "purity" (§4.3). I conclude by demonstrating that confession and forgiveness are the discursive forms that are not only necessary to correct this flawed conception of purity (§4.4), but also to

---

[8] *PhG* 277/¶510. I return to this example in §4.1.
[9] See in this connection Kukla and Lance's (2009, 194–195 esp.) pragmatic alternative to Darwall's contractarianism.

provide the forms of moral repair necessary to sustain relations of reciprocal recognition in light of moral disagreement (§4.5).

4.1 Morality as a Shape of Spirit

Morality is the inheritor of the idea that emerged in the world of culture that purity is constitutive of the self. In culture, that idea found expression in the opposition between the actual self and its world of power and wealth, on the one hand, and the pure self and its world of thinking. As Hegel's account of the experience of spirit migrates from the France of the terror at the conclusion of chapter VIB to the "other land of self-conscious spirit," the German-speaking lands of Kant's philosophical revolution, at the outset of chapter VIC, it certainly sounds as though "morality" will retain the limitations that stem from an exclusive focus on the "pure" self and its world of thinking. In this "other land," "absolute freedom ... counts as the true in this inactuality [*Unwirklichkeit*], refreshes itself with its thought insofar as it *is* and remains *thought*, and knows this being enclosed within self-consciousness as the perfect and complete essence."[10] In short, morality seems condemned at the outset to repeat the shortcomings that stemmed from the partial perspectives of faith and pure insight, the "pure" shapes of consciousness of the world of culture.

This appearance, however, is misleading. And we can appreciate the core difference between the forms of pure consciousness that we found in the world of culture and that which emerges in the world of morality by considering the developments that we have found in the account of the self. We have seen that the self of the world of culture shares with that of the world of ethical life the idea that the self is an "atom," a "point" that exists independent of our attitudes and activities. To be sure, in the world of culture, selfhood was understood to be a status that we achieve only by transforming our given and natural existence, but the purposes that directed those activities of self-transformation were understood to be fixed and given, either from within the actual world of culture, or from the pure thought-worlds of faith and pure insight. And the claim that the self exists as a given point found expression in the explicit conception of the self that emerged in the experience of the world of culture, absolute freedom.

While morality certainly does identify the basic character of the self in terms of the idea of purity, it rejects the atomism of the prior shapes

---

[10] *PhG* 323/¶595.

of spirit. The new, moral understanding of the basic character of the self emerges from the experience of absolute freedom. Recall that absolute freedom identified the self with the universal will, the knower and instituter of shared norms. Its experience, however, was that "absolute negativity," the transcendence of any particular determinacy belonging to self-consciousness, is equally an essential aspect of its constitution. As a result, instead of being able to claim immediate knowledge of the deliverances of the universal will, absolute freedom had to acknowledge the need for mediation and justification of its claims to know. As Hegel will argue, it needs to identify ultimately with the "concept," the intelligible structure in which distinguished terms can be related, and that can comprehend within itself objectivity and otherness, rather than simply destroying them or separating them off.

This experience gives rise to a new way of mediating its individuality, the characteristic of being *this* self, and its universality, the characteristic of having shared knowledge and understanding with others:

> For consciousness, the immediate unity of itself with the universal will, its requirement to know itself as this determinate point in the universal, transforms itself into its opposite. What disappears for it is the abstract *being* or the immediacy of the substanceless point, and this lost immediacy is the universal will itself, which it now knows itself to be insofar as it is *sublated immediacy*, insofar as it is pure knowing or pure willing. It thereby knows [the universal will] as itself and knows itself as the essence, but not as the *immediately existing* essence, not as the revolutionary government, as anarchy striving to constitute anarchy, or as the middle point of this or that faction or one opposed to it, rather the *universal will* is its *pure knowing and willing*, and it is universal will as this pure knowing and willing. It does not lose *itself* in [the universal will], for pure knowing and willing is it much more than is the atomic point of consciousness. It is therefore the reciprocal interaction of pure knowing with itself; pure *knowing* as *essence* is the universal will, but this *essence* is simply pure knowing. Self-consciousness is therefore the pure knowing of the essence as pure knowing.[11]

The moral self, then, is one for whom its object and its truth is its own knowing. As a form of self-consciousness, the moral self does not seek to know itself in terms of something other than itself, either in terms of the this-worldly determinations of wealth, power, or wit or in terms of the otherworldly determinations of faith as an eternal soul or of pure insight as pure matter or utility. Instead, its effort to achieve self-knowledge

---

[11] *PhG* 322–323/¶594.

takes as its object its own knowing, so that the "essence" of moral self-consciousness, what it takes to be true, is just its own knowing of the truth. The Kantian resonances of this moral conception of the self ought to be clear since they give expression to core aspects of the ideas of epistemic and moral autonomy. In considering the "essence" or the "true" to be self-consciousness's own "knowing," Hegel is offering a characterization of Kant's transcendental project more broadly, in which the ideas of truth and of moral obligation find their ground in an investigation of the structure of pure reason. Kant vindicates our claims to knowledge of what is true and what is right by identifying reason itself as an essential source, where the pure concepts of the understanding structure *a priori* our experience of the world, and where the moral law stems from pure practical reason itself. Kant's efforts to identify the pure grounds for our knowledge in reason itself assign an essential role to autonomy, so that what is true and right should not be understood to be completely determined from outside of the knowing and willing subject, but rather to be products of the self-determination of their own reason.[12]

Hegel's account of pure knowledge, however, is importantly distinct from Kant's. Kant conceives of the pure concepts of understanding and the moral law to be transcendental in character, given independent of experience, but responsible for determining it. By contrast, Hegel accounts for pure knowing by construing it as the product of a specific process. To be sure, Hegel suggests that there is a certain immediacy that belongs to pure knowing, but that immediacy is an achieved standpoint, the product of an activity of purification or refinement:

> The knowing of self-consciousness is for it the *substance* itself. It is for it equally *immediate* as absolutely *mediated* in an undivided unity. *Immediate* – like the ethical consciousness, it knows and does duty itself and belongs to it as its nature; but it is not *character*, as the ethical consciousness is, which is, because of its immediacy, a determinate spirit, belonging only to one of the ethical essentialities, and containing the side of *not knowing*. It is *absolute mediation*, like the self-forming and faithful consciousness; for it is essentially the movement of the self, of sublating the abstraction of *immediate existence*, and becoming universal – but neither through the pure alienation and division of the self and its actuality, nor through fleeing. Rather it is *immediately present* in its substance, for the substance is its knowing, it is the intuited pure certainty of itself; but precisely *this immediacy*, which is its own actuality, is all actuality, for the immediate is *being* itself, and it is pure immediacy

as purely refined [*geläuterte*] through absolute negativity, it is *being* in general or *all being*.[13]

Or, as Hegel puts this point at the outset of chapter VIC.b:

> In the moral worldview, we see [...] consciousness *itself consciously constitute* its object [*das Bewußtsein* selbst *seinen Gegenstand mit* Bewußtsein erzeugen]; we see it neither discover [*vorfinden*] the object as something alien, nor become it unconsciously; rather it proceeds in general according to a reason [*Grunde*], from which it *posits* the *objective being*; it knows it as itself, for it knows itself as *active*, that it *constitutes* [erzeugt].[14]

In treating pure knowing as a product of the activity of self-consciousness, Hegel is, in a sense, picking up a prominent thread that emerges in Kant, that which stresses the active, spontaneous, and apperceptive character of forms of theoretical and practical knowledge.[15] In linking it with this activity of purification that is in turn the source of its pure knowing, Hegel's account of the moral self appears closer than we might expect to the strand of Kantianism that Korsgaard has designated "constitutivism."[16] Korsgaard's idea draws on both senses of the term "constitution," both as a specific arrangement or configuration of parts that gives unity to a thing, and also as the activity that gives rise to that arrangement. The constitution that is appropriate to a person is the one that gives them unity and coherence, and its achievement requires the acknowledgment of certain principles that govern or give rise to it, most importantly the principles of practical reason, and hypothetical and categorical imperatives. And it is deliberative action in accordance with those principles that, in turn, "constitutes" the individual into "a single unified agent," so that "deliberative action is self-constitution."[17] Korsgaard's constitutivist conception fits well with the idea of the self with which Hegel's account of "morality" begins since, in both cases, the self is identified as the product of an activity that constitutes it, where that constitutive activity is governed by standards whose source lies within the individual themselves.[18]

The conception of the self that we find in *Phenomenology of Spirit* shares in common with Korsgaard's idea that selves are not, as Hegel puts it, simply

---

[13] *PhG* 324/¶597.
[14] *PhG* 332/¶616.
[15] On the link more generally, see Pippin 1989.
[16] See the initial overview in Korsgaard 1999, and the fuller account provided in Korsgaard 2009.
[17] Korsgaard 1999, 22.
[18] Of course, one significant difference between these accounts merits note at the outset. Hegel does not argue that the principles or ideas that give structure to and that constitute the self are also the principles of moral action, a claim that is central to Korsgaard's project. *Phenomenology of Spirit* does not present us with determinate ethical principles.

"discovered" but rather "constituted" or "engendered" (*erzeugt*) through the activities of self-conscious beings, and that the being so constituted is not a simple thing, but rather a specific configuration of parts. For Hegel, the idea of the self is a *linking* idea that establishes determinate bonds between the individual's knowledge, their actions, and others. However, the greatest difference between their accounts is that Hegel offers us a *social* constitution conception of the self, so that determinate relations to others are partly constitutive of the self.

This idea has been implicit throughout Hegel's account of spirit, where "self" is the designation for self-conscious beings as participants in a shared social world. However, we have also seen that the first two conceptions of the self that emerged in chapter VI, the person and absolute freedom, do not actually acknowledge the ways in which the self is constituted through engagement with others in a world. Instead, both conceptions of the self are atomistic, committed to the claim that the existence of the self does not depend on relations to others. By contrast, it is only in Hegel's account of morality that we find a conception of the self that acknowledges that the self is not "discovered" but rather "created," and that this process of creation is one that is worldly and intersubjective.

Given morality's starting point, the "moral worldview," it may be surprising that it is in the world of morality that we find this idea of self-conscious social constitution. Even if the language of constitution – of the self as "constituted" or "engendered" through activity – is prominent from the outset, it may seem that the moral self is just as individualistic or just as atomized as those that preceded it. It is certainly true that the social dimension of the moral self only emerges in the course of the experience of the moral world. The initial arguments that Hegel offers with respect to the moral worldview aim to draw out a contradiction within it, a contradiction that the social conception of the self ultimately addresses.

Again, we can see Hegel's argumentative strategy here as a *reductio* whose aim is to demonstrate that the moral self actually requires a shared social world in which it is constituted. Stressing that the moral self is defined by its "purity," Hegel's starting point is to situate that self within a world that would give as little definition to the self as possible so that the self is understood as "free" from its world, and the world, in turn, exists as similarly free from the self, defined by its own constitutive laws. Hegel identifies this minimal world-conception as that of "nature," an "actuality *without significance*," the mere "negative object" of moral consciousness.[19]

[19] *PhG* 325/¶599.

In chapter VIC.a–b, Hegel argues that this "moral worldview" gives rise to a series of contradictions. The moral conception of the self carries over from absolute freedom the idea that a "universal will" is essential to the self, so that the moral self identifies its essential character in terms of an idea of "duty," being bound by that law. However, if the objective world in which the agent acts is really alien to the demands of duty that are essential to the self, then the actualization of those demands will not be possible in the moral world. The moral view of the world addresses this challenge by "postulating" that we find the actualization of morality instead in a "beyond," separate from the moral self as it actually is. Hegel argues that instead of solving the problem, however, this postulate actually generates a contradiction within the moral worldview. On the one hand, the moral worldview holds that morality is something actual in the knowing and willing of the moral agent, but on the other, it holds that the moral agent's knowing and willing are bound to be incomplete and so not a moral "actuality," requiring for their completion and perfection a relation to another, "holy moral legislator."[20] The idea of a condition in which morality and nature exist in harmony, so that there is an actual moral consciousness is, Hegel stresses, a mere "representation" of the moral worldview. However, Hegel argues that morality cannot be "in earnest" in holding that this harmony is *merely* represented. Playing on the cognates of the verb "*verstellen*," Hegel instead holds that morality must actually "dissemble" with respect to the claim that we find actual moral consciousness only in a "beyond," simply because the actions of real moral agents themselves constitute the "actualization" (*Verwirklichung*) of the demands of duty,[21] and moral agents justifiably claim genuine knowledge of the demands of morality.[22]

The more basic contradiction that we find in the moral worldview, then, is that morality exists as a shape of spirit, but denies a constitutive aspect of the idea of spirit, that the world makes claims on us by providing us with the purposes with which we identify, and that we make actual in our actions. Overcoming this initial "moral worldview," then, requires rejecting the idea of the world as a free and separate world of nature, indifferent to agents and their aims, and instead identifying the world as a world of action, not alien to the purposes that agents take up, or to the claims that they hold are binding on them.

---

[20] For a concise statement of this contradiction, see *PhG* 331–332/¶615.
[21] *PhG* 333/¶618.
[22] *PhG* 337–338/¶626.

The worldly conception of the moral self that acknowledges that the self is socially constituted is conscience. On its face, this claim might seem absurd. After all, Hegel stresses that, on acknowledging the contradictions inherent in the moral worldview, the moral self "retreats" from those contradictions, and "returns to itself," holding that "what is *actual* is just its *pure knowing* and *pure duty*."[23] And in understanding the self to be the "moral genius which knows the inner voice of its immediate knowing as the divine voice," conscience seems simply to internalize the moral worldview's otherworldly postulate of a "holy moral legislator."[24] Moreover, conscience's conception of the objective world in which it acts seems to be equally as impoverished as the moral worldview's idea of nature, an indifferent domain of "an absolute plurality of circumstances."[25] So it may seem that conscience makes little progress with respect to the issue of the character of worldliness in comparison to the moral worldview. This impression is no doubt at play in the expectation that many interpreters have for a return of the world of ethical life, of concrete institutions, an expectation that *Phenomenology of Spirit* never satisfies.

Of course, one of Hegel's primary aims in the "Conscience" chapter is to demonstrate that the idea of a self insulated from the shared social world is an instance of what Pippin calls a "fantas[y] of self-sufficiency."[26] However, Hegel advances the argument by appealing to features inherent in the world of conscience, not one beyond it. The world of conscience – unlike the world of the moral worldview – is a world of *others*, who make claims about what is right and true on and before us. And the claim that the other makes on me need not depend for its justification on any particular social or political institution or set of institutions. Moreover, not only does conscience have a world, the shared world of participants in moral discourse, Hegel also demonstrates that that participation is actually *constitutive* of the self. Conscience, for Hegel, does not exist independent of my engagement with others in the project of making and acting on moral claims.

4.2 Conscience as a Conception of the Self

What does it mean to be conscientious? In the first instance, conscience individualizes. My conscience addresses its demands to me. As Heidegger

---

[23] *PhG* 341/¶632.
[24] *PhG* 352/¶654.
[25] *PhG* 346/¶642. Compare 328–329/¶605.
[26] Pippin 2004, 264.

writes, "conscience is in its ground and essence *in each case mine*," and it is only when I attend to its call that it becomes possible for me "to become the 'conscience' of the other."[27] However, as its etymology suggests – *con-scientia, syn-eidesis* – conscience also designates a form of shared knowing, a knowing along with others. This tension between individualization and sharedness might seem to threaten the coherence of the idea of conscience, prompting us either to give up the idea that conscience's knowing can really be shared, or that there is anything distinctively or ultimately individualized in it.[28]

It is a distinctive feature of post-Kantian idealism that it not only identifies this tension between what is individual and what is shared but makes it productive. For Fichte, the concept of the "individual" (*Individuum*) is not original, but instead the product of a synthesis of the "I" and the "you," so that individuality only emerges through a special sort of interaction with others.[29] We find a similar tension in Hegel's idea of the self. On the one hand, selfhood is a status that is universal, that I know to be shared with others who are also selves. On the other hand, I am always, as Hegel expresses the idea, *this* self, a particular individual. Self-knowledge will require acknowledging both of these dimensions of my constitution. As the final conception of the self that emerges in the course of the experience of spirit, and the one that makes possible relations of reciprocal intersubjective recognition, "conscience" (*Gewissen*) is no less animated by this productive tension between what belongs specifically and uniquely to the individual, and what can be shared with others.[30]

I have been suggesting so far that being conscientious requires participation in the practices of moral discourse, of making claims about what is right and good, where those are claims that are made both before others, stated outwardly to them, but also claims that are made on others, concerning as they do those actions that are duties. The core to understanding Hegel's account of conscience in *Phenomenology of Spirit* is to understand it as an account of "the self." I've argued, starting in §3.1, that conceptions

---

[27] Heidegger 1972, 278, 298.

[28] With respect to the latter possibility, see Hill's account of the conceptions of conscience as "God-given instinctual access to moral truth" and as "mere internalized social norms." Hill 1998.

[29] See *SW* I, 502.

[30] While many interpreters take Hegel to be primarily a critic of conscience, recent work by Siep (see 1998, 2008, 2010, and 2014, 142–148 especially) and Moyar (2011) articulates the positive contribution that the account makes in *Phenomenology*. While I contest their accounts on particular points in what follows, they rightly articulate the centrality of conscience to Hegel's account of reciprocal recognition.

of the self establish determinate relations between the individual, their actions, and others.[31] And this is equally true for conscience.

4.2.1 Knowledge and Action

When the individual is understood as conscience, knowledge is what establishes the link between them and their actions. Conscience's knowledge takes the form of "conviction" (*Überzeugung*). In contrast to the "moral worldview," in which "pure duty" was understood to be opposed to actuality and actualization, in conscience, moral knowledge is actual within the individual themselves:

> Conscience has *for itself* its truth in the *immediate certainty* of itself. This *immediate* concrete certainty of itself is the essence; considered according to the opposition of consciousness, its own immediate *singularity* [Einzelnheit] is the content of the moral deed; and the *form* of that deed is equally this self as pure movement, namely as *knowing* or as *its own conviction*.[32]

The knowledge that conscience claims does not distinguish between a pure self and an alien actuality. Instead, as conscience, "This self constitutes [*macht…aus*] the content of the hitherto empty essence, for it is the *actual*, which no longer has the significance of being an independent nature alien to the essence with its own laws."[33] Even though it belongs to the individual understood as a singular agent, conscience's knowledge is nonetheless understood to be "the *simple universal*, so that this knowing *as its own* knowing, as conviction, is equally duty."[34] Conscience, therefore, entails a rejection of the strict division between the particular knowledge of this individual and the "pure" knowledge of duty. Instead, what conscience knows is a universal that is "concrete," actual within individual agents.[35]

---

[31] Schlösser 2011 notes the general connection between self-knowledge, action, and language. But his account does not acknowledge the distinction between the three conceptions of the self that emerge in chapter VI, and he does not link this development to the problem of recognition.

[32] *PhG* 343/¶637.

[33] *PhG* 344/¶638.

[34] *PhG* 344/¶639.

[35] The language of concreteness predominates in *PhG* 342/¶634. Pinkard rightly stresses the concrete character of conscientious knowledge but understands this knowledge in an excessively subjective way: "[T]he romantics turned away from the idealist account of making representations one's own in favor of a more concrete sense of making something one's own by looking inward and exploring one's *own* subjectivity in the hope of finding therein the grounds for a truly free and non-alienated human life." Pinkard 1994, 209. If we construe the concreteness of conscience's knowledge as the idea that it is "situated," we need not accept this subjectivistic interpretation.

In this conception, the "proper" subject matter of moral consideration is not an independent space of special values, or a domain of distinctively moral principles or ideas, separate from the particular concerns and modes of thinking of particular agents. The universals that the individual knows in the form of their convictions do not require vindication by a separate set of pure principles. Instead, conscience involves a double-movement from the moral worldview. First, duty is, we might say, brought down to the level of the individual agent, so that it is actual within them as their own knowing. Second, conscience also entails an elevation of the individual and their knowing so that these are not considered moral second-bests in comparison to "pure duty" or moral principle. Rather, as the sole site for the realization of moral ideals, the individual and their knowledge are understood to be essential to moral action and practice, simply on their own, or "immediately," not requiring justification by a set of higher principles insulated from them and from their particular actuality.[36]

In one prominent line of interpretation, for Hegel, conscience identifies the standard for right action in the individual's subjective certainty, in the form of emotion or feeling.[37] In this account, the position that Hegel is sketching resembles Fichte's, where conscience is the higher faculty of feeling, through which we have an immediate awareness of the most fundamental drive that constitutes us as agents, the drive for self-sufficiency.[38] However, while Hegel stresses the role of certainty (*Gewissheit*) in conscientious knowing, nowhere in his discussion does he account for that certainty in terms of feeling (*Gefühl*).[39] And Hegel's core claim about certainty is much weaker than Fichte's claim about conscientious feeling. In *Phenomenology*, the central claim of morality is that my knowledge and capacity for certainty is a necessary condition for an action to be a duty for me, not a sufficient one. As we shall see, this view entails the possibility

---

[36] As the conception of the self that overcomes the divisions between the domains of pure reason and nature, conscience need not understand the demands of duty to be opposed to those of nature, or to think that the essence of the self is something that transcends nature and sensibility. The "determination and content" of the conscientious agent's certainty can be "*natural* consciousness, that is, drive and inclination" just because conscience does not draw a hard and fast distinction between the self as something pure and the natural world. *PhG* 346–347/¶643. Rather, conscience can incorporate the individual's nature instead of demanding its repression.

[37] See for example Halbig 2008 and Pinkard 1994, 209–213.

[38] *SW* IV, 147. Wood (1990, chapter 10) reads the *Phenomenology* account of conscience alongside the account in the *Philosophy of Right* as a criticism of Fichte's normative ethics. Kosch 2014 and 2018, and Ware 2017 and 2020 argue that Hegel's account misses the mark as a critique of Fichte. According to my interpretation, the *Phenomenology* account of conscience is primarily concerned with ontological questions rather than normative ethical ones.

[39] For an account of the role of feeling in Fichte's account of conscience, see Brownlee 2022.

that my initial claims to certainty may prove false, subject to correction in light of the competing claims of others.

A more promising account of conscience's knowledge takes its point of departure from the fact that this knowledge is concrete. For example, Russon considers conscience's knowledge to be a knowledge of its "situation," an insight into what is required or right to do in particular circumstances.[40] Moyar's account of conscience's knowledge clearly brings together both dimensions of subjective certainty and objective insight. Moyar draws on Moran's account of "transparency": "The claim of transparency is that from within the first-person perspective, I treat the question of my belief about P as equivalent to the question of the truth of P."[41] In this account, conscience's certainty is not rooted in "'psychological evidence' about myself," but rather in a commitment to the truth of its conviction.[42] What makes that conviction true need not be any feeling or emotion within me. Indeed, Hegel stresses that conscience includes the content that has oriented all of the shapes of spirit, only, unlike those prior forms, this substantial content is not a predicate attaching to the individual's knowing, but rather as a dimension of their subjectivity.[43]

Indeed, Hegel does not give us a positive account of what makes particular moral claims true in *Phenomenology*. While understanding the self does require considering morality and its distinctive "world," so that being a self requires acknowledging that I have obligations, *Phenomenology of Spirit* does not present us with a determinate ethical theory. The question of what the self is is in an important sense a prior and more basic question than the ethical question of how I should live or the moral question of what I have an obligation to do. Stating that I have duties or obligations, that these are essential to being a self, is, however, very different from stating what those duties or obligations are.[44]

At the same time, this elevation of individual moral knowledge also bears with it an acknowledgment of the contingency of that knowledge: "It is for

---

[40] Russon 2004, 162.
[41] Moran 2001, 62–63, quoted in Moyar 2011, 19.
[42] Moyar 2011, 20.
[43] In this connection, see *PhG* 345/¶641.
[44] It is another question whether Hegel's characterization of conscience is an instance of understanding morality as a "peculiar institution" that assigns excessive weight to the claims of obligation. See B. Williams 1985, chapter 10. Duty is but one of the ideas that conscience invokes to make sense of its actions, along with "right" and "virtue." Since Hegel is not here interested in providing us with a particular normative ethical view, he need not be committed to the claim that understanding obligation is the primary ethical task. But he also emphasizes the importance of obligation at the level of understanding the self, which is, in some respects, deeper.

itself what is completely valid in its contingency [*das in seiner Zufälligkeit Vollgültige*], that knows its immediate certainty as pure knowing and acting, as the true actuality and harmony."[45] As the limited knowledge of this particular individual, moral knowledge is contingent, but, as conscience, this knowledge retains its full "validity" and the knower *counts* as such. The knowledge characteristic of conscience is, therefore, in important respects a "situated knowledge," not divorced from the actual world of real agents, and Hegel's rejection of a stance of moral epistemic "purity," supposedly insulated from actuality, bears much in common with recent criticisms of self-avowed "intellectualist" accounts of knowledge.[46]

Action is the form through which conscience's convictions undergo a process of "actualization."[47] (*Verwirklichung*) It is only through action that conscience comes to be an existent actuality, to have *Dasein*. The claim that action makes moral knowledge something actual or real emerged centrally in the experience of the moral worldview.[48] Hegel makes this point quite directly in his account of the "beautiful soul," to whom we will return again later, who is unable to realize their convictions by acting, out of the fear of tarnishing the perfection of their moral knowledge. The beautiful soul lacks

> determinate existence [Dasein], for …. the self does not arrive at actuality. It lacks the power of externalization [*Kraft der Entäußerung*], the power of making itself into a thing, and of bearing being. It lives in the anxiety of besmirching the magnificence of its inner through action and determinate existence, and in order to preserve the purity of its heart, it recoils from the touch of actuality.[49]

Moral knowledge must be actualized through action in order to count as such.[50]

While action is necessary for the realization of the agent's convictions, those convictions, in turn, determine the essence of the action. When an agent acts, they bring themselves into a unique relation to an actuality that is opposed to them, that is, as Hegel says, "the negative of consciousness."[51]

---

[45] *PhG* 341/¶632.
[46] For a helpful account, in an explicitly Hegelian vein, see Kukla 2021.
[47] *PhG* 342/¶635.
[48] "Action is nothing other than the actualization of the inner moral purpose, nothing other than the production of an *actuality determined* through *the purpose*, or the harmony of the moral purpose and of actuality itself." *PhG* 333/¶618.
[49] *PhG* 354/¶658.
[50] Compare Kant on the claim that, even if the individual fails to fulfill their aim through action, "the good will… would still shine in itself as something that has its full worth within itself." *AA* 4: 394.
[51] *PhG* 346/¶642.

That actuality is a "manifold... an absolute plurality of circumstances." The moral worldview was unable to come to terms with this plurality of the world of actuality, which required acknowledging that the same situation seems to demand of the agent the fulfillment of many, perhaps conflicting determinate duties. By contrast, Hegel holds that, for conscience, we can identify the action that properly belongs to the agent in the particular circumstance by appeal to conviction. What the agent knows they are doing, what they know to be a duty is supposed to fix the meaning of their deeds: "What is *positive* in the action, its content, as the form of duty and the essence of the action, belongs to the self, to its certainty of the action."[52]

Conscience, therefore, sustains, in important respects, the commitment to autonomy that is characteristic of "morality" more broadly. When I act conscientiously, my action gives expression to (*drückt ... aus*) the moral knowledge that I have in the form of conviction.[53] And that knowledge, in turn, does not depend for its validation on something outside me, but is rather understood to be original to me as this individual. As a conception of the self, conscience links the agent to their actions through their moral knowledge, and this link accords with the autonomy of the agent.

4.2.2 *Knowledge and Recognition*

In addition to linking agents and their actions, conceptions of the self also relate individuals to one another in determinate ways. As conscience, the individual agent can be recognized by others because their moral knowledge is a shared knowledge.[54] Hegel is explicit that what is recognized is not the action simply, but rather that others recognize the agent in virtue

---

[52] *PhG* 349/¶646. See also *PhG* 346/¶643. The tension that emerges within the experience of conscience is that between the conviction of the agent, and those of others. Since my conviction is supposed to be a shared and universal knowledge, this experience points to the need for means for arriving at shared agreement regarding the meaning of the action.

[53] In general, Hegel holds that actions are best understood to be "expressive" of the self, a point central to the readings of C. Taylor 1985 and Pippin 2008. However, the expressive dimension of action is distinct from that of language, a point that, we will see, is central to his account of conscience. To capture the expressive aspect of action, he uses the verb *ausdrücken* and its cognates, while he uses *aussprechen* and related term to identify the expressive aspect of language. For such uses, see, for example, *PhG* 350/¶649 and 353/¶656.

[54] For this reason, I disagree with the contrast between individual knowledge and the shared knowledge of the community that Pinkard offers, where the conscientious community respects "the right of conscience," according to which "each would be allowed to go his own way, to explore his own self, knowing that others affirm this for him instead of forcing him into some social mold." Pinkard 1994, 210. See also Rush's characterization of the relation between conscientious individuals as a "respectful, hands-off attitude toward the other's introspective quest for individual moral authenticity." Rush 2016, 134.

of the moral knowledge that their action actualizes.⁵⁵ That is, the conscientious agent is recognized by others insofar as they count for them as a
knower, which they do by establishing that their knowledge is really a
universal and shared knowledge. To be sure, they must be an agent – they
must act on their convictions – but they are recognized not directly for
what they do, but for the moral knowledge expressed in their action:

> Conscience has not abandoned pure duty or the *abstract in-itself*, rather it is,
> as *universality*, the essential moment of conducting itself in relation to others.
> It is the common [*gemeinschaftliche*] element of self-consciousness, and this
> substance, in which the deed has *persistence* and *actuality*, the moment of *being-
> recognized* by others... The *existent actuality* of conscience is one that is *self*, that
> is, existence [*Dasein*] conscious of itself, the spiritual element of becoming-
> recognized. The deed is therefore only the translation of a *singular* content
> into the *objective* element in which it is universal and recognized, and precisely
> this, that the action is recognized, makes the action into an actuality. Action
> is recognized, and thereby actual, because the existent actuality is immediately
> bound to conviction or knowing, or the knowing of its purpose is immediately
> the element of existence, universal recognizing. For the *essence* of action, duty,
> consists of the *conviction* of conscience concerning it; this conviction is equally
> the *in-itself* itself; it is the self-consciousness that is *universal in itself*, or *being-
> recognized*, and so actuality. That which is done with the conviction of duty is
> immediately something that has persistence and existence.⁵⁶

While action "actualizes" (*verwirklicht*) a moral knowledge that would otherwise remain abstract, it is the recognition of others that lends the action itself
"actuality" (*Wirklichkeit*), that renders it an existence that expresses an essence.
And when others recognize me as conscience, they recognize me as a knower.
The status of being a knower, of possessing convictions regarding duty, is what
establishes the relation of equality on which reciprocal recognition depends.
This shared status of being knowers, central to conscience as a conception of
the self, is what mediates relations between the agent and others.

   However, establishing that others do in fact share moral knowledge
with me is a fraught matter. The challenge emerges from the distinctive
character of action. The contact with a reality distinct from the agent that
action necessarily entails can also threaten the relation to conviction that is
supposed to comprise the essence of action, and so to undermine the possibility of recognition. Unlike knowing, which remains within or returns

⁵⁵ "The self-certain spirit exists as such for another; its *immediate* action is not what counts and is
actual [*was gilt und wirklich ist*]; what is recognized is not the *determinate*, what *exists in itself*, but
only the self-knowing *self* as such." *PhG* 351/¶651.
⁵⁶ *PhG* 344–345/¶640.

to the medium of the conscious knower, the "medium" (*Medium*) of action is that of determinate existence or "being." Consequently, actions involve a "distinction" from the knower – both from the agent, and from others – and this distinction creates a challenge for the achievement of relations of recognition: "In *being*, the distinction is posited as persisting, and the action as a *determinate* one, unequal with the element of the self-consciousness of all, and therefore not necessarily recognized."[57] Action is necessary to the actualization of claims to moral knowledge, but, at the same time, it seems to be a necessarily imperfect vessel for that realization, since it involves a fundamental distinction between knowers and the medium of action, being, that action by itself cannot overcome.[58]

It is not sufficient, then, for others simply to assume that I have genuine conscientious convictions, or that my actions really give expression to them. Recognition rather requires, in addition to knowledge and action, specific forms of language, and, more broadly, participation in moral discourse.

4.2.3 Language

We have already seen (in §3.1.3) an important sense in which language is necessary to the self. First, for Hegel, language fulfills the general role of making individuals intelligible to one another. It is an "*existence*, an objectivity, which has the I's true nature in it. *I* is *this* I – but equally universal."[59] When Hegel introduces language into his account of conscience, this function is central:

> We see here again *language* as the existence of spirit [*Dasein des Geistes*]. It is self-consciousness existing *for another*, which is immediately *present as such* but still universal as *this* [self-consciousness]. It is the self that separates itself from itself, that becomes objective as pure I=I, but equally maintains itself in this objectivity as *this* self, as it coalesces with the others and is *their* self-consciousness; it hears itself as it is heard by the others, and this hearing [*Vernehmen*] is just *existence that has become the self.*[60]

---

[57] *PhG* 350/¶648.
[58] Hegel goes so far as to say that it is not only possible for others to doubt that my action is morally good, but that they "must" take it to be evil. Since it is a determinate reality distinct from them and their own moral knowledge, in which the self of another is expressed, they must "dissolve it in their own consciousness, to make it nothing through judgment and explanation, in order to maintain their self." *PhG* 350/¶649.
[59] *PhG* 276/¶508.
[60] *PhG* 351/¶652. As Stekeler-Weithofer (2014, 2, 682) observes, conscience is often portrayed as a voice whose call the individual must hear. For Hegel, this dynamic of call and response in conscience is one that we find between individuals as participants in moral discourse.

Conscience requires language specifically to make its status as a knower intelligible to others:

> Language emerges as the medium [*Mitte*] of independent and recognized self-consciousness, and the *existent self* is immediately universal, plural, and in this plurality simple being-recognized. The content of the language of conscience is *the self that knows itself as the essence.*[61]

Second, for the individual, language makes intelligible the link between the agent and their actions. The different forms that language assumes in the "spirit" chapter specify distinct links between the agent and their deeds. The language of the ethical world, whose predominant forms are "law and simple command" and "lament" give expression to the immediate relation between the individual and the customs and laws of the ethical world, and to the inevitably tragic implications of that immediacy.[62] Likewise, the content of the language of the world of culture, that of the "inverted and inverting and disrupted self," gives expression to the waylessness of the self of that world stemming from the loss of apparent authoritativeness of state power and wealth.[63] The language of conscience is distinctive in articulating a novel understanding of the relation between the individual and their actions.

The predominant form of the language of conscience is distinctive. Hegel identifies it broadly as "expression" (*Aussprechen*), which I will gloss as "expressive speech," to preserve its distinctiveness as a form of expression. In this role, language presents the individual's convictions, their distinctive and individual moral knowledge, in a form that is accessible and intelligible to others:

> The content of the language of conscience is *the self that knows itself as essence.* Language expresses [*spricht … aus*] this alone, and this expression is the true actuality of the deed, and that in which the action counts [*das Gelten der Handlung*]. Consciousness expresses its *conviction*; this conviction is that in which the action is a duty; the action only *counts* as a duty insofar as the conviction is *expressed.* For the universal self-consciousness is free from the *merely existent determinate* action; for [the universal consciousness, the *action*] doesn't count at all as *existence*, but only the *conviction* that [the action] is a *duty* [counts]; and this duty is actual in language.[64]

Expressive speech in particular best fulfills the general role that language plays, namely of making individuals intelligible to one another in a way that

---

[61] *PhG* 351/¶653.
[62] *PhG* 351/¶653.
[63] *PhG* 351/¶653.
[64] *PhG* 351/¶653.

does not compromise or sacrifice individuality. It makes manifest for others my individual convictions, and so communicates to them my conscientiousness, that I have moral knowledge. For this reason, the expressive speech of conscience is distinct from the witty talk of the world of culture. That former self possessed rich linguistic resources, but lacked conviction, the moral knowledge that is central to conscience. Moreover, the way in which I articulate my duties makes intelligible the actions that are properly mine, since my expressive claims offer a determinate account of what I do, and explicitly link those deeds to my conscientious convictions. This feature of the language of conscience distinguishes it from the two forms of language that predominated in the ethical world, command and lament. Agents in that world understood themselves to be subject to rigid commands, but lacked knowledge of the source and justification for those commands.[65] Likewise, in lamenting their subjection to fate, they admit to the absence of autonomy, to being subject to ethical powers lying beyond their control.[66]

We can clarify some significant elements of Hegel's account of conscience's language by considering one of the forms that expressive speech assumes, that of assurance (*Versicherung*).[67] Assurance aims to show to others that the conscientious agent is really convinced that they have a duty to act:

> Actualizing the action does not mean translating its content from the form of a *purpose* or *being-for-self* into the form of *abstract* actuality, but rather translating out of the form of the immediate *certainty* of itself, that knows its knowing or its being-for-self as the essence, into the form of *assurance*, that consciousness is convinced [*überzeugt*] of its duty, and, as conscience, knows duty *from itself*; this assurance assures, therefore, that it is convinced that its conviction is a duty.[68]

As a form of expressive speech, assurance does not simply aim to provide evidence to others that the agent really is convinced. For that to be possible,

---

[65] See again *PhG* 236/¶436.

[66] *PhG* 255–256/¶469.

[67] Assurance is only *one* of the forms of expressive speech. As I suggest later, one of the core arguments that Hegel advances in the second part of the "Conscience" chapter is that expressive speech must assume other forms than assurance – confession and forgiveness – in order to vindicate conscience's claim to moral knowledge. Bernstein (1996, 44) suggests that the language of conviction "disowns its expressive dimension by wanting what is expressed to play a formal role, validating the goodness of the self in acting in a certain manner," and that confession, which "aims simply at solidarity, commonality," "replaces the language of conviction." (See also Moyar 2011, 166.) By contrast, in my account, all of these forms of language – assurance, confession, and forgiveness – fit within the expressive rubric of conviction.

[68] *PhG* 351/¶653.

there would have to be some condition in the agent, distinct from those of others, to which assurance gives them access. But for the individual's conscience to be separate from others in that way would undermine the claim that conscience is essentially a shared form of knowing.[69] Instead, Hegel holds that, as a form of expressive speech, assurance is better understood as a form in which the self of the individual becomes manifest, not as this singular individual, but rather as a self, equal to others:

> The expression [*Aussprechen*] of this assurance sublates in itself the form of particularity; it recognizes therein the *necessary universality of the self*, because it calls itself *conscience*, it calls itself pure self-knowing and pure abstract willing, that is, it calls itself a universal knowing and willing, that the others recognize, that is *equal* to them, for they are equally this self-knowing and -willing, and so are also recognized by the others.[70]

For this reason, conscience's expressive speech is best understood as a form of illocution, an act that it undertakes to bring about a condition of equality and sameness with the others, to make public for others its status as a knower. As Richard Moran shows, telling someone something ought to be understood as a form of assurance,[71] an act that is "expressive" in a distinctive way, namely that it is "an intentional act of self-representation, an act of the person as such, directed to some other person."[72] Hegel stresses the expressive dimension of assurance, in linking it explicitly to securing the recognition of others. Assurance does not simply provide evidence to others of my convictions that could be communicated to them otherwise, outside of my illocutionary acts. Instead, those acts are necessary to what

---

[69] See Hegel's argument against the idea that there is a "particular" aspect to the conscience of the individual that is separate from the "will of the universal and pure consciousness." *PhG* 352/¶654.

[70] *PhG* 352/¶654. It is on these points that we should situate Hegel's account of the self in relation to Dahlstrom's (2017) account of authenticity.

[71] "When someone tells me it's cold out, I don't simply gain an awareness of her beliefs, I am also given an *assurance* that it is cold out." Moran 2018, 44. So Moran argues that assurance does not simply aim to provide someone with evidence for what I really do believe. Instead, it is an essentially "social act of mind" (the phrase is Thomas Reid's), whose aim is a distinctive sort of self-presentation.

[72] Moran 2018, 128. Moran accounts for the distinctive characteristics of assurance and self-presentation in terms of ideas of authority and responsibility: When I tell you that it's cold out, I present myself as having the authority to make the claim, and I also take on responsibility for the action, e.g. if my claim turns out to be false, you might be justified in being irked at me when you overdress. Moran explicitly links his account of the pragmatics of telling to Brandom's deontic scorekeeping model, where the ideas of authority and responsibility are prominent and basic. Brandom has recently presented his own account of the conscience chapter where these ideas again loom large. See Brandom 2019, chapters 14–16. For an earlier account, see Farneth 2017, chapter 4. I will argue that the ontological interpretation of conscience which understands it to be a conception of the self helps us better to make sense of Hegel's text than the constellation of authority and responsibility concepts central to Brandom's approach.

Hegel calls "the *necessary universality of the self*," the fact that being a self does not simply mean being this, singular individual, but rather means equally sharing that being with others.[73] In short, language, in particular expressive speech as a dimension of moral discourse, is partly constitutive of the self.

If the idea that language might not only give expression to the self but also contribute essentially to its constitution seems novel to the account of conscience, it merits note that Hegel has already acknowledged this constitutive role. It emerges initially in Hegel's account of the illocutionary act of naming, which constitutes an individual as a "monarch." The flattery and speech of the noble "constitutes the spiritual ... medium" (*macht die geistige ... Mitte aus*) through which it "makes universal power" into "the singularity of self-consciousness" by establishing it as embodied within an individual: "In the name, the individual *counts* [gilt *der Einzelne*] as a pure individual not only in their own consciousness, but in the consciousness of all."[74] The example of the monarch shows that Hegel acknowledges that particular illocutionary acts can not only themselves be efficacious, but that they can be constitutive and generative. Of course, even if being the monarch is a product of activities of recognition, that status will be a limited one, insofar as it is exclusive: only one person gets to be the monarch, and monarch-subject relations cannot be relations of reciprocity. Moreover, we have also seen that the conception of the self that predominates in the world of culture is *atomistic*, premised on the assumption that what I am is something given and determined independent of the activities of others.

By contrast, the language of conscience is distinct in several respects. First, as we have seen is true generally, from the standpoint of "morality" the self is not understood to be an "atom," existing in advance of the activities of the self-conscious beings, but rather as something that is constituted through those activities. As conscientious, I *become* a "universal self" only through engagement in moral discourse, through acts of expressive speech, of avowing and acting on particular convictions. Moral discourse is not incidental to moral practice, but is rather the essential dimension of moral practice that makes possible relations of equality among the practitioners.

---

[73] It is important not to confuse Hegel's appeals to expressive speech here with an endorsement of emotivism or expressivism. Hegel's view is not emotivist, since, as we have seen, he assigns no special role to emotions and feelings in moral practice. Likewise, his appeals to expressive speech need not be deflationary in the way that expressivism is. It is better to understand the illocutionary acts of conscience as avowals, since avowals can express propositions that can be true or false. See on this issue Moran 2001, 100–107.

[74] *PhG* 277/¶510.

Second, unlike the act of naming a monarch, participation in moral discourse is not supposed to be exclusive. With the act of naming, something has gone very wrong if, at the conclusion of the practice, more than one person claims the title of absolute monarch. By contrast, when the self is understood as conscience, because moral knowledge is not understood to be the exclusive property of this or that individual, but rather a knowledge that is universal and shared, engagement in moral discourse will not be limited to one or a few individuals. Instead, it will be inclusive of everyone who can be construed to be a moral knower and agent. And finally, unlike the naming of the monarch, whose outcome is the institution of hierarchy, the aim of moral discourse is to make explicit shared understanding and to secure relations of equality among those who claim to be moral knowers.

For Hegel, two forms of expression are therefore central to conscience. Action is the immediate expression (*Ausdruck*) of the agent's moral knowledge, in which their convictions are first actualized and existent. But being a self requires a second form of expression, and a second actualization: When the agent speaks their convictions to others in the form of expressive speech (*Aussprechen*), they show themselves to be a moral knower to others, who lend their deeds a second sort of actuality, giving them persistence and "validity." This latter form of expression is not reducible to the first.[75] For Hegel, linguistic expression is therefore essential to being a self, and participation in moral discourse, particularly discourse whose subject matter is duty and right, is necessary to secure the status of equality that is necessary to reciprocal recognition:

> Whoever therefore says they act out of conscience speaks truly, for their conscience is the knowing and willing self. But it is essential that they *say* this, for this self must equally be the *universal* self. This [self] is not in the *content* of the action, for this is, because of its *determinacy*, indifferent: Instead, universality lies in the *form* of this content; it is this form which is posited as actual; it is the *self* which is actual as such in language, which expresses [*aussagt*] itself as the true, but precisely therein recognizes all selves and is recognized by them.[76]

[75] See again *PhG* 351/¶651: "The element of persistence is the universal self-consciousness; what emerges in this element cannot be the *effect* of action, because action does not endure there, and does not remain [*erhält kein Bleiben*], but only self-consciousness is what is recognized [*das Anerkannte*] and secures actuality."

[76] *PhG* 352/¶654. I therefore disagree with Benhabib's claim that "In Hegel's *Phenomenology*, 'externalization',", whose primary forms are labor and production, "becomes the primary model of human activity." Benhabib 1985, 66. Of course, Hegel is not, in *Phenomenology*, in the business of supplying us with a "discourse ethics" of the Habermasian type (see Habermas 1983), or any particular ethics. In particular, we need not understand him to be arguing that there is a transcendental structure of

Conscience, therefore, corrects the shortcomings in the prior two conceptions of the self that emerge in the development of spirit. Like the person, conscience is a status that can be affirmed universally of participants in moral discourse, insofar as they show themselves to be capable of moral knowledge and so it satisfies the equality condition for reciprocal recognition. Unlike the person, however, conscience is not alienating. Conscientious actions express my moral knowledge as this self, in this situation, with my own characteristic insight. And expressive speech makes manifest the convictions that I hold to matter in a way that makes them shareable with others, so that being conscientious does not exclude the "content" with which I identify, which is instead an essential dimension of my selfhood.

4.3 Purity and Evil

Unlike its predecessors, conscience is the conception of the self that is adequate to secure relations of reciprocal recognition, and my account of it has, so far, been largely a positive one, aimed at drawing out the central features of conscience, especially those most significant for recognition. I have not yet attended to one of the features of Hegel's account that is central for many interpreters, the fact that it is critical. On a related note, my discussion so far has focused on the first half of Hegel's account of conscience – in which he claims to set out the elements of conscience's "*abstract* consciousness" – neglecting the second half – which tracks the emergence of conscience's "*self-consciousness*" through its concrete objective development.[77] In the methodological terms Hegel sets out in his "Introduction," I have not yet considered the "experience" of conscience, the development it undergoes through the enactment of its claim to know.

The generic problem that animates the experience of conscience is the ambivalent status of the idea of "purity" that is essential to morality. As we have seen, it is central to the idea of conscience that we cannot make sense of the idea of purity by appealing to a rigid distinction between duty

communication and shared understanding that can provide us with a clue to the content of moral norms. For this reason, his appeals to the need for shared understanding do not run afoul of the criticisms of Habermas's Kantian position that we find, for example, in Geuss 2019. However, Hegel does understand discursive practice and communication to be an essential dimension of morality. And some form of agreement is necessary to secure relations of recognition among individuals. On this issue, see §§5.4–5.

[77] *PhG* 353/¶656. In my reading, this paragraph marks the division between Hegel's account of the general elements of conscience – its "abstract consciousness" – and its concrete experience of itself – its "self-consciousness." Compare Harris 1997, 2, 467.

and nature, a distinction that conscience collapses by seeing duty as something actual within the knowing, acting, and speaking of conscientious individuals. However, conscience retains a commitment to the core claim of morality, namely that its own pure willing and knowing is the essence, is what is true. The experience of conscience is animated by the attempt to make sense of the idea of purity in the absence of the strict divisions of the moral worldview. The contradictions that emerge within conscience and among conscientious individuals arise from failed attempts to make sense of the role that the idea of purity might play in conscience.

The first concrete stance that conscience assumes is that of the "beautiful soul."[78] The beautiful soul is committed to a specific claim about the purity of knowing and willing that is constitutive of the moral self. That claim entails a radical division between what is "inner," what belongs to it as an "I," which it deems to be the essence, and any form of "externality," which it takes to be inessential. However, because of its commitment to the purity of its own inwardness and knowing, as we have seen, it is incapable of action, the only form in which conscientious knowing can be actualized. It understands attempts to realize its knowledge through action to be ones that undermine the purity of its knowing. It is capable of expressive speech, but because it does not act, its knowledge remains inactual, so that its speech lacks proper content and is without significance. By consequence, the only world it can "create" is one of its empty "*discourse* [Rede], which it has immediately heard, and whose echo only returns to itself."[79]

The second stance that conscience assumes in its experience acknowledges this shortcoming in the beautiful soul, its inability to actualize its knowing, and corrects that shortcoming through action.[80] However, while it acknowledges the need for action, it understands its knowing to belong to it exclusively *qua* individual, and so in distinction from other selves.[81]

---

[78] Hegel's references here are literary. As Rush 2016, 121 observes, "Because Hegel refrains on principle from naming names in *Phenomenology*, it can become a parlor game to match up individual philosophers or schools of philosophy with various forms of consciousness." For this reason, my account focuses primarily on the figures sketched in the text rather than their possible real-world counterparts. However, there is a rich and deep literature on the significance of Hegel's allusions. On the beautiful soul generally, see Norton 1995. In Hegel's account, see Speight 2001, chapter 4 and Speight 2008. Siep 2000, 211–216 offers a concise account of the stakes and of the interpretations on offer. See also Harris 1997, 2, 478–487.

[79] *PhG* 354–355/¶658.

[80] This figure is often interpreted as an embodiment of the irony of the early romantics, especially F. W. Schlegel. See in this connection Pinkard 1994, 213ff and Rush 2016, 129–139.

[81] "It replenishes empty duty with a *determinate* content *from itself*," so that "it has positive consciousness of duty, that it makes for itself the content as *this* self." *PhG* 355/¶659.

It, therefore, retains the beautiful soul's conception of moral purity, but dismisses that purity as inessential, as a mere moment of its action. For it, "pure duty" is a "*superficiality*" (Oberfläche) that "lies only in words and counts as a being-for-others." While it expresses its convictions to others, it understands its individual knowledge of duty to supersede any possible shared or universal knowledge. But in so doing, it undermines the possibility of recognizing and being recognized by them: "The language in which all recognize one another reciprocally as acting conscientiously, this universal equality, disintegrates into the inequality of singular being-for-itself...; the opposition of individuality to other individuals and to the universal thereby necessarily emerges."[82]

Both stances, therefore, share a conception of purity as a trait that is a merely inward property of knowledge and is independent of externalization or actualization, but simply disagree about its value. However, neither is capable of reconciling the three essential elements of conscience. The beautiful soul claims moral knowledge, and speaks about it, but is incapable of actualizing its knowledge through action. The acting conscience actualizes its individual convictions, but treats moral discourse as inessential empty talk, and so undermines the possibility of vindicating its claim to know as something universal, shared with others.[83]

Within conscience's experience, the incoherence of each stance is expressed in the fact that each counts as "evil" (*Böse*).[84] For Hegel, an *agent* is evil when they act with knowledge of their duties, but assign these an "unequal value" in comparison to their own individuality, so that duty counts for them, but only as "a moment," not as "the essence" of their action: "Because of this holding-fast to duty, the first consciousness counts as *evil*, because it is the inequality of its *being-in-itself* with the universal, and because this consciousness expresses its deed as equality with itself, as duty and conscientiousness, it counts as *hypocrisy*."[85] The evil agent does not fail completely to be conscientious, because if they did, they would fail entirely to be a moral self. Instead, the evil agent shows that they are a moral knower, in particular in their expressive speech, which is why they are a hypocrite.[86]

---

[82] *PhG* 355/¶659.
[83] Pinkard (1994, 217) helpfully observes one of the core traits shared between both stances: "Both are hypocrites, in that both make duty a matter merely of words."
[84] In Brownlee 2013, I work to articulate the elements of Hegel's moral concept of evil, and its significance for his ethics more broadly.
[85] *PhG* 356/¶660.
[86] Contrast generally Fichte on moral evil, where evil arises as a failure of reflection and rational knowledge of the character of the drive for self-sufficiency. *SW* IV, §16.

However, there is also a sense in which the beautiful soul, whose characteristic activity is that of passing judgment (*urteilen, beurteilen*) on the
acting conscience, is evil.[87] To be sure, Hegel notes that we need to distinguish between action and judgment. As the activity of the beautiful
soul, judgment does not "actualize" any convictions, and insofar as our
moral activity is limited to mere judgment, we do not contribute to the
realization of moral knowledge. Instead, the judge is guilty of their own
sort of hypocrisy, that "wants judgment to be taken for an *actual* [wirkli-
che] deed, and proves its rectitude through the expression [*Aussprechen*] of
admirable sentiments instead of through action," so that, for it too, "duty
lies only in its discourse."[88] Hegel identifies this stance of judgment as "the
vanity of … knowing-better," whose aim is to distinguish the judge from
others, in particular those who take on the real work of actualizing the
demands of morality. For such judges, too, moral discourse, which ought
to contribute to the establishment of shared relations with others, becomes
a tool for the judge to demonstrate their elevation above, and so inequality
with, others.[89]

Each stance manifests an essential point about action, namely that all
actions embody the moment of "particularity": "As every action is capable
of consideration according to its consistency with duty, it is equally capable of this other consideration according to its *particularity*; for as action
it is the actuality of the individual."[90] What is lacking, at least according
to conscience's "abstract conception" of itself, is a means of affirming the
particularity necessary for action and agency, alongside the universality
that is required for moral knowing. From the standpoint of the beautiful
soul, particularity and determinacy are a "blemish" (*Makel*), that undermine the capacity for *any* action to count as really conscientious.[91] From

---

[87] To be sure, he only suggests that the judge might present "an *other manner* [Manier] of being evil."
   PhG 359/¶666. However, it is clear that he thinks the judge is equally a hypocrite (they judge the
   agent according to their own conception of duty while accusing the agent of acting according to the
   same, they treat mere judgment as though it were an actual deed, and they claim to be high-minded
   in their concern with pure duty but only dwell on the base motives of the agent).
[88] *PhG* 357/¶664.
[89] There is an unfortunate interpretive tendency to read the conscientious judge as though they in fact
   speak for the "universal" or the community as a whole. See, for example, Siep's (2000, 213) account,
   according to which the claims of the acting conscience are measured against those of a "judging,
   universal moral consciousness." However, when we recognize the judge's stance as evil, we see, by
   contrast, that conscience undermines the pretension of any one individual to speak exclusively on
   behalf of the universal. Shared forms of knowing are links that are forged through discursive interaction, not the default property of any one individual or group independent of that interaction.
[90] *PhG* 358/¶665. Russon (2004, 164) notes well the essentiality of particularity to any action.
[91] *PhG* 348/¶645.

the standpoint of the acting conscience, particularity and determinacy are *all* there is to action, and the project of shared knowing is mere empty talk. Of course, expressive speech in the form of moral discourse is what is supposed, according to conscience's "abstract conception" of itself, to address these challenges by presenting the inwardness of the agent in a public form available to others. Indeed, conscience's experience points to the limitations of the only form of expressive speech that is initially available to it, namely "assurance." The evil agent "assures" others in speaking about their action, subordinating the universal demands of moral discourse to their own particular interests and knowledge. The moral judge claims to speak from the standpoint of shared moral knowledge, but their speech is equally just an expression of their own narrow standpoint. Because it begins with a flawed conception of the purity of moral knowledge, at least according to its "abstract consciousness" of itself, the only form of moral discourse that conscience requires is assurance, in which I express to others my own inward certainty. But a moral discourse limited to assurance will be incapable of performing the essential task of moral discourse, securing shared understanding.

Moreover, if assurance is the only form of moral discourse that is available, dutiful actions will be indistinguishable from ones that are actually evil.[92] Evil shows that my assuring others of my good moral intentions and noble moral motivations is compatible with my acting out of base self-interest and judging on the basis of my own vanity. It should not surprise us that the link between conscience's initial, flawed conception of purity and its limited moral discourse generates inconsistencies in the course of its experience. Indeed, Hegel has already suggested that, considered only

---

[92] Of course, saying that there is no way of distinguishing evil actions from dutiful ones is clearly different from saying that all actions ought to count as evil. Russon 2004 follows Bernstein 1996 in holding that this particularity of action will entail that every action is also "transgressive" of existing moral understanding, and so, presumably, evil. Similarly, in these accounts, forgiveness is simply a matter of affirming the necessarily particular character of each action. Compare Hoff 2018, 7. While particularity is essential to action for Hegel, it is a mistake to hold that all actions are evil because they are particular. To affirm this is to adopt the flawed stance of the beautiful soul, for whom particularity is necessarily opposed to shared moral understanding. Such interpretations make it difficult to understand why forgiveness is even appropriate in this context. As Jeffrie Murphy writes: "[W]e may forgive only what it is initially proper to resent; and, if a person has done nothing wrong or was not responsible for what he did, there is *nothing to resent* (though perhaps much to be sad about). Resentment – and thus forgiveness – is directed toward *responsible wrongdoing*." Murphy 1988, 20. If particularity is essential to any action, the agent has done nothing wrong in simply acting, so there is nothing to forgive. Rather, it is the beautiful soul who needs to get over themselves, and acknowledge that it is their own standard of judgment that is flawed. (See in this connection Rush's remark that the accusation of evil is "unfair." Rush 2016, 133.) We ought to seek instead an alternative account according to which evil is a distinctive feature of extreme moral failure.

according to the "abstract" consciousness of conscience, prior to its development through experience, the conscientious community is an unrealistic moral idyll: "The spirit and substance of their association [*Verbindung*] is therefore the reciprocal assurance of their conscientiousness, good intentions, delight at this mutual purity and refreshment at the magnificence of knowing and expressing, of looking after such excellence."[93] Moreover, it would be difficult to consider conscience an adequate conception of the self if it depended on the actuality of the sort of moral community entailed by conscience's "abstract" conception of itself. Given the reality of extreme moral failure, any moral conception of the self will have to be able to come to terms, in some sense, with evil, to demonstrate that that moral conception of the self remains a robust one worth affirming even in spite of the threat that evil poses to moral practice.

However, evil also creates a deep challenge to the possibility of relations of reciprocal recognition. If what binds us is shared moral knowledge, realized through action, and secured through participation in moral discourse, what sort of tie is it possible for us to sustain with the evil agent or judge? If participation in moral discourse is a necessary dimension of selfhood, what additional forms of moral discourse are necessary to overcome the limitations of mere assurance? If a conscience committed to the idea that purity is only a characteristic of its own "inwardness," opposed to any externalization and determinacy, is incoherent, what conception of purity can incorporate both the particularity of action and the demands of shared knowing?

4.4 Confession and Forgiveness

Resolving the contradiction in the stances of the beautiful soul and the acting conscience will require a change in their conceptions of moral purity. In brief, instead of understanding purity to be a property of the inwardness of the moral subject, incapable of externalization – and so as an unblemished perfection to be insulated from the world of action or as a mere currency worthless in itself to circulate indifferently in the moral economy – conscience comes to understand purity as emergent from a process of "refinement" through which it comes to know the other as itself: "Both sides are refined to this purity [*zu dieser Reinheit geläutert*], in which there is no more selfless existence in them, no negative of consciousness."[94]

---

[93] *PhG* 353/¶656.
[94] *PhG* 362/¶671.

The purity constitutive of the self is then generated through the activities of the two consciences when, through their own actions, they overcome the opposition of the inactual beautiful soul and the evil agent.[95] Conscience's initial conception of its purity as inwardness opposed to externalization corresponds to a distinctive form of expressive speech, namely assurance, which gives expression to what conscience claims to know in advance of its action. So this new conception of purity as an achievement generated through interaction corresponds to new and richer forms of expressive speech, confession (*Geständnis, gestehen, eingestehen, bekennen*), and forgiveness (*Verzeihung*), which arise as responses to particular deeds, and are oriented toward the restoration of the standing of conscientious individuals by situating them anew in relation to their actions. Confession and forgiveness contribute to the achievement of fully reciprocal recognition because they instantiate relations of reconciliation between the opposed consciences by making manifest the distinctive flaws in the stances of both the conscientious agent and the conscientious judge, and establishing the equality of the parties on which reciprocal recognition depends. As discursive practices that instantiate that recognition, they also secure the selfhood of both parties by reestablishing the relation between the individual and their deeds, and between the individual and their fellows.

Confession and forgiveness are important for two reasons, then. First, they contribute to correcting the flawed conception of purity with which conscience begins, showing how purity is better understood as a product of dynamic interaction.[96] However, their significance is not exhausted by the role that they play in the experience of conscience. As I demonstrate (in §4.5), they are also essential elements of any conception of moral practice that can both make possible relations of reciprocal recognition and secure the selfhood of its participants.

Within the experience of conscience, confession and forgiveness make manifest and enact the equality of the opposed consciences, an equality

[95] I argue that confession and forgiveness produce shared understanding, and that this shared understanding is partially constitutive of the self. My account, however, is agnostic with respect to the issue of value realism and constructivism. Farneth 2017, 70 attributes to Hegel the latter view, holding that the confessing community "recognizes that content is constructed intersubjectively." My claim regarding shared understanding is, I think, less controversial, and it does not entail constructivism, only that we come to a *shared understanding* with respect to moral questions only through discursive interaction, though what we understand may either have its reality independent of that interaction or be constructed through it. My claim regarding the self is, by contrast, constitutivist.

[96] Harris has in mind this role for forgiveness in proposing the possibility of a "*logical* forgiveness" of the merely "one-sided" character of action and judgment. See Harris 1997, 2, 503. By contrast, I argue (in §4.5) that real moral forgiveness is necessary for the achievement of reciprocal recognition.

that is necessary for reciprocal recognition.[97] Within Hegel's account, reciprocal recognition emerges only when both parties acknowledge that they embody distinct but complementary forms of evil. The evil agent's confession is, Hegel insists, not an "abasement, humiliation, or casting aside" on the part of the confessor, "a one-sided form of expressive speech, through which it posits its *inequality* with the other." Instead, their confession is rooted in and gives voice to an intuition of their "equality" or "likeness" (*Gleichheit*) in relation to the conscientious judge.[98] As an illocution, confession aims to enact that relation of equality by generating a shared understanding that has up to now been lacking. This understanding would be essentially social and shared. In its confession, the evil agent

> intuits itself as this *simple knowing of the self* in the other [einfaches Wissen des Selbsts *im Andern*] in such a way that the external shape of this other is not, as was the case with wealth, something essenceless, a thing. Rather, it is the thought, knowing itself, that answers it. It is the absolutely fluid continuity of pure *knowing* that refuses communication with it. In its confession, it already disavowed its *separate being-for-self*, and posited itself as sublated particularity and so as continuity with the other, as universal.[99]

In confessing, the evil agent seeks to establish a genuinely shared form of knowing with the other, which it understands to be not given in advance, but rather a "universal" that is the result of a process, a "sublated particularity."[100]

---

[97] Hegel is explicit that reciprocal recognition does not emerge simply through the agent demonstrating their respect for duty and virtue (they already avow a moral motive and justification for their action in their assurance [*PhG* 356/¶661]); through the agent's own one-sided insistence that their knowledge as this individual is what duty is, just because they do not acknowledge this stance as evil ("It confesses itself as evil through the assertion that it, in opposition to the recognized universal, acts according to *its* inner law and conscience" [*PhG* 356–357/¶662]); or through the insistence of the conscientious judge (who demonstrates that their standard of duty is specifically *not* shared by the acting conscience, and so is not actually universal [*PhG* 357/¶663]). A merely *one-sided* action on either of their parts would not secure the equality of the parties, since it would demonstrate that one of them had failed to be a knower, and so failed to be conscientious.

[98] The agent's confession "expresses ... its intuition of its *equality* with the other, in its confession it expresses *their equality* from its own side, because language is the *existence* of spirit as the immediate self; it expects, therefore, that the other contributes its own to this existence." *PhG* 356/¶661.

[99] *PhG* 359/¶667.

[100] Hegel will therefore agree a fair bit with Foucault that confession is not simply an act of personal freedom, but one that, by giving expression to a truth otherwise unexpressed, binds us to one another, and so "constitut[es us] as subjects in both senses of the word." Foucault 1980, 60. Likewise, for both, the practice of confession derives its significance from the broader scheme of social practices of which it is a part. Of course, Hegel thinks that those social practices constitute us as selves, and so contribute essentially to enabling us to make sense of ourselves. By contrast, for Foucault, rituals of confession are procedures for producing truth, and so are effects of power-knowledge. See in this connection Comay 2011, 135.

However, as is clear from the refusal of the other, that shared understanding is not immediately forthcoming. The impediment stems from the asymmetry in the stances of the evil agent and the beautiful soul arising from the different values that they have assigned to purity up to now. The beautiful soul who refuses the confession of the evil agent is now the "hard heart," who holds fast to their conception of purity as a merely inward condition, insulated now from intersubjective engagement. Of course, as we've seen, this stance is ultimately incompatible with their status as conscience, since it entails a refusal of action, which requires externalization. As Hegel expresses this contradiction, their supposed "pure being" is really indistinguishable from an "empty nothing," and so is the "poorest shape" of consciousness.[101] It is only with the "breaking of the hard heart" that they are "raised to universality."[102] Their change is analogous to that of the acting conscience. Just as the latter acknowledged the necessity of shared understanding, and so the admission that their particularity is merely a "moment" of their constitution, so the hard heart must acknowledge that "the knowing that, through judgment, determines and fixes the distinction of the universal and the singular side of the action" is itself merely an element of conscience.[103]

The breaking of the hard heart is enacted in the act of forgiveness, which is, like the confession of the acting conscience, rooted in an intuition of their own equality with the other. Its forgiveness is

> the renunciation [*Verzichtleistung*] of itself, of its *inactual* essence which it posited as equal with what was other to it, the *actual* action, and it recognizes as good that determination that the action maintained in thought which it called evil, or rather it lets go of this distinction of the determinate thought and its determining judgment existing for itself, as the other lets go of its determining of the action existing for itself.[104]

Hegel characterizes the new intersubjective relationship that forgiveness makes possible as a distinctive kind of knowing: "The word of reconciliation is the *existent* spirit that intuits pure knowing of itself as *universal* essence in its opposite, in the pure knowing of itself as *singularity* existing absolutely in itself – a reciprocal recognition that is *absolute spirit*."[105]

---

[101] *PhG* 360/¶668, 354/¶657.
[102] *PhG* 360/¶669.
[103] *PhG* 361/¶669.
[104] *PhG* 361/¶670. Hegel says very little about what sort of act forgiveness actually is. Speight 2005 suggests some helpful links between Hegel's and Butler's conceptions of forgiveness.
[105] *PhG* 361/¶670.

In the account that I've offered, the primary progress that we find within conscience's experience is the correction of a flawed conception of purity. Both the beautiful soul and the acting conscience begin with the view that purity is a characteristic that exists prior to and independent of action. For this reason, the beautiful soul rejects action, while the acting conscience rejects the idea that universal and shared forms of knowing are necessary at all. Both learn through experience the incoherence of their stances, and the result is a new conception of the purity that is constitutive of morality and the moral conception of the self, according to which moral knowledge is the product of a process of purification enacted through a dynamic of intersubjective interaction. Confession and forgiveness are necessary elements of that dynamic, since they are forms in which conscientious individuals can acknowledge the limitations of their initial claims to moral knowledge, and still achieve a shared understanding.

The confession and forgiveness of the two consciences enact an actual relation of reciprocal intersubjective recognition. Such relations are, as we have seen, relations of equality, rooted in the intuition common to both individuals, of their likeness. More broadly, the status of being conscientious – of being a moral knower capable of realizing one's convictions through action and engaging in practices of moral discourse that establish moral knowledge as a shared knowledge – is one that can be shared equally. The relation is one that is reciprocal since it is reversible. As common participants in a shared practice, each is equally engaged in the acts of recognizing and being recognized by the others as a moral knower and agent. Moreover, the relation of recognition as conscience is nonalienated, in the sense that confession and forgiveness explicitly acknowledge the particularity of the individuals so related. The two individuals recognize one another not simply as bearers of a common but abstract status, but rather as having given expression to convictions that belong properly to them, and as having realized those convictions in determinate ways through their own actions. I recognize you as conscientious not simply insofar as I consider you, in general, to be a source of claims, but insofar as I engage with the particular claims that you make, and the specific actions that realize those claims.

4.5 Moral Discourse and Moral Repair

Within the experience of conscience, confession and forgiveness make possible relations of reciprocal intersubjective recognition by correcting the faulty conception of purity with which the beautiful soul and the acting conscience operate. We might worry, however, that confession and for-giveness are only necessary for reciprocal recognition because conscience begins from that flawed conception. First, it may be the case that both figures count as evil only from the standpoint of the other, so that the action of the acting conscience counts as evil only because the beauti-ful soul regards all particularity to compromise the agent's moral stand-ing. Likewise, it may be the case that the judgment of the beautiful soul appears to be evil only to the acting conscience, for whom the "universal" on whose behalf the beautiful soul claims to speak is empty. Once we acknowledge that particularity is an essential moment of action and judg-ment, it may seem that there is no longer any evil to be confessed or for-given.[106] Confession and forgiveness may be necessary in Hegel's account of the emergence of reciprocal recognition, but once we acknowledge the necessity of particularity to action and judgment, it seems possible that recognition may no longer require them.

Second, we have also seen that the reciprocal recognition that emerges through confession and forgiveness marks the emergence of a new form of spirit, absolute spirit. Hegel expresses the significance of this devel-opment in theological terms: "The reconciling 'Yes' in which both I's discharge their opposed *existence* is the *existence* of the *I* expanded to two-ness that remains self-same therein, and has certainty of itself in its com-plete externalization – it is the appearing God in the midst of those who know themselves as pure knowing."[107] Since this development also marks the conclusion of Hegel's treatment of "spirit," and the transition to the emergence of "religion," a range of interpreters understand it in specifi-cally theological or religious terms.[108] We might therefore be concerned that religion can secure the conditions for the shared self-understanding that recognition requires better than the actions of confession and for-giveness do.

In contrast to these approaches, I shall argue that confession and for-giveness are activities that Hegel understands to be essentially moral, and

---

[106] Hegel states that, in forgiving the acting conscience the beautiful soul "recognizes as good the determination that the action maintained in thought, which it called evil." *PhG* 361/¶670.

[107] *PhG* 362/¶671.

[108] On these grounds, Pippin 2004 dismisses the resolution as irrelevant to understanding the political question of the significance of recognition. Of course, his objection presupposes that the primary significance of recognition lies in its contribution to political understanding, a conclusion that, of course, we need not accept. Farneth 2017, 75–76 stresses the sacramental character of confession and forgiveness within Lutheran Protestantism. Though in her account, "Hegel draws on the struc-ture and logic of Luther's sacramental theology, but … he naturalizes it in his account of absolute spirit."

that they are vital ones for the continued realization of relations of recognition and so for our continuing standing as selves. I begin by considering Robert Stern's recent account which identifies a robust religious dimension in Hegel's account.

Stern argues that Hegel's conception of confession and forgiveness is deeply Lutheran. Rejecting Brandomian accounts of recognition in terms of relations of the authority and responsibility we possess as co-legislators of norms,[109] Stern argues that Hegelian forgiveness does not consist of waiving an authority over another that I would otherwise be entitled to claim. Instead, for Stern

> I forgive you because I precisely see that I *cannot* judge you or hold you to account; and in confessing, you do not recognize me as a judge, but as a fellow sinner, who therefore cannot stand in judgement over you, so again this is not a second-personal relation of authority, as authority is exactly what is suspended in this situation, once our shared sinfulness is acknowledged.[110]

Instead of each individual standing as judge over the other, Stern interprets Hegel's claim that spirit is the "Master" (*Meister*) standing over each, to entail that it is spirit that *does* have the authority to pass judgment on them.[111] For Stern's Hegel, the primary challenge to securing relations of recognition is not one of navigating conflicting claims to authority, but rather of affirming a "shared ontological status." This characterization fits very well the account of recognition that we have been tracking throughout chapter VI, where the primary challenge is to arrive at a shared conception of the self that can be affirmed equally of both the parties, but which each party is equally capable of affirming of itself.

Since it ties the achievement of recognition to a conception of the self that is anchored in a specific religious community, Stern acknowledges that his account leaves open the question of how "a shared sense of our moral infirmities [could] be accomplished in a more secular manner,"[112] and so leaves open the question of the continuing significance of confession and forgiveness to moral practice. Of course, something like confession and forgiveness – actions in which we make manifest to one another our moral imperfection, but can nonetheless establish intersubjective bonds with them – must remain necessary for recognition. But Stern does not fill in the form that that bond must take, aside from saying that it must

---

[109] See in this connection Farneth 2017, 76–77.
[110] Stern 2021, 611.
[111] Stern 2021, 612.
[112] Stern 2021, 613.

be "a community of rather different sort" than that of mutually account-
able and equal persons, and pointing out that it will require individuals
reciprocally to see one another as they see themselves.[113]
However, the text does not oblige us to adopt Stern's reading. First,
Hegel does not displace the activity of judgment from individuals to
God as Stern suggests he does. While Hegel does characterize spirit as the
Meister standing over both the beautiful soul and the acting conscience,
as Molly Farneth notes, this is not the same as ascribing the authority of a
lord (*Herr*) to God.[114] Indeed, Hegel does not explicitly ascribe the role of
judge to spirit in these passages, stressing instead the ways in which spirit
can affect and transform our actions.[115] Second, it is evil and not sin that is
the primary form of moral failure that Hegel considers in the text,[116] and
even if evil has a theological or religious significance for Hegel, it is the
moral significance of evil that he explores in his account of conscience.[117]
Perhaps most importantly, while it is the case that, in Hegel's text, confession and forgiveness are rooted in a shared intuition of equality or likeness
among individuals, this intuited equality does not by itself constitute the tie
of community among them. Rather, the illocutionary dimensions of confession and forgiveness are what form or inaugurate that tie. For this reason,
we need not assume that Hegel is appealing to a specific form of religious
community that already exists, since it is these actions that first constitute
the bond of reciprocal recognition that is "absolute spirit." Instead, he is
specifically presenting ways in which those bonds can be built and rebuilt.[118]

---

[113] Stern 2021, 618, 619. See also Harris 1997, 2, 502–504. By contrast, Rush 2016, 138n49 argues that
the confession that we find in the experience of conscience is better understood in juridical than
theological terms.

[114] Farneth 2017, 71–72.

[115] When Hegel says that *Geist* is "the *Meister*" over all deed and actuality," he takes this to mean that
Geist can "discharge and make them un-happen" (*sie abwerfen und ungeschehen machen kann*). *PhG*
360/¶667. Similarly, when he says that "The wounds of *Geist* heal and leave no scars behind," he
glosses this to mean that "the deed is not imperishable [*das Unvergängliche*], but is withdrawn by
spirit into itself, and the side of singularity that is present in it, whether as aim or as existent negativity and limitation is what disappears immediately." *PhG* 360–361/¶669.

[116] Terminological choices make a difference here. Notably, Hegel identifies the moral failure under
consideration as evil (*Böse*), not as sin (*Sünde*), or even as guilt/debt/trespass (Luther translates the
opheilêmata of Matthew 6:12 as *Schuld*).

[117] See, for example, the distinction that Hegel draws between moral and religious conscience in
Philosophy of Right (*GW* 14.1, 120/§137R).

[118] So I also disagree with Siep (2000, 214) that, in his account of conscience, Hegel has "not developed
the concrete forms of [the] reconciliation" generated through forgiveness, and that he suggests only
that we find these "in forms of rational morality." It is the moral practice of claim-making, which
has to include the social acts of confession and forgiveness, in which reconciliation is actual. We
need not think that we only understand the "concrete forms" in which that recognition is possible
if Hegel presents us with a theory of specific institutions.

In this connection, it is important to recall that confession and forgiveness are, in Hegel's account, responses to the reality of moral evil. For this reason, it is a mistake to think that these are activities that we can leave behind following the turn from morality to religion, since evil remains a continuing reality in moral life. It is true that, with the correction of the beautiful soul's view of purity, not all actions will count as evil for it. But the affirmation of particularity as a necessary moment of action by no means entails that *no* action will be evil, since, as the abuse of moral ideas and discourse for self-serving ends, evil remains an enduring possibility for conscientious agents. Confession and forgiveness derive their continuing importance for moral practice from the role that they can play in what Margaret Urban Walker has identified as the project of "moral repair," whose aim is to "affirm values and standards ... as shared among those with whom we deal, ... stabilize trust in ourselves and others to be responsive to those standards, and ... restore or instill a hopeful view of our moral values, ourselves, and each other."[119] Walker notes that moral wrongdoing can damage not only the particular relationship between the wrongdoer and their victim, but can also undermine the ties of trust that bind us in community more broadly, and so also the sense of the individual's own standing in the eyes of others.[120]

In Hegel's account of conscience, establishing or reestablishing these ties is so important because of the role that they play in constituting the self. We have seen that merely assuring others of our commitments is not alone sufficient to establish the ties of shared knowledge, since even the evil agent offers such assurances. However, confession and forgiveness are acts that are both rooted in an intuition of our equality or sameness with the other, but that also acknowledge the reality of evil, of profound moral failure. Their primary significance for Hegel is performative, since they make manifest for others that intuition and knowledge, even in acknowledging the ways in which agents have failed to live up to moral standards in the past. They contribute to constituting the tie to others that makes me a self. Confession and forgiveness, therefore, do not just affirm an already-existing "shared ontological status," but rather secure it in the first place. They are essential dimensions of the moral practices that constitute individuals as selves, as conscience.

Indeed, the new conception of moral purity that we find at the conclusion of the experience of conscience, where moral knowledge is the

[119] Walker 2006, 162.
[120] Walker 2006, 88–98.

product of shared interaction with others, suggests an even more robust need for reparative practices, since there are no guarantees that I can get it completely right with respect to my duties prior to that interaction. If the moral community depends on shared moral knowing, then it will have to include practices of moral repair, through which individuals can admit to moral failure and enact a commitment to correct it.

Likewise, the achievement of that shared understanding need not depend on an already-founded form of community or institutions, because the ties of the moral community just are ties of recognition, enacted in reparative practices. As Andreas Wildt expresses this point, the reciprocal recognition that emerges from confession and forgiveness is "trans-institutional."[121] This fact, however, does not entail that confession and forgiveness only promise, in some distant "postmodern" community, the actuality of reciprocal recognition.[122] That recognition is existent, actual, in the intersubjective ties that we establish through shared participation in moral practice, in which we articulate and act on our convictions, and accept and challenge the like activities of others. Just as my convictions need not be limited by the norms that predominate in extant institutional forms, nor does recognition need to be deferred to some indefinite future. Practices of moral repair are not just necessary in cases where I realize I have violated an existent legitimate norm in my action. They are equally important when I see that my judgment of an other has been rooted in a norm whose time has past, and that I am the one who needs to seek forgiveness.

---

[121] Wildt 1982, 22. This feature of Hegel's account of reciprocal recognition is important for allaying concerns like that of Deligiorgi 2012, for whom "What is 'real', for Hegel, turns out to be what is social; that is, the notions and rules that are sustained at any one time by specific social practices," (188) so that "Hegel's thick intersubjective model results in the absorption of action-ascriptions to evaluation according to rules that are nothing over and above what is socially current at any one time; it is this that I see as the absorption of morality to social etiquette." (190)

[122] Brandom 2019, 540, 647. For Brandom, this new form of community is projected into the future, so that the account of forgiveness serves only as an "allegory," not as recounting existent human actualities: "Our task, as it has so often been, is to read the allegory – in this case, so as to understand the nature of this final form of mutual recognition as reciprocal confession and forgiveness. Unlike the earlier stories, this one outlines something that has not happened yet: a future development of Spirit, of which Hegel is the prophet: the making explicit of something already implicit, whose occurrence is to usher in the next phase of our history." Brandom 2019, 584.

CHAPTER 5

Conclusion

5.1

Hegel introduces the activity of recognition into his text to address a question about self-knowledge, so that recognizing and being recognized by others are necessary for the achievement of self-knowledge. The requirement that relations of recognition be reciprocal stems from the fact that recognition becomes a structure of self-consciousness – of consciousness's knowledge of itself, mediated through its relation to an other – only when my act of recognizing you is completed by your act of recognizing me. Consequently, self-knowledge necessarily requires intersubjective relationships. By contrast, the deepest truth about my own constitution that I can learn from the standpoint of individual reflection in abstraction from relations to others is that it is "absolute negativity," the absence of anything that could count as content for self-knowledge. At the same time, Hegel also argues that the negativity characteristic of self-conscious beings, their capacity to transcend any particular determination, can also become productive, not only of the material realities that labor generates, but also of distinctively social reality, "universal consciousness," the world of shared norms that can mediate relations between self-conscious beings.

The achievement of self-knowledge, and so of relations of recognition, depends on our engagement in shared social reality. That shared reality is produced and reproduced through our ongoing activity. It provides the positive content on the basis of which individuals make sense of themselves. And, because it is normatively structured, at least some forms of social reality will secure the relations of equality necessary for reciprocal recognition. Of course, not all forms of social reality will do this. In some cases, predominant norms will institute and reinforce relations of domination and inequality. However, in others, those norms will make it impossible for anyone to be recognized. Relations of recognition instead require a shared conception of the self that is embodied in social reality, and that serves as a norm that governs and shapes our activities of recognition.

The self is, for Hegel, socially constituted. It is only articulated and actual within a shared social world. A conception of the self is a linking idea, binding the individual to their actions and to others in determinate ways. While there are a variety of ways in which I can relate to my actions and to others, and so a variety of different conceptions of the self, in order to secure relations of reciprocal recognition, conceptions of the self must satisfy two criteria. First, it must be possible to affirm a conception of the self of every participant in shared social life. Even if I might identify with social roles that I do not share with others, such social roles themselves cannot comprise a conception of the self, and would have instead to be comprehended under a universal idea of what I am that could be affirmed equally of all. Second, conceptions of the self must satisfy a "fulfillment" criterion, so that you and I must each be able to affirm them as comprehending those features of our constitution that we take to matter. Consequently, conceptions of the self that exclude these dimensions of our constitution will be alienating.

The condition of alienation is a pervasive one for Hegel. While there are a variety of candidates for conceptions of the self that satisfy the equality criterion, overcoming alienation requires giving up atomistic conceptions of the self – according to which being a self is simply a matter of possessing a property or realizing a purpose that does not depend essentially on relations to others – in favor of an understanding of the self as partially constituted through intersubjective relations. The conception of the self that satisfies both the equality and fulfillment criteria is conscience. As conscience, moral knowledge in the form of conviction links the agent to their actions, and moral discourse in the forms of assurance, confession, and forgiveness links them to others. Conscience is a conception of the self that can be affirmed equally of all who count as moral knowers, and it is not alienating since it is (ultimately) inclusive of my particularity, of my specific moral insight and experience, of the determinate actions that I take in realizing my convictions, and of my natural individuality. Reciprocal recognition becomes possible when our activities of recognition are governed by the concept of conscience, that is, when we act on our convictions, declaring them by participation in moral discourse, and when we hold others to the standard of our best conception of what is right, and, in turn, answer in earnest to their judgments.

Since the self is socially constituted, self-knowledge must be a form of social knowledge. We might be inclined to think that self-knowledge simply depends on a grasp of the concept of the self, that is, in understanding what it means to be conscience. However, Hegel insists instead that we achieve that knowledge only by enacting that concept, by governing ourselves and treating one another in accord with its demands. Participation in moral practice governed by this conception of the self contributes decisively to self-knowledge by providing me with a distinctive intuition, the intuition of myself in the other.[1] And that intuition is an essential dimension of the knowledge that is actual only in reciprocal recognition: "The word of reconciliation is the *existent* spirit that intuits pure knowing of itself as *universal* essence in its opposite, in the pure knowing of itself as *singularity* existing absolutely in itself – a reciprocal recognition that is *absolute spirit*."[2] Put succinctly, a conception of the self gives structure to the activities of reciprocal recognition within which the intuition of equality can emerge between individuals. And it is within those recognitive relations that the self is actually constituted, and so experienced and known by those who recognize one another.[3]

5.2

Of course, if recognitive relations actually constitute the self, then their absence will undermine it. We can identify at least two ways in which failures to achieve recognition will undermine selfhood, which correspond to two ways in which we can fail to meet the normative demands stemming from the idea of conscience.

As we have seen, when we recognize one another as conscience, we recognize them as moral knowers who realize their convictions through action, and who give expression to their knowledge in the medium of moral discourse. The first way in which we can fail to recognize others is to treat them as deficient in their capacity for moral knowledge, to assign their moral agency a diminished value, or to ignore or disavow their participation in moral discourse. A few examples: The form of epistemic injustice that Fricker identifies as "testimonial injustice" compromises the conditions under which agents can participate in moral practice as equals, since it entails prejudicially assigning diminished credibility to the speaker based on a stereotype, rather than admitting them as an

---

[1] *PhG* 359/¶666, 360/¶668, 361/¶669.
[2] *PhG* 361/¶670.
[3] In this relation, we find "the *actual* I, universal *self*-knowing [sich selbst *Wissen*] in its absolute opposite, in knowing existing *in-itself* [*in dem* insichseienden *Wissen*], that is, because of the purity of its isolated being-in-itself is itself the perfect universal." *PhG* 362/¶671.

equal to the domains of moral discourse and practice.[4] Certain forms of the critique of ideology will also undermine the conditions under which others can count as equals in moral practice. Specifically, if such a critique prompts me to assume an objective, explanatory stance toward the claims of the other that is oriented solely to showing how their claims are the products of their participation in a given social system, then I am not treating them as conscientious, as a moral knower engaged in a shared practice.[5] This first form in which recognition is absent is one in which the conditions set out by the concept of the self are not fulfilled.

However, even if we treat the other as conscientious, there is a second way in which we can fail to achieve the recognition of others, and so fail to secure the conditions for selfhood. As we have seen, within conscience, the commission of evil generates a rift between selves whose overcoming requires participation in reparative practices. It is significant that evil remains an enduring possibility for conscientious agents, so that the challenge to shared understanding that evil creates is one that cannot be eliminated in principle. While Hegel points to confession and forgiveness as reparative practices that can contribute to "healing" the "wounds of spirit," he does not argue for the necessity – either moral or historical – of such reconciliation.[6] Moreover, there is no position within the community that conscience is to establish that is insulated from the possibility of evil. We might think of evil action as the primary threat to the establishment of such a community. However, since shared moral understanding is a product of discursive interaction, Hegel shows us that it is a mistake to identify the conscientious judge as a default moral authority, since their activity of judging, too, can subordinate the demand of achieved shared understanding to their own vanity. The actions that undermine the achievement of reciprocal recognition persist as possibilities, and the reparative actions that can restore that achievement in the face of evil, while real, are not necessitated.[7] Recognition requires the establishment of a shared moral understanding, but the picture with which Hegel presents us is one in

---

[4] See Fricker 2007 and, on the connection between epistemic injustice and recognition, Fricker 2018.

[5] Of course, it is possible for claims to moral knowledge to be false for Hegel, and, in turn, for us to hazard some explanations of their falsity. But what conscience requires is a good-faith effort to engage with the other as a candidate knower – to engage them as a partner in moral discourse, to take up the participant standpoint – and not simply to treat their claims as a symptom to be explained and accounted for – to withdraw and assume the objective standpoint. Among the core ideas of conscience is that the participant standpoint is unavoidable for maintaining the integrity of the self.

[6] *PhG* 360–361/¶¶669, 670.

[7] See Bernstein 1996, 53ff on the unforgivable.

which that shared understanding cannot at any moment be guaranteed, and in which its achievement is always a tenuous one.[8]

Both of these failures of recognition, and so failures to establish the conditions for the experiential dimension of self-knowledge, suggest that self-knowledge might be a relatively rare achievement. While, again, I might know, in general terms, what it means to be conscientious, and how I might recognize others as such, Hegel suggests that self-knowledge requires a reciprocal intuition of oneself in the other. When that intuition is lacking, we find, instead of self-knowledge, a condition of self-doubt. Circumstances in which we fail to achieve reciprocity in our relations with others are ones in which we will be unable to make sense of ourselves. In some respects, this might seem a modest cost to bear for refusing reciprocity, especially when we weigh it up against the possible benefits of domination and the agony of subjection, or even the cheerfulness that might come from ignorance. And, of course, it leaves aside consideration of actual moral reasons that we might invoke to ground a demand to recognize others. However, insofar as recognition bears on the experience of being a self, its primary significance lies in making it possible for us to overcome the self-doubt that the failure to achieve moral understanding with others generates.

5.3

The reconciliation and reciprocal recognition with which Hegel's account of "Spirit" concludes is, of course, not the end of his account of spirit in *Phenomenology*. And nor does it mark the end of his account of the self. Consider one of the text's most famous programmatic statements from the "Preface," which Hegel wrote after having completed the remainder of the book: "Everything depends on grasping and expressing the true not only as *substance*, but equally as *subject*."[9] Central to this conception of truth is a novel conception of subjectivity, which Hegel explains both in terms of "the concept" and "the self": "Because the concept is the proper self [*das eigene Selbst*] of the object, [a self] that presents itself as [the object's] *becoming*, it is not a resting subject, that bears accidents unmoved, but is instead the self-moving concept that takes its determinations back into itself."[10] This conception of the relation between subjectivity, the concept,

---

[8] I return to the specific sort of understanding required in §5.5.
[9] *PhG* 18/¶17.
[10] *PhG* 42/¶60.

and the self emerges as a dimension of "absolute knowing," the final configuration of spirit in *Phenomenology*.[11] As Alfredo Ferrarin points out, the
connection between the self and the concept is also at the heart of the
project of the later *Science of Logic*.[12]

Indeed, a study aiming to provide a complete account of the self in
Phenomenology would have to devote more attention to these developments and to the account of religion than I have here. As Harris observes,
Phenomenology – and, we might add, the account of the self – does not
end with the resolution of conscience's experience, since Hegel has not yet
shown "just how the social substance became a subject" and, for Harris at
least, "that is just what Hegel cares most about."[13]

For some interpreters, that latter account, in particular, is actually necessary for understanding the dynamic of recognition in the text, namely
when the confession and forgiveness that contribute to reciprocal recognition are understood to be essentially religious.[14] By contrast, I've argued
that we need not understand the confession and forgiveness that make
possible reciprocal recognition as the practices of any particular religious
community,[15] but are instead the moral activities that make a community
of reciprocal recognition possible. The specific conception of the self that
is necessary for such recognition is conscience.

However, it also bears noting just how much Hegel's account of
conscience and its experience contribute to the account of the self that
he offers in the text. When, in his discussion of "Absolute Knowing,"
Hegel seeks to recapitulate the core development that his book tracks,
he appeals most centrally to conscience, in particular to the scene of

---

[11] We find there the "equality" of certainty and truth, sought after throughout the text (see *PhG*
57/¶80 on the correspondence of object and concept): "*Ich* is not only the self, but it is the
equality of the self with itself; this equality is, however, complete and immediate unity with
itself, or *this subject* is equally *the substance*." (*PhG* 430–431/¶803) And this equality depends
on articulating the true in terms of "the concept": "This equality exists in the fact that the
content maintains the shape of the self. What the essence itself is has come to be the element
of determinate existence or the *form of objectivity* for consciousness, namely the *concept*." *PhG*
427–428/¶798.

[12] Ferrarin 2019, 50–52, esp. "As *science* truth is pure self-developing self-consciousness, and has the
shape of the self [*die Gestalt des Selbsts*], so that *what exists in and for itself* is the conscious concept
existing in and for itself, the concept *as such*." *GW* 21, 33.

[13] Harris is here taking issue with Shklar's claim that "the *Phenomenology* might well have ended"
(Shklar 1976, 203) with the reconciliation between the conscientious agent and judge. Harris 1997,
2, 519.

[14] As we have seen is the case for Harris 1997, Farneth 2017, and Stern 2021.

[15] Even Harris's "rationally enlightened 'Lutheran' community which is now an invisible Church,
deeply impregnated by hypocritical self-deception, but so widespread that its sounds are hard to
find." Harris 1997, 2, 503.

reconciliation with which the account of conscience concludes.[16] Indeed, he points to the way in which one of the core developments of religion, how the substance becomes a subject, has already happened in the experience of conscience, only not as the deed of the substance, but rather as the

> proper deed of the *self*, the concept links [*verbindet*] it, so that the *content* is the proper deed of the self – for this concept is, as we see, the knowing of the deed of the self in itself as all essentiality and all determinate existence, the knowing of *this subject* as the *substance*, and the knowing of the substance as this knowing of its deed.[17]

And it is the externalization of conscience in its actions, and its subsequent recognition that embodies the structure of the concept, in which "the I is with itself in its otherness."[18] So even if there remain dimensions of the idea of the self that are developed only in Hegel's accounts of religion and absolute knowing, as his recapitulation makes clear, the most significant elements of that conception are already on the table in his account of conscience.

5.4

In the account that I have offered, the achievement of reciprocal recognition depends on shared participation in a normatively structured world. As I have presented it, the world of conscience is primarily a world of other moral knowers and agents, and the central norm that structures it is that of conscience itself, which establishes the joint expectations that others will realize their knowledge in their actions, make claims on and before others, and respond to the claims of others, in the medium of moral discourse. Importantly, this account of reciprocal recognition does not depend on a specific theory of rational institutions of the sort that Hegel sets out in

---

[16] See *PhG* 424–425/¶793. Moyar 2017a offers an interpretation of absolute knowing that stresses the role of conscience. His account emphasizes the role of practical issues connected to value. While action is certainly an important theme in "Absolute Knowing," Moyar's orientation to value is less prominent. By contrast, if we consider conscience as a conception of the self, then we can make sense of the connection between conscience, absolute knowing, and the standpoint of science in the text.

[17] *PhG* 427/¶797. That confession and forgiveness are deeds of the self marks an important distinction from the theology of the reconciliation with evil that Hegel tracks in his account of revealed or manifest religion. See especially *PhG* 415–417/¶780. We already find this shift from substance to subject within the account of conscience, only, again, as an action of the self, rather than an action of the substance. See *PhG* 345/¶640.

[18] *PhG* 428/¶799. Hegel stresses the link between the concept and the distinctive community that is established through forgiveness in *PhG* 361–362/¶671.

his mature philosophy of objective spirit.[19] And nor is it any worse off for it. Instead, the reciprocal recognition that emerges within the world of morality, specifically that of conscience, is "trans-institutional."[20] To be sure, social forms that make individuals intelligible to one another – most importantly language – are necessary for that recognition. But the sort of contestation over the meaning of moral norms that Hegel dramatizes in his account of conscience can be an engine for transformation at a range of levels, from the individual transformation that comes from the admission of error and renewed commitment to the shared project of morality, to the social transformation that comes from the actions of the "moral revolutionary" whom we considered in §1.1.[21]

It should not surprise us that recognition can play this transformative role. It is central to Honneth's prominent account that the struggle for recognition provides the "grammar of social conflict."[22] Dean Moyar identifies a central role for conscience in that dynamic. Moyar draws two distinctions with respect to recognition. First, he distinguishes between recognition as a process and as a relation. While he claims that Hegel's aim in *Philosophy of Right* is to set out a structure of value in which we find stable relations of recognition, he argues that *Phenomenology of Spirit* foregrounds recognition as a process in which values change over time through challenges to the justifications that individuals offer for their actions.[23] Second, he distinguishes between indirect and direct recognition. The immediate

---

[19] Of course, there are a variety of different accounts of the relation between the early conceptions of recognition and Hegel's mature philosophy of spirit, from accounts like Habermas's, according to which recognition loses its significance in the later work, to accounts like Pippin's, according to which the mature theory of ethical life is simply the completion of Hegel's account of recognition. A complete account of the relation between *Phenomenology of Spirit* and the mature system would require significantly more space than I have here. I can say briefly, though, that I believe that the account of recognition that I've offered here is compatible with the view that Hegel sets out in his mature work. The two projects have basically different aims. The early account aims to present a social ontology of the self that addresses the ontological question of what I am where activities of recognition lie at the heart of Hegel's view. By contrast, the later account aims to present the materials for an ethics, addressing concretely questions about how it is good to live, where the concept of freedom plays a programmatic role. The primary position that my own account here rules out is the one according to which the early account remains incomplete or dependent on the mature one.

[20] Cobben's (2009, chapters 7–9) account aims both to establish continuity between the early conception of recognition and the later philosophy of right, while also pointing to ways in which the early view entails the need for specific corrections in the later one. In particular, he argues that the role of conscience, in particular as it is articulated in *Phenomenology of Spirit*, is reduced in the later work, where acknowledging the claims of conscience would require significant modifications to the institutional structures that Hegel sets out in *Philosophy of Right*.

[21] And it is this transformation and novelty that Hegel comes to stress increasingly in his discussion of "Absolute Knowing" and in the work's "Preface." See again *PhG* 14/¶11.

[22] See again §1.2 for the distinction of my own account from Honneth's.

[23] Moyar 2011, 144.

object of indirect recognition is the purpose realized in an action, where we indirectly recognize the competence of the free agent when we affirm that purpose. By contrast, direct recognition emerges in situations where we challenge an individual's action, demanding a justification for it. For Moyar, this recognition is a driver of social change because it can bring to light new justifications, requiring a transformation of existing norms.[24]

The account of *Phenomenology of Spirit* and of the role of conscience that I've offered here differs from Moyar's in at least two respects. First, if we take the "spirit" chapter to track a historical process of social change, inter-subjective challenges to action-justifications that generate new normative orders are not prominent in that development. Instead, we find a process through which the statuses necessary for reciprocal recognition, articulated conceptions of the self, only emerge at the conclusion of a given develop-ment. And those conceptions do not transform the normative order in a direct way, but instead emerge as their "truth." Moreover, in all but the last case, conscience, those conceptions of the self prove inadequate to secure the conditions for reciprocal recognition, and it is their failure that induces the collapse of a given world, and the rise of a new one. Of course, we can, retrospectively, understand the emergence of a new world to correct the failure of recognition that brought about the downfall of the prior shape. But those who embody the new stance belong to a different world than those who experienced the possibility and failure of recogni-tion. Moyar insists that "At most (non revolutionary) points in time, the values in a society will demonstrate stable *relations* of recognition."[25] But in the picture that Hegel presents in *Phenomenology*, while each world has its own sort of stability, his argument is that the conditions for achiev-ing reciprocal recognition are precisely what is lacking in prior historical worlds. Indeed, it is only with the articulation of an adequate conception of the self, conscience, that genuinely reciprocal recognition becomes pos-sible within Hegel's account.

Once conscience becomes the predominant conception of the self, the sort of challenge-response model of normative change that Moyar presents looks very plausible.[26] But that means that the articulation of this novel

---

[24] Moyar 2011, 145.
[25] Moyar 2011, 149.
[26] Stekeler-Weithofer (2014, 2, 650–651) argues that conscience is basically distinct from the "revolutionary" self of absolute freedom, which aims to remake the entire world from the ground up. Instead, with conscience, "the freedom of the person does not consist of autonomistic self-legislation, but of the critical recognition [*Anerkennung*] of inherited forms of cooperation, their critical observance, and the *common* development of 'the concept,' including all practical, that is,

conception of the self entails a basic transformation in the process of normative change, whose medium and engine will be moral practice, with discursive interaction playing a central role.

At the same time, it is not obvious that what Moyar calls "direct recognition" will play the prominent role that he ascribes to it. Moyar argues that generally "the recognition of the actions of conscience should be conceived as a form of indirect recognition," since it is primarily a matter of affirming the purposes the agent realizes through their actions.[27] However, as we have seen, Hegel is explicit that recognition is not simply an effect of my action, but depends rather on my declaring what I am doing to others.[28] In this sense, all moral recognition will be linguistically mediated and dependent on engagement not just in moral action, but participation in moral discourse.

Nor is it obvious that Hegel countenances what Moyar calls "direct recognition." For Moyar, this is a recognition of my "ability" or "competence" as a free agent.[29] However, it is not clear where this recognition might have a place within conscience. As conscience, the way that I demonstrate something like my competence is by showing that I am a moral knower, that I realize my convictions through actions, and that I can account for what I do in the medium of expressive speech. In the simplest cases, what others directly affirm when they recognize me is the moral content that I claim to have realized through my action. But the recognition that I win and administer from this engagement is thoroughly mediated since it depends entirely on my actually knowing what it is right to do, and likewise with others.

Moyar's idea of direct recognition may be more promising in cases of moral disagreement, since these are cases in which I might be called directly to account for what I have done. He interprets the resolution of conscience's experience, the mutual forgiveness between the agent and

---

ethically thick action-determining concepts." Of course, saying that we should not expect the transformation of established social forms to be total does not mean that it cannot be radical, or that conscientious practice works only if there are not existent practices that are radically wrong. See, in this connection, the remarks in Novakovic 2017, 157–160, reflecting on the significance of the example of Elizabeth Costello for understanding Hegel's account of social criticism.

[27] Moyar 2011, 151.

[28] *PhG* 351/¶651. Since Moyar understands "avowal" to be essential to conscience's knowing, it seems there is a sense in which he will accept this claim. However, he suggests that the challenge raised by the multiple interpretability of our actions will only emerge in some cases. Moyar 2011, 155–156. By contrast, I have argued that language is an essential dimension of conscience and a necessary element of any recognition as conscience.

[29] Moyar 2011, 150.

the judge, to provide an instance of direct recognition of our humanity, specifically of "the direct mutual recognition of each other as a source of value."[30] Of course, Hegel does not account for this reconciliation either in terms of value or humanity. In the account that I've offered, within the experience of conscience, confession and forgiveness are important because of the role that they play in modifying the moral idea of purity, so that shared understanding is understood to be a product of discursive interaction. I've also argued that, as practices of moral repair, they are essential dimensions of moral practice more broadly. But do they require a "direct recognition" of the "humanity" of the other? Or are they also forms of recognition that are mediated through shared moral knowledge?

<h2 style="text-align:center">5.5</h2>

We can sharpen the question here by considering another account of moral community in which intersubjective discourse plays a central role. Fichte argues that, as rational beings, we have an obligation to seek agreement with respect to the content of our duties, and that participation in communicative practices is, therefore, a duty. For Fichte, the goal of that practice is the achievement of agreement with others regarding the ultimate ends of moral action.[31] Even if that agreement is "unattainable," it is a necessary "idea," comprising "the whole final purpose of the human being insofar as that they are considered an individual."[32] On one interpretation, the achievement of agreement with respect to our convictions is, for Hegel, not an unattainable task, but a necessary condition for participation in the community of moral knowers.[33] And in this account, I recognize you as conscientious only insofar as we attain actual agreement with respect to our expressed convictions. All forms of moral disagreement will undermine the possibility of reciprocal recognition.

There are, of course, other models of community aside from those that are based on shared goals or substantive values. In the liberal tradition,

---

[30] Moyar 2011, 166. Moyar also says that the two "are now aware that value is not created from scratch by individuals" but that "they must recognize a valuable world as always already there." Earlier, he writes, "As a *process*, recognition should be construed as a *source of value*, for value is invested in certain actions and social practices based on the ability of individuals to recognize each other within them. We do not invent or construct value on this picture, but the values in society are transformed through process in which societies and individuals discover how they are able to flourish." 2011, 149. The account is ambiguous as to whether it is individuals or recognition that are the source of value.

[31] See *SW* IV, §18.V. See also the discussion in Wood 2016, 203–209.

[32] *SW* IV, 253.

[33] It bears noting that, in *Phenomenology*, recognition ultimately requires shared participation in forms of moral community. By contrast, for Fichte, recognition relations are ones of right, not of morality.

toleration derives its significance in large part from its power in sustaining political ties in the face of moral disagreement. However, at least in certain accounts, my tolerating the other seems to entail a weaker tie than that in which I recognize them as a moral knower. And in any case, understanding recognition in terms of toleration would require shifting from a moral to a political conception of community. Forms of community that incorporate, at their foundations, a conception of their participants as imperfect (Robert Stern's account of the Protestant community as a community of sinners, for example) would seem to provide models of intersubjective relation in which moral failure is not an impediment to the achievement of ties of recognition. But of course, within such a community, moral failure emerges only against the backdrop of substantive and institutionally embodied agreement, a shared *credo* or "comprehensive doctrine."

Is it possible to achieve reciprocal recognition in the absence of agreement with respect to the content of our convictions? Does recognition really require the achievement of the community that, for Fichte at least, is a mere ideal?

In addressing this question, we should consider the specific way in which the bond of recognition emerges between the agent and the judge in Hegel's account, namely through the confession and forgiveness of evil. A certain sort of agreement is necessary in response to evil, but that is not a complete agreement in ends that we ought all to pursue, but rather an agreement about evil, about what we ought at all costs to avoid. Of course, that agreement emerges as a result of confession, which certainly entails an admission of my frailty, that I have done what I should not have. But in the account that Hegel offers, that confession equally entails a commitment on my part no longer to be that way. Moreover, in contrast to complete agreement regarding our ultimate ends or our values, the commitment not to do evil can be piecemeal, based on a knowledge of particular evils, rather than on a comprehensive understanding of the good as a whole. So recognition need not depend on full moral agreement or an articulation of shared values in a community like a church, since, as a response to wrongdoing, it requires only agreement about the evil to be avoided. And while it is possible to recognize the agent who has confessed to evil, that recognition is not a "direct" recognition of their humanity (either as their capacity for moral action or their being a source of value), competence, authority, or even their frailty, but rather of their acknowledgment of and conscientious commitment not to do evil.

Given the persistence of the possibility of evil, of profound moral failure, in human life, it will remain a threat to the achievement of relations of

recognition and so to the experience of the integrity of selfhood. The case
of Elizabeth Costello dramatizes the failure even to achieve the relatively
modest agreement on which recognition depends. For Costello, it is precisely the shared assumptions held by the majority – specifically concerning the appropriate treatment of nonhuman animals – that are the source
of her estrangement from others. What moral repair (at least as Walker
understands it) would require is a transformation of those broadly shared
assumptions. Simply affirming her right or her capacity to articulate competing moral claims would only accentuate the rift, since that affirmation
does not address directly the claims that she makes. Like recognizing her
merely as a person, an act indifferent to the actual content with which the
individual identifies, it would be an act of "disrespect." Costello's case is
one in which we find not only disagreement about the good, but rather
disagreement about evil, about what should not be done, and where it is
evil that creates the primary impediment to the achievement of relations
of recognition, and that generates the greatest threat to Costello's selfhood. In comparison to Hegel's narrative, Coetzee's story ends in a state of
suspension. Even if we might claim to know what would establish the tie
of community between Costello and others – confession and forgiveness –
those actions are not forthcoming. In the absence of moral transformation,
either on the part of others or by Costello, it is not obvious what sort of
recognition is possible for her.

    To see the sense in which recognition need not depend on more robust
agreement or thicker forms of institutionally embodied community, consider a contrasting case from the first series of the Phoebe Waller-Bridge
television program *Fleabag*. The series documents the estrangement and
loneliness of its main character, who is never named and whom the program's scripts identify only as "Fleabag," following the deaths of her
mother, and her friend and business partner, "Boo." We learn early on
in the series that Boo has died after learning that her boyfriend has had
an affair (intending only to injure herself by stepping into a bicycle lane,
she causes a multiple-casualty accident). But in the series' final episode, it
is revealed that Fleabag is the other party to this affair. Fleabag's gradual
estrangement from her family and former partners is therefore rooted in
part in her own experience of guilt at the betrayal of her friend, and the
drama of the final episode, on which I'd like to focus here, is moral, concerned with Fleabag's coming to terms with her own actions.

    Ultimately, that drama resolves with a scene of recognition following
confession and forgiveness. But it does not come from reconciliation with
her significant others – Fleabag admits fault in her recent behavior by

apologizing to her father who hard-heartedly rebuffs her effort at reconciliation (the recognition scene is not between a Lear and a Cordelia) – and nor does it come from participation in a distinctively moral community. Instead, the other who recognizes her and overcomes her estrangement is a relative stranger, "Bank Manager," whom we meet early in the series when he denies Fleabag a loan for her struggling café. While an apparently minor character – he appears in just three scenes over the course of the series – his role in the confession and forgiveness scene is central. He, too, finds himself in a condition of disgrace, having sexually harassed a colleague and become estranged from his family as a result. During a chance encounter in an earlier episode, he confesses his own actions to Fleabag, expressing a desire to restore the relationships he has damaged. In the show's final scenes, he discovers Fleabag standing at the curb, in the same place Boo did immediately prior to her own self-destructive act. He accompanies Fleabag into her café, where she breaks down and confesses her actions and deep anxieties at her various forms of estrangement, which she ultimately expresses in terms of a radical desolation.[34] His initial response to her confession seems to mirror Fleabag's father's, but after leaving Fleabag alone in the café and walking to his car, he returns, and before sitting down opposite Fleabag states simply "People make mistakes." The episode resolves with a scene of forgiveness, where the affirming "yes" consists of the two beginning Fleabag's loan application again.

The moral resolution of the story is therefore very different from that of the "Lives of Animals" since it depends on the mutual confession and forgiveness of evil: Fleabag and Bank Manager both acknowledge that they have committed wrongs, and their reconciliation stems in part from an intuition of their equality, rooted in a common awareness of their fallibility, and their shared commitment to begin again. There is a sense in which their reciprocal recognition derives from their participation in shared institutions, but those institutions are not those of a set of explicitly shared or thick values, since they meet as market participants. And we cannot account for the significance of their actions simply in terms of the norms typically at work in those institutions. Their joint act of completing a loan application does not derive its significance from the fact that both demonstrate respect for one another as persons possessing legal rights. Rather, that activity is so meaningful because of the way that it contributes to restoring a threatened experience of selfhood. There is reciprocal recognition

---

[34] "Either everybody feels like this a little bit and they're just not talking about it, or I'm completely fucking alone." *Fleabag* 2016.

grounded in a shared understanding of what it means to be a self, and it is for this reason that the otherwise prosaic activities and speech in the scene come to bear such deeply personal significance. Likewise, I'm drawn to say that the humanity of both agents of recognition is on display here. But that humanity is not simply their dignity, authority, competence, or any other property distributed separately among them as individuals. Instead, it is in the way in which their knowledge and experience of disgrace and estrangement are shared between them, and where the intuition of each in the other is the bond that draws them back from desolation.

Works Cited

Adorno, Theodor W. 1970. *Negativ Dialektik*. In *Gesammelte Schriften*, Vol. 6. Eds. Rolf Tiedemann, Gretel Adorno, Susan Buck-Morss, and Klaus Schultz. Frankfurt a. M.: Suhrkamp. 7–412.

Alznauer, Mark. 2017. "Spirit in the *Phenomenology of Spirit*." In Moyar 2017b, 126–147.

Ameriks, Karl. 2000. *Kant and the Fate of Autonomy*. New York: Cambridge University Press.

Arendt, Hannah. 1958. *The Human Condition*. Chicago: University of Chicago Press.

Baier, Kurt. 1958. *The Moral Point of View: A Rational Basis for Ethics*. Ithaca, NY: Cornell University Press.

Benhabib, Seyla. 1985. *Critique, Norm, and Utopia: A Study of the Foundations of Critical Theory*. New York: Columbia University Press.

Bernasconi, Robert. 1989. "Persons and Masks: The *Phenomenology of Spirit* and its Laws." *Cardozo Law Review* Vol. 10, Nos. 5/6: 1695–1711.

Bernstein, Jay. 1996. "Confession and Forgiveness: Hegel's Poetics of Action." In *Beyond Representation: Philosophy and Poetic Imagination*. Ed. Richard Eldridge. New York: Cambridge University Press. 34–65.

2015. *Torture and Dignity*. Chicago: University of Chicago Press.

Brandom, Robert B. 2007. "The Structure of Desire and Recognition: Self-Consciousness and Self-Constitution." *Philosophy and Social Criticism* Vol. 33, No. 1: 127–150.

2019. *A Spirit of Trust: A Reading of Hegel's Phenomenology*. Cambridge, MA: Belknap Press.

Brinkmann, Klaus. 2003. "Hegel on Forgiveness." *Hegel's Phenomenology of Spirit: New Critical Essays*. Eds. A. Denker and M. Vater. Amherst, NY: Humanity Books. 243–264.

Bristow, William. 2007. *Hegel and the Transformation of Philosophical Critique*. New York: Oxford University Press.

Brownlee, Timothy L. 2013. "Hegel's Moral Concept of Evil." *Dialogue: Canadian Philosophical Review* Vol. 52, No. 1: 81–108.

2022. "Conscience, Conviction, and Moral Autonomy in Fichte's Ethics." *British Journal for the History of Philosophy* Vol. 30, No. 4: 626–645.

Butler, Judith. 2004. *Undoing Gender*. New York: Routledge.

Bykova, Marina F. 2008. "Hegel's *Phenomenology* as a Project of Social Ontology." *Proceedings of the XXII World Congress of Philosophy* Vol. 18: 27–35.

2009. "Spirit and Concrete Subjectivity in Hegel's *Phenomenology of Spirit*." In Westphal 2009, 265–295.

2019. "On Hegel's Account of Selfhood and Human Sociality." In *Hegel's Philosophy of Spirit: A Critical Guide*. Ed. Bykova. New York: Cambridge University Press. 164–185.

2020. "Hegel's Philosophy of *Bildung*." In *The Palgrave Hegel Handbook*. Eds. Bykova and Kenneth R. Westphal. Cham: Palgrave Macmillan. 425–449.

Calhoun, Cheshire. 2016. "Moral Failure." In *Moral Aims: Essays on the Importance of Getting it Right and Practicing Morality with Others*. New York: Oxford University Press. 27–46.

Cassam, Quassim. 1994. "Introduction." In *Self-Knowledge*. Ed. Cassam. New York: Oxford University Press. 1–18.

Cavell, Stanley. 1969. "Knowing and Acknowledging." In *Must We Mean What We Say?* New York: Scribner.

Ciavatta, David V. 2009. *Spirit, the Family, and the Unconscious in Hegel's Philosophy*. Albany: State University of New York Press.

Clarke, James Alexander. 2014. "Fichte, Hegel, and the Life and Death Struggle." *British Journal for the History of Philosophy* Vol. 22, No. 1: 81–103.

Cobben, Paul. 2009. *The Nature of the Self: Recognition in the Form of Right and Morality*. Berlin: De Gruyter.

Coetzee, J. M. 1999. *The Lives of Animals*. Ed. and introduced by Amy Gutmann. Princeton, NJ: Princeton University Press.

2004. *Elizabeth Costello*. London: Vintage.

Comay, Rebecca. 2011. *Mourning Sickness: Hegel and the French Revolution*. Stanford, CA: Stanford University Press.

Dahlstrom, Daniel O. 2013. "The Self Before Self-Consciousness: Hegel's Developmental Account." *Hegel Bulletin* Vol. 34: 135–158.

2017. *Identity, Authenticity, and Humility*. Milwaukee, WI: Marquette University Press.

Darwall, Stephen. 1977. "Two Kinds of Respect." *Ethics* Vol. 88, No. 1: 36–49.

2006. *The Second Person Standpoint*. Cambridge, MA: Harvard University Press.

2013. "Respect as Honor and Accountability." In *Honor, History, and Relationship: Essays in Second-Personal Ethics II*. New York: Oxford University Press. 11–29.

2021. "Recognition, second-personal authority, and nonideal theory." *European Journal of Philosophy* Vol. 29: 562–574.

Dawn, Karen and Peter Singer. 2010. "Converging Convictions: Coetzee and his Characters on Animals." In Leist and Singer 2010, 109–118.

Deligiorgi, Katerina. 2012. *The Scope of Autonomy: Kant and the Morality of Freedom*. New York: Oxford University Press.

Diamond, Cora. 2003. "The Difficulty of Reality and the Difficulty of Philosophy." *Partial Answers* Vol. 1/2: 1–26.

Düsing, Klaus. 1993. "Hegels 'Phänomenologie' und die idealistische Geshichte des Selbstbewusstseins." *Hegel-Studien* Vol. 28: 103–126.

Farneth, Molly. 2017. *Hegel's Social Ethics: Religion, Conflict, and Rituals of Reconciliation*. Princeton, NJ: Princeton University Press.

Ferrarin, Alfredo. 2019. *Thinking and the I: Hegel and the Critique of Kant*. Evanston, IL: Northwestern University Press.

Fleabag. 2016. Episode #1.6. Dir. Harry Bradbeer. Written Phoebe Waller-Bridge. Aired September 16.

Forster, Michael. 1998. *Hegel's Idea of a Phenomenology of Spirit*. Chicago: University of Chicago Press.

Foucault, Michel. 1980. *The History of Sexuality, Volume I: An Introduction*. Trans. Robert Hurley. New York: Vintage Books.

Fraser, Nancy. 2003. "Social Justice in the Age of Identity Politics: Redistribution, Recognition, and Participation." In *Redistribution or Recognition? A Political-Philosophical Exchange*. Eds. Nancy Fraser and Axel Honneth. New York: Verso. 7–109.

Fricker, Miranda. 2007. *Epistemic Injustice: Power & the Ethics of Knowing*. New York: Oxford University Press.

2018. "Epistemic Injustice and Recognition Theory: A New Conversation." *Feminist Philosophy Quarterly* Vol. 4, No. 4: Article 8.

Gadamer, Hans-Georg. 1976. *Hegel's Dialectic: Five Hermeneutical Studies*. Trans. P. Christopher Smith. New Haven, CT: Yale University Press.

Geuss, Raymond. 2019. "A Republic of Discussion: Habermas at Ninety." *The Point*, June 18. https://thepointmag.com/politics/a-republic-of-discussion-habermas-at-ninety.

Gottlieb, Gabriel. 2016. "Fichte's Developmental View of Self-Consciousness." In *Fichte's Foundations of Natural Right: A Critical Guide*. Ed. Gabriel Gottlieb. New York: Cambridge University Press. 117–137.

2018. "A Family Quarrel: Fichte's Deduction of Right and Recognition." In *Kant and His German Contemporaries*. Ed. Daniel O. Dahlstrom. New York: Cambridge University Press. 170–192.

Habermas, Jürgen. 1967/1968. "Arbeit und Interaktion. Bemerkungen zu Hegels Jenaer Philosophie des Geistes." *Technik und Wissenschaft als Ideologie*. Frankfurt a.M.: Suhrkamp. 9–47.

1971. "Hegels Kritik der Französischen Revolution." In *Theorie und Praxis*, 4th Ed. Frankfurt a.M.: Suhrkamp. 128–147.

1981. *Theorie des kommunikativen Handelns*, 2 Vols. Frankfurt a.M.: Suhrkamp.

1983. "Diskursethik - Notizen zu einem Begründungsprogramm." In *Moralbewußtsein und kommunikatives Handeln*. Frankfurt a.M.: Suhrkamp. 53–126.

1990. *Strukturwandel der Öffentlichkeit*, New Edition. Frankfurt a.M.: Suhrkamp. Original edition published 1962.

Hacking, Ian. 1999. *The Social Construction of What?* Cambridge, MA: Harvard University Press.

Halbig, Christoph. 2008. "Die Wahrheit des Gewissens." In Vieweg and Welsch 2008, 489–503.

Harris, H. S. 1995. *Hegel: Phenomenology and System*. Indianapolis, IN: Hackett.

1997. *Hegel's Ladder*, 2. Vols. Indianapolis, IN: Hackett.

Haslanger, Sally. 2012. *Resisting Reality: Social Construction and Social Critique*. New York: Oxford University Press.

Heidegger, Martin. 1972. *Sein und Zeit*, 12th Ed. Tübingen: Max Niemeyer.

Henrich, Dieter. 1982. "Fichte's Original Insight." Trans. D. R. Lachterman. *Contemporary German Philosophy* Vol. 1, No. 9: 15–52. German original published 1967.

Hill, Thomas E., Jr. 1998. "Four Conceptions of Conscience." *Nomos* Vol. 40: 13–52.

Hoff, Shannon. 2018. "The Right and the Righteous: Hegel on Confession, Forgiveness, and the Necessary Imperfection of Action." In *Phenomenology and Forgiveness*. Ed. Marguerite La Case. Lanham, MD: Rowman & Littlefield. 3–23.

Honneth, Axel. 1992. *Kampf um Anerkennung*. Frankfurt a. M.: Suhrkamp.

2001. *Leiden an Unbestimmtheit*. Stuttgart: Reclam.

2003. "Unsichtbarkeit. Über die moralische Epistemologie von 'Anerkennung.'" In *Unsichtbarkeit, Stationen einer Theorie von Intersubjektivität*. Frankfurt a. M.: Suhrkamp. 10–27.

2008. "From Desire to Recognition: Hegel's Account of Human Sociality." In Moyar and Quante 2008, 76–90.

2011. *Das Recht der Freiheit*. Berlin: Suhrkamp.

2018. *Anerkennung. Eine europäische Ideengeschichte*. Berlin: Suhrkamp.

Hoy, Jocelyn. 2009. "Hegel, Antigone, and Feminist Critique: The Spirit of Ancient Greece." In Westphal 2009, 172–189.

Hyppolite, Jean. 1974. *Genesis and Structure of Hegel's Phenomenology of Spirit*. Trans. Samuel Cherniak and John Heckman. Evanson, IL: Northwestern University Press.

Ikäheimo, Heikki. 2007. "Recognizing Persons." *Journal of Consciousness Studies* Vol. 14, No. 5–6: 224–247.

2011. "Holism and Normative Essentialism in Hegel's Social Ontology." In Ikäheimo and Laitinen 2011a, 145–209.

2014. "Hegel's Concept of Recognition—What is it?" In *Recognition—German Idealism as an Ongoing Challenge*. Ed. Christian Krijnen. Boston: Brill. 11–38.

Ikäheimo, Heikki and Arto Laitinen. 2007. "Analyzing Recognition: Identification, Acknowledgement, and Recognitive Attitudes Toward Persons." In *Recognition and Power: Axel Honneth and the Tradition of Critical Social Theory*. Eds. Bert Van Den Brink and David Owen. New York: Cambridge University Press. 33–56.

Eds. 2011a. *Recognition and Social Ontology*. Leiden and Boston: Brill.

2011b. "Recognition and Social Ontology: An Introduction." In Ikäheimo and Laitinen 2011a. 1–21.

Ikäheimo, Heikki, Kristina Leopold, and Titus Stahl, Eds. 2021. *Recognition and Ambivalence*. New York: Columbia University Press.

Jaeggi, Rahel. 2005. *Entfremdung: Zur Aktualität eines sozialphilosophischen Problems.* Frankfurt a.m.: Campus.
2014. *Kritik von Lebensformen.* Berlin: Suhrkamp.
Jenkins, Scott. 2009. "Hegel's Concept of Desire." *Journal of the History of Philosophy* Vol. 47, No. 1: 103–130.
Kelly, George Armstrong. 1972. "Notes on Hegel's Lordship and Bondage." In MacIntyre 1972, 189–217.
Klotz, Christian. 2008. "Kritik und Transformation der Philosophie der Subjektivität in Hegels Darstellung der Erfahrungen des Selbstbewußtseins." In Vieweg and Welsch 2008, 171–186.
Köhler, Dietmar and Otto Pöggeler, eds. 2006. *G. W. F. Hegel, Phänomenologie des Geistes.* Berlin: Akademie.
Kojève, Alexandre. 1980. *Introduction to the Reading of Hegel.* Eds. Raymond Queneau and Allen Bloom. Trans. James H. Nichols, Jr. Cornell, NY: Cornell University Press.
Korsgaard, Christine. 1996. *Creating the Kingdom of Ends.* New York: Cambridge University Press. 106–132.
1999. "Self-Constitution in the Ethics of Plato and Kant." *The Journal of Ethics* Vol. 3: 1–29.
2009. *Self-Constitution: Agency, Identity, and Integrity.* New York: Oxford University Press.
Kosch, Michelle. 2014. "Practical Deliberation and the Voice of Conscience in Fichte's 1798 System of Ethics." *Philosopher's Imprint* Vol. 14, No. 30 (October): 1–16.
2018. *Fichte's Ethics.* New York: Oxford University Press.
Kukla, Quill. 2021. "Situated Knowledge, Purity, and Moral Panic." In *Applied Epistemology.* Ed. Jennifer Lackey. New York: Oxford University Press. 37–66.
Kukla, Rebecca. 2000. "Myth, Memory, and Misrecognition in Sellars' Empiricism and the Philosophy of Mind." *Philosophical Studies* Vol. 101, No. 2/3: 161–211.
2018. "Slurs, Interpellation, and Ideology." *Southern Journal of Philosophy* Vol. 56, Supplement: 7–32.
Kukla, Rebecca and Mark Lance. 2009. *"Yo" and "Lo": The Pragmatic Topography of the Space of Reasons.* Cambridge, MA: Harvard University Press.
Leist, Anton and Peter Singer, eds. 2010. *J. M. Coetzee and Ethics: Philosophical Perspectives on Literature.* New York: Columbia University Press.
MacIntyre, Alasdair, Ed. 1972. *Hegel: A Collection of Critical Essays.* New York: Anchor.
Markell, Patchen. 2003. *Bound by Recognition.* Princeton, NJ: Princeton University Press.
Marx, Karl. 1953. *Das Kapital,* Erster Band. Berlin: Dietz.
McBride, Cillian. 2013. *Recognition.* Malden, MA: Polity.
McDowell, John. 2009a. "The Apperceptive I and the Empirical Self: Towards a Heterodox Reading of 'Lordship and Bondage' in Hegel's Phenomenology." In McDowell 2009b, 147–165.

2009b. *Having the World in View: Essays on Kant, Hegel, and Sellars*. Cambridge, MA: Harvard University Press.

2009c. "Towards a Reading of Hegel on Action in the 'Reason' Chapter of the Phenomenology." In McDowell 2009b, 166–184.

Moran, Richard. 2001. *Authority and Estrangement: An Essay on Self-Knowledge*. Princeton, NJ: Princeton University Press.

2018. *The Exchange of Words: Speech, Testimony, and Intersubjectivity*. New York: Oxford University Press.

Moyar, Dean. 2008. "Self-Completing Alienation: Hegel's Argument for the Transparent Conditions of Free Agency." In Moyar and Quante 2008, 150–172.

2011. *Hegel's Conscience*. New York: Oxford University Press.

2017a. "Absolute Knowing and the Ethical Conclusion of the Phenomenology." In Moyar 2017b, 166–196.

Ed. 2017b. *The Oxford Handbook of Hegel*. New York: Oxford University Press.

Moyar, Dean and Michael Quante, eds. 2008. *Hegel's Phenomenology of Spirit: A Critical Guide*. New York: Cambridge University Press.

Murphy, Jeffrie. 1988. "Forgiveness and Resentment." In *Forgiveness and Mercy*. Eds. Jeffrie Murphy and Jean Hampton. New York: Cambridge University Press. 14–34.

Neuhouser, Frederick. 2000. *Foundations of Hegel's Social Theory*. Cambridge, MA: Harvard University Press.

2009. "Desire, Recognition, and the Relation between the Bondsman and Lord." In *Blackwell Guide to Hegel's Phenomenology of Spirit*. Ed. Kenneth Westphal. Malden, MA: Blackwell Publishing. 37–54.

Ng, Karen. 2020. *Hegel's Concept of Life: Self-Consciousness, Freedom, Logic*. New York: Oxford University Press.

Norton, Robert E. 1995. *The Beautiful Soul: Aesthetic Morality in the Eighteenth Century*. Ithaca, NY: Cornell University Press.

Novakovic, Andreja. 2017. *Hegel on Second Nature in Ethical Life*. New York: Cambridge University Press.

Patterson, Orlando. 1982. *Slavery and Social Death: A Comparative Study*. Cambridge, MA: Harvard University Press.

Pinkard, Terry. 1994. *Hegel's* Phenomenology: *The Sociality of Reason*. New York: Cambridge University Press.

2012. *Hegel's Naturalism: Mind, Nature, and the Final Ends of Life*. New York: Oxford University Press.

2017. *Does History Make Sense? Hegel on the Historical Shapes of Justice*. Cambridge, MA: Harvard University Press.

Pippin, Robert B. 1989. *Hegel's Idealism*. New York: Cambridge University Press.

1993. "You Can't Get There from Here: Transition Problems in Hegel's Phenomenology of Spirit." In *Cambridge Companion to Hegel*. Ed. Fred Beiser. New York: Cambridge University Press. 52–85.

2000. "What is the Question for which Hegel's Theory of Recognition is the Answer?" *European Journal of Philosophy* Vol. 8, No. 2 (August): 155–172.

2004. "Recognition and Reconciliation: Actualized Agency in Hegel's Jena Phenomenology." *Internationales Jahrbuch des Deutschen Idealismus* Vol. 2: 249–267.

2008. *Hegel's Practical Philosophy.* New York: Cambridge University Press.

2011. *Hegel on Self-Consciousness. Desire and Death in the* Phenomenology of Spirit. Princeton, NJ: Princeton University Press.

Pöggeler, Otto. 1961. "Zur Deutung der Phänomenologie des Geistes." *Hegel-Studien* Vol. 1: 255–294.

1966. "Die Komposition der Phänomenologie des Geistes." *Hegel-Studien* Vol. 3: 27–74.

2006. "Selbstbewußtsein als Leitfaden der Phänomenologie des Geistes." In Köhler and Pöggeler 2006, 129–141.

Quante, Michael. 2010. "'The Pure Notion of Recognition': Reflections on the Grammar of the Relation of Recognition in Hegel's Phenomenology of Spirit." In Schmidt am Busch and Zurn 2010, 89–106.

Railton, Peter. 1984. "Alienation, Consequentialism, and the Demands of Morality." *Philosophy and Public Affairs* Vol. 13, No. 2 (Spring): 134–171.

Rawls, John. 1955. "Two Concepts of Rules." *The Philosophical Review* Vol. 64, No. 1 (January): 3–32.

1980. "Kantian Constructivism in Moral Theory." *The Journal of Philosophy* Vol. LXXVII, No. 9 (September): 515–572.

1999. *A Theory of Justice,* Revised Edition. Cambridge, MA: Harvard University Press.

2005. *Political Liberalism,* Expanded Edition. New York: Columbia University Press.

Redding, Paul. 1996. *Hegel's Hermeneutics.* Ithaca, NY: Cornell University Press.

2005. "Fichte's Role in Hegel's Phenomenology of Spirit, Chapter 4." https://philpapers.org/archive/REDFRI.pdf.

2007. "Hegel, Fichte, and the Pragmatic Contexts of Moral Judgement." In *German Idealism: Contemporary Perspectives.* Ed. Espen Hammer. New York: Routledge. 225–242.

2008. "The Independence and Dependence of Self-Consciousness: The Dialectic of Lord and Bondsman in Hegel's Phenomenology of Spirit." In *The Cambridge Companion to Hegel and Nineteenth-Century Philosophy.* Ed. Frederick C. Beiser. New York: Cambridge University Press. 94–110.

Rose, Gillian. 1981. *Hegel Contra Sociology.* Atlantic Highlands, NJ: Humanities Press.

Rush, Fred. 2016. *Irony and Idealism: Rereading Schlegel, Hegel, and Kierkegaard.* New York: Oxford University Press.

Russon, John. 2004. *Reading Hegel's Phenomenology.* Bloomington, IN: Indiana University Press.

2015. *Infinite Phenomenology: The Lessons of Hegel's Science of Experience.* Bloomington, IN: Indiana University Press.

Sandel, Michael. 1984. "The Procedural Republic and the Unencumbered Self." *Political Theory* Vol. 12, No. 1 (February): 81–96.

1998. *Liberalism and the Limits of Justice*, Second Edition. New York: Cambridge University Press.

Saunders, Joe. 2016. "Kant and the Problem of Recognition: Freedom, Transcendental Idealism, and the Third-Person." *International Journal of Philosophical Studies* Vol. 24, No. 2: 164–182.

Schacht, Richard. 1984. *Alienation*. Lanham, MD: University Press of America.

Schlösser, Ulrich. 2011. "Self-Knowledge, Action and the Language of Confession in Hegel's Phenomenology of Spirit." *Bulletin of the Hegel Society of Great Britain* Vol. 63: 269–283.

Schmidt am Busch, Christoph and Christopher Zurn, eds. 2010. *The Philosophy of Recognition: Historical and Contemporary Perspectives*. Lanham, MD: Lexington Books.

Shklar, Judith N. 1976. *Freedom and Independence: A Study of the Political Ideas of Hegel's* Phenomenology of Mind. New York: Cambridge University Press.

Siep, Ludwig. 1974. "Der Kampf um Anerkennung. Zu Hegels Auseinandersetzung mit Hobbes in den Jenaer Schriften." *Hegel-Studien* Vol. 9: 155–207.

1998. "Die Bewegung des Anerkennens in Hegels Phänomenologie des Geistes." In Köhler and Pöggeler 2006, 107–128.

2000. *Der Weg der Phänomenologie des Geistes*. Frankfurt a. M.: Suhrkamp.

2008. "Practical Reason and Spirit in Hegel's Phenomenology of Spirit." In Moyar and Quante 2008, 173–191.

2010. "Recognition in Hegel's Phenomenology of Spirit and Contemporary Practical Philosophy." In Schmidt am Busch and Zurn 2010, 107–128.

2014. *Anerkennung als Prinzip der praktischen Philosophie*. Hamburg: Meiner. Original edition published 1979.

Speight, C. Allen. 2001. *Hegel, Literature, and the Problem of Agency*. New York: Cambridge University Press.

2005. "Butler and Hegel on Forgiveness and Agency." *Southern Journal of Philosophy* Vol. 43, No. 2: 299–316.

2008. "Was ist das Schöne an der schönen Seele? Hegel und die ästhetischen Implikationen der letzten Entwicklungsstufe des Geistes." In Vieweg and Welsch 2008, 504–519.

Stekeler-Weithofer, Pirmin. 2008. "Wer ist der Herr, wer ist der Knecht? Der Kampf zwischen Denken und Handeln als Grundform des Selbstbewußtseins." In Vieweg and Welsch 2008, 205–237.

2014. *Hegels Phänomenologie des Geistes, Ein dialogischer Kommentar*, 2 Vols. Hamburg: Felix Meiner.

Stern, Robert. 2002. *Hegel and the Phenomenology of Spirit*. New York: Routledge.

2017. "Freedom, Norms, and Nature in Hegel: Self-Legislation or Self-Realization?" In *Hegel on Philosophy in History*. Eds. Rachel Zuckert and James Kreines. New York: Cambridge University Press. 88–105.

2021. "Is Hegelian recognition second-personal? Hegel says 'no.'" *European Journal of Philosophy* Vol. 29, No. 3: 608–623.

Taylor, Charles. 1972. "The Opening Arguments of the Phenomenology." In MacIntyre 1972, 151–187.

1985. "Hegel's Philosophy of Mind." In *Philosophical Papers, Vol. 1: Human Agency and Language*. New York: Cambridge University Press. 77–97.

1994. "The Politics of Recognition." In *Multiculturalism*. Ed. Amy Gutmann. Princeton, NJ: Princeton University Press.

Taylor, Paul. 2013. *Race: A Philosophical Introduction*, Second Edition. Malden, MA: Polity.

Testa, Italo. 2008. "Selbstbewußtsein und zweite Natur." In Vieweg and Welsch 2008, 286–307.

Thompson, Michael. 2004. "What is it to Wrong Someone? A Puzzle about Justice." In *Reason and Value: Themes from the Moral Philosophy of Joseph Raz*. Eds. R. Jay Wallace, Philip Pettit, Samuel Scheffler, and Michael Smith. Oxford: Clarendon Press. 333–384.

Thompson, Michael J. 2011. "Enlarging the Sphere of Recognition: A Hegelian Approach to Animal Rights." *Journal of Value Inquiry* Vol. 45, No. 3: 319–335.

Vieweg, Klaus and Wolfgang Welsch, Eds. 2008. *Hegels Phänomenologie des Geistes. Ein kooperativer Kommentar zu einem Schlüsselwerk der Moderne*. Frankfurt a. M.: Suhrkamp.

Walker, Margaret Urban. 2006. *Moral Repair: Reconstructing Moral Relations after Wrongdoing*. New York: Cambridge University Press.

Ware, Owen. 2017. "Fichte on Conscience." *Philosophy and Phenomenological Research* Vol. XCV, No. 2 (September): 376–394.

2020. *Fichte's Moral Philosophy*. New York: Oxford University Press.

Westphal, Kenneth, Ed. 2009. *The Blackwell Guide to Hegel's Phenomenology of Spirit*. Malden, MA: Blackwell.

Wildt, Andreas. 1982. *Autonomie und Anerkennung. Hegels Moralitätskritik im Lichte seiner Fichte-Rezeption*. Stuttgart: Klett-Cotta.

Williams, Bernard. 1981. "Persons, Character, and Morality." In *Moral Luck*. New York: Cambridge University Press. 1–19.

1985. *Ethics and the Limits of Philosophy*. Cambridge, MA: Harvard University Press.

Williams, Robert R. 1992. *Recognition: Fichte and Hegel on the Other*. Albany, NY: State University of New York Press.

1997. *Hegel's Ethics of Recognition*. Berkeley and Los Angeles: University of California Press.

Wood, Allen W. 1990. *Hegel's Ethical Thought*. New York: Cambridge University Press.

2016. *Fichte's Ethical Thought*. New York: Oxford University Press.

Index

CPSIA information can be obtained
at www.ICGtesting.com
Printed in the USA
BVHW052129120123
656187BV00002BA/7